THE QUILTER'S
COMPANION

KATHARINE GUERRIER

THE QUILTER'S COMPANION

THE COMPLETE GUIDE TO MACHINE AND HAND QUILTING

CREATIVE
PUBLISHING
international

CHANHASSEN, MINNESOTA

First published in the USA in 2003
by Creative Publishing international, Inc.

18705 Lake Drive East
Chanhassen, Minnesota 55317
1-800-328-3895
www.creativepub.com

President/CEO: Michael Eleftheriou
Vice President/Publisher: Linda Ball
Vice President of Sales & Marketing: Kevin Haas

A QUINTET BOOK

ISBN 1-58923-243-7

This book was designed and produced by
Quintet Publishing Limited
6 Blundell Street
London N7 9BH

Managing Editor: Diana Steedman
Editor: Clare Tomlinson, Sue Richardson
Photography: Jeremy Thomas, John Melville, Keith Waterton
Diagrams and illustrations: Jenny Dooge
Design: Steve West, Sharanjit Dhol
Creative Director: Richard Dewing
Publisher: Oliver Salzmann

Important
The author and publishers have made every effort to ensure
that all instructions given in this book are safe and accurate.
They cannot accept liability for any resulting injury or loss or
damage to either property or person, whether direct or
consequential and howsoever arising.

Color separation by Pica Colour Separation Overseas Pte Ltd
Printed in Leefung-Asco Printers Ltd

10 9 8 7 6 5 4 3 2 1

Contents

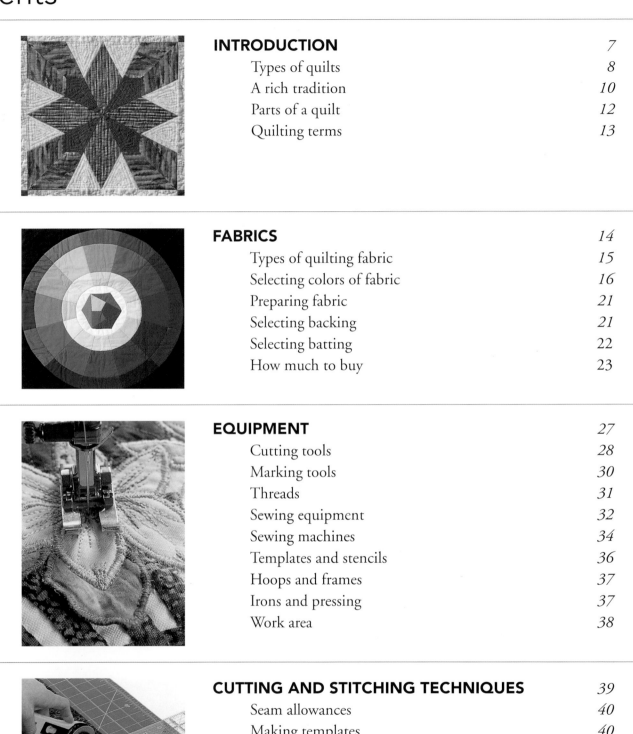

Contents

Introduction

The appeal of color, pattern, and texture is perhaps the first thing to attract a newcomer to the craft of patchwork and quilting. When it becomes apparent that it is possible to produce beautiful quilts for the home that are both decorative and useful, using basic sewing skills and a few readily available items of equipment, the interest is further engaged and before you know it, you are being creative and making a quilt for yourself.

Once begun, an interest in quilts will often endure for life as quilts, quilt making, and its associated world opens up. Many quilt makers say that while working on one quilt, they are already planning the next, which is in itself an illustration of how compulsive an occupation it can become. Hundreds of visitors to quilt shows across the world demonstrate just how popular the needlecraft is, and the fact that quilt making is so accessible to the beginner, while offering challenges to the more experienced explains its abiding appeal. Together with that satisfaction and creativity, there is a world of new friends sharing a common interest, through quilting bees and guilds which organize classes, speakers and courses for all levels of interest and ability across the different techniques.

Quilt shops today offer probably the widest variety of fabrics ever, giving infinite choices to plan and design our quilts; even following a prescribed pattern every quilt can be unique just by the choice of fabrics used.

This book combines the foundation techniques in patchwork, quilting and appliqué, with contemporary styles so that, whether you are new to patchwork or already an accomplished quilter, you will find here a resource to stimulate and spark creativity. The first-time quilter can gain insight into selecting fabrics in a chosen color scheme, and enjoy sewing together arrangements of geometric squares, maybe using scraps saved from other needlecraft projects. As skills are developed and new challenges sought, the more complex techniques of appliqué and intricate methods of piecing are explained, along with a variety of specialty techniques that will maintain interest and promote experimentation. Here is your companion and reference as you enter the unique fascination of quilting.

Types of quilts

The definition of a quilt is that it is composed of three layers: the top, which can be made using a variety of different techniques; the filler, known as batting (or wadding), which provides warmth and loft; and the backing. These layers are fastened together with stitches that are often both functional and decorative.

There are three main categories by which quilts are usually classified: *patchwork*, in which the top is made of pieces of fabric stitched together in geometric patterns; *appliqué*, in which fabrics are stitched to a background to make a top layer of decorative and often realistic designs; and *quilting*, which is the stitching used to fasten the three layers of a quilt together. The quilting can become the main focus of decoration when the stitching is done on a plain piece of fabric in elaborate designs, resulting in what is called a wholecloth quilt. The crafts of patchwork, appliqué and quilting encompass many diverse techniques and decorative styles, which go a long way to explaining their popularity, both for the makers and for quilt owners.

Patchwork (pieced) quilts

Pieced quilts fall into a number of different categories according to how the designs are organized. Probably the most enduring classics are patchwork blocks, in which squares are subdivided into a number of geometric shapes like squares, triangles, and rectangles and then repeated over the surface of the quilt top. The variety of designs possible is wide ranging and they can be used in a large number of ways. Set edge to edge, exciting secondary designs appear, and when the blocks are separated with strips of fabric called sashing, each

block is individually framed. Alternating each block with a solid square of fabric provides the maker with space to show off quilting skills. The blocks can also be presented as squares or set "on point" so that they appear as diamonds. The repeated unit need not be a square—rectangles, hexagons, or diamonds can be subdivided to create more intricate blocks, and the "strippy" quilt, in which the repeated designs are used to create long strips running the length of the quilt, creates another possibility.

Another form of pieced quilt is the frame, or medallion quilt. Here, there is a central square or rectangle, often with a large pieced or appliquéd motif, that is surrounded by borders in concentric

A pieced quilt by Becky Knight, *Thinking of You*.

frames. The "one patch" uses just one repeated shape—simple squares or rectangles, or more complex shapes such as hexagons or diamonds. The repetition, and the often wide variety of fabrics used, gives the whole surface of these quilts a rich visual texture.

A sampler quilt is composed of a number of different block designs which can be both pieced and appliquéd, and are then separated by sashing strips.

Appliqué quilts

The term appliqué derives from the French verb *appliquer*, meaning to put or lay on. Pieces of fabric are secured onto a background with hand or machine stitches. The technique of appliqué can lend itself to an organic or pictorial style of design in which naturalistic forms can be more accurately depicted. Popular motifs include fruit, flora and fauna. Also, the more organic, abstract motifs, in which curved shapes are used, can be more easily achieved with appliqué than with piecing. Appliqué quilts can be made in repeated units or blocks, or with one large motif covering the whole surface of the quilt.

Quilting

Quilting is the device that fastens the three layers of the quilt together in whatever method is chosen. It can be simply achieved with tied knots placed at regular intervals, or more elaborately with running stitches worked by hand or machine in a number of different ways. A simple quilting design may be composed of a grid worked in straight lines, whereas more intricate patterns can be achieved by using designs inspired by feathers, cables, fans, shells, and heart motifs.

Wholecloth quilts exploit the texture these stitches give to a quilt, as they form the principal decoration when there is no patchwork or appliqué. Additional texture is sometimes added by padding selected parts of the quilt in a technique known as "trapunto." Within these traditional categories, there are many variations and, of course, the possibility of your own creative input. The choice in fabrics, techniques, and colors makes this a fascinating craft for anybody who has an interest in needlework and a desire to make unique pieces of work that are useful and decorative.

An appliquéd quilt by Mary Kent, *Mary's Quilt.*

A wholecloth quilt by Sandie Lush, *Flame.*

A rich tradition

An interest in quilts, whether as a maker, collector, or student of textiles will almost inevitably lead to an interest in the history of the related crafts of patchwork, appliqué, and quilting, embracing as they do social history and the aesthetics of design and color, combined with practical sewing skills.

Evidence of the craft has been found in Egyptian tombs and in archeological remains on the Silk Road—an ancient trade route between China and India—in the form of carvings and pictures, as well as actual examples of patchwork. The word "quilt" itself derives from the Latin word *culcita*, meaning a mattress or pillow filled with something soft and warm, such as feathers, wool, or hair. Patchwork items are recorded as having been brought from the East by the Crusaders, but it was in the seventeenth and eighteenth centuries, when fine printed cottons were exported to the west by the East India Company, that patchwork became a popular pastime for ladies of the leisured classes with time on their hands.

Imported fabrics were considered a threat to British textile manufacturers and trade restrictions were imposed, making them scarce and expensive. Even tiny scraps were hoarded to be used in patchwork and appliqué, making a little go a long way. The surviving quilts from this period are the fine chintz appliqué and patchwork mosaic quilts, one of which, dated 1708, can still be seen at Levens Hall in Cumbria, Great Britain.

The luxuries of time for fancy needlework and expensive materials were afforded by only a few, and alongside these fine quilts, another type of patchwork was being made for utilitarian purposes. From homespun and less expensive cotton fabrics, simple shapes such as squares,

Baltimore album quilt, c.1840s.

rectangles, and triangles were pieced together with a running stitch—taking less time than the laborious "paper piecing" or "English" method that allowed for more intricate shapes.

A significant factor in the development of the quilt was the settlement of North America by Europeans. On arrival in the New World, basic supplies for the pioneers were short, and conservation and recycling of fabrics was a necessity. Trade restrictions decreed that fabrics must be bought from Britain, making them expensive, and at times unobtainable, so every scrap of fabric was hoarded to be used and reused in those first American quilts.

From basic beginnings, quilt makers began to develop traditions and designs which were to become uniquely American.

Quilt classics, such as geometric blocks, Baltimore appliqué, richly textured crazy quilts, and picture and story quilts, bear witness to the ingenuity and creativity of these early quilt makers.

Once the tops were ready, they were often quilted by groups of women at "quilting bees." The tops were set up with the batting and backing on a large quilting frame, and as many women as could fit around the edges stitched the three layers of the quilt together, often in just one day. Others helped by threading needles and preparing food for the party that often followed; these were events eagerly anticipated for communities often isolated through the winters by rough roads and bad weather.

In the early years of the twentieth century, machine-made bedding and work for women outside the home led to a decline in interest in quilt making. There was no longer the time nor the necessity for quilts to be made by hand.

After a period of decline, during which time quilts were seen as old-fashioned and consigned to attics or garages, there came a

Sunburst, American quilt, nineteenth century.

revival of interest. This was sparked partly by the exhibition of quilts staged at the Whitney Museum in New York in 1971 by Jonathan Holstein and Gail van der Hoof, and by American Bicentennial celebrations in 1976.

This renewed interest has inspired many people to push the design boundaries beyond tradition and to experiment with the medium of fabric and thread to produce not just quilts for beds but "art" quilts designed to be hung on walls. The possibilities in quilt making for working with color, patterns, and textures have been extended by the array of materials and equipment made available by contemporary designers and textile manufacturers.

The reasons for making quilts today have gone beyond the bounds of necessity. Quilt making remains one of the most accessible forms of creative expression. It is based on comprehensible design principles, uses the most elementary materials, and results in something with great visual impact that is both decorative and useful.

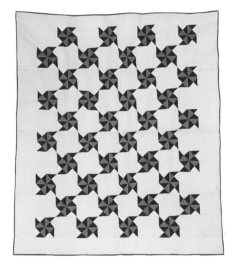

Pinwheel, American quilt, nineteenth century.

Lady of the Lake, Amish quilt, c.1930.

Parts of a quilt

The quilt consists of three layers in a "sandwich" of fabrics. Combinations of techniques, such as piecing and appliqué, are common in forming the top layer, and some form of quilting is necessary to secure the top layer to the middle layer of batting, and the backing fabric. Variations are endless, from the simple nine-patch to complex appliquéd quilts that are a challenge to the maker.

Quilting
The means of securing the three layers of the quilt together. There are a variety of ways of doing this, such as tying with decorative knots and stitching by hand or machine.

Quilt top
The top layer of the quilt. This can be pieced patchwork, appliqué, or cut as a single piece of fabric, as in wholecloth quilts.

Block
A design unit that can be pieced, plain, or appliquéd. Repeated over the surface of the quilt, it forms the decorative elements of a patchwork quilt. Blocks can be square, rectangular, hexagonal, or any geometric shape that will fit together either in repeat shapes or combinations.

Border
The final frame of fabric that surrounds the quilt top. This can be pieced, appliquéd, or plain. The outer edges of the border can also be shaped into scallops with rounded corners.

Batting
The middle layer or filling that will provide warmth and weight. This can be made from cotton, wool, silk, or synthetic fibers.

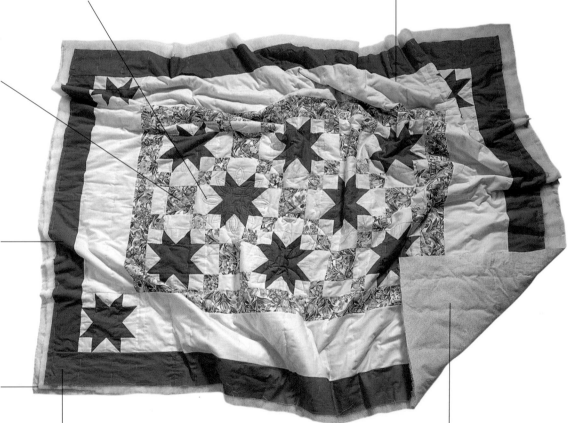

Square or butted corner
Border or binding strips sewn at right angles.

Backing
The back or bottom layer of the quilt sandwich. This is often one large piece of fabric, or it can be pieced from a variety of fabrics.

Quilting terms

Basting
Temporary stitches used to hold fabrics together with large hand or machine stitches or pins.

Bearding
The migration of fibers from the batting through to the quilt top. This causes a fuzzy coating on the quilt surface.

Bias
The diagonal grain of the fabric. Bias grain will stretch and is best used when making binding that will be applied to curves. True bias is at a 45° angle to both the lengthwise and crosswise grains. Woven fabric has the greatest amount of stretch on the bias.

Binding
The edging of a quilt which covers and holds all raw edges. Bindings may be plain or decorative.

Block
The design unit made from either patchwork or appliqué or a combination of the two repeated to make the quilt top. These can be straight or "on point."

Blocking
If a quilt has become misshapen or wrinkled in the making, blocking it out by applying steam, heat, and pressure will cure this.

Border
Decorative or plain fabric strips that run around the edges of a quilt top. Borders may be straight, curved, flowing, swagged, and may be pieced or quilted or both.

Design wall
A means of putting work in progress on a vertical surface to assess the design qualities. This can be a large pin board or a flannel wall.

Embroidery
Stitches applied to fabric to decorate and embellish the surface. Frequently used on crazy quilts.

Fat quarters
Pieces of fabrics, prints and solids, sold in color-coordinated bundles tied with ribbon or raffia. The fabric pieces measure about 18" × 22" (50 × 57 cm) and are a half yard (meter) cut in half down the fold. The size is more useful than the traditional quarter yard (meter).

Filling or filler
Another term for the batting; the middle layer of a quilt.

Finger-press
Rather than use an iron, seam allowances are pressed using the underside of a thumbnail.

Foundation
A base onto which patches can be stitched. Log Cabin and Crazy quilts were traditionally stitched to a foundation. This method has been developed to make the construction of intricate and small scale blocks easier.

Grain
The direction of the thread in a woven fabric. The lengthwise grain runs parallel with the selvage, the crosswise grain runs across the width, and the bias grain runs diagonally.

Hem
Finishing of the edge of a quilt or garment by folding over the fabric to the wrong side and slip stitching it in place. Stitches should not show on the right side.

Isometric paper
A graph paper marked out in a grid of equilateral triangles. Useful for drafting patterns with diamonds, hexagons, and octagons.

Loft
Refers to the thickness and springiness of the batting.

Miter
Finishing of a corner of a border or binding by joining at a 45° angle.

Pilling
The tendency for some fabric to form tiny balls of fiber on the surface with wear. This is more associated with synthetic rather than natural fabrics.

Press
The application of heat, steam, and pressure to flatten and smooth fabrics.

Reducing glass
The opposite of a magnifying glass. Useful to get an overall view of patchwork to determine the position of values and design elements in work in progress.

Rotary cutter
A sharp circular blade set in a handle that, when used in conjunction with the rotary ruler and mat, speeds up the cutting process and improves accuracy. With the use of the rotary cutting set, the need for many templates can be eliminated.

Sashing
Strips of fabric, plain or pieced, that are sewn between the square block units of a quilt.

Selvage
The finished edges that run the length of the fabric bolts on each side.

Sleeve
A fabric casing stitched to the back of the quilt at the top so that it can be hung.

Template
Pattern for marking fabrics for patchwork, appliqué, and quilting. These can be purchased ready made or you can make them from stiff card or template plastic.

Value
The lightness or darkness of a color. In a quilt, the arrangement of dark, medium, and light values are important in the definition of the pattern.

Window template
A template that is the outline of the patchwork or appliqué shape with a $1/4$" (0.75 cm) seam allowance. This is useful when centering a motif or using fabric in a directional way.

Fabrics

Quilt makers tend to be obsessive collectors. Not only do they buy fabric with a particular quilt in mind, they just collect fabric. It is a good idea to create a personal palette by sorting fabrics according to color. This exercise can produce some interesting results. It will clearly indicate your own preferences, and will undoubtedly reveal gaps in the range and suggest the variety of prints that you need for a complete palette.

The combination of prints and solid colors can also create particular styles and moods. Pastels of soft ice blue, soft pink, pale yellow, mint green, lavender, and apricot, combined with large floral prints will create a "shabby chic" look favored by many interior designers. In contrast, an Amish style uses rich, dark, solid fabrics. Country quilts can be achieved with the use of blues,

reds, golds, and greens in both geometrics and florals, with accents of purple together with strong beiges and tans. A taste of the East can be conjured up with the introduction of an Asian print as a focus, picking up on the strong color content for supporting fabrics.

As quilters come to own a vast array of fabrics, scrap quilts are possible. Scrap quilts of the nineteenth century are much admired for the stunning effects they achieve, incorporating an apparently random collection of fabric, that is, on closer inspection, carefully considered. Typically, browns, reds, black, greys, mustards, and indigoes, together with sharp accents of acid green and bubble-gum pink, are set against a background of varying light neutrals. Experiment with combining your scraps, using old quilts that you admire as inspiration.

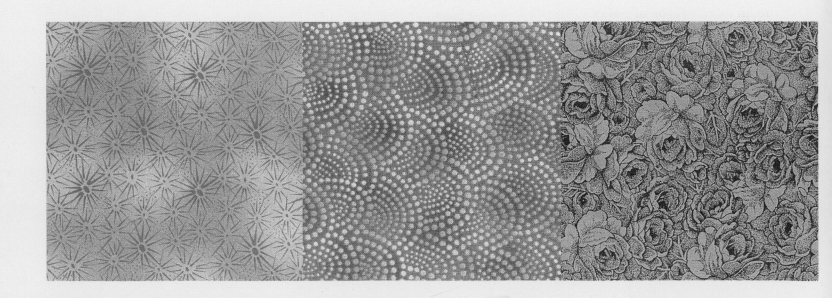

Types of quilting fabric

When selecting the type of fabric to use for quilt making, the first thing to consider is the fiber content. The favored fabric for a pieced quilt is 100 percent cotton. However, this is a rule that may be broken; for example, Victorian needlewomen were innovative designers who often used silks to fine effect.

Fabrics manufactured with "easy care" in mind contain a high polyester content but they are not easy to work, and are therefore not recommended for piecing and quilting. Wholecloth quilts give wonderful results with 100 percent cotton, although a variety of other fabrics will react with the light across the surface of the quilt to show off the mastery of the design and stitching.

Piecing or appliqué is easier with cotton as it retains its pressed form, which is an advantage when a crisp seam or a sharp appliqué edge is required, whereas polyester blends are manufactured to resist pressing. Cotton is more opaque than polyester, therefore reducing the problem of seams showing through to the front of the quilt. Cotton fibers do not pill as a result of wear so that quilts will not be covered by unsightly fiber balls that can result from abrasion of fabrics with some polyester content. Needles and pins pass through cotton fibers much easier than through polyester blends, and cotton fabrics stick to each other and do not slip while being pieced in small patches.

It is important to understand the structure of the fabric when cutting out your pieces.

Fabrics are woven by laying threads down lengthwise and weaving threads crosswise through them. The number of threads in a square section indicates the thread count. High thread counts appear when the component threads are fine, and

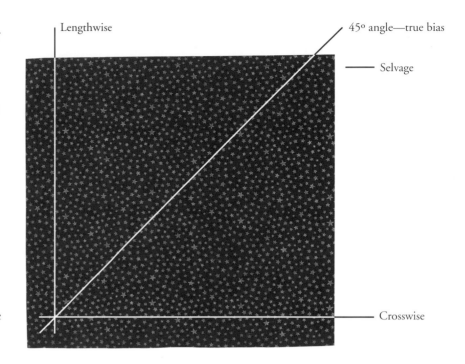

a lower thread count appears when the thread is coarser or more openly woven. Openly woven fabric will shrink when washed and should be avoided for quilting.

The woven threads comprise three parts: the selvage, the grain, and the bias. The selvage is the lengthwise edge of the fabric where the threads are doubled when woven. It is difficult to sew through these threads because they are woven extremely tight, so the selvage edges are never used for blocks and piecing.

The lengthwise grain runs parallel to the selvage edges of the fabric. This has the least amount of stretch. Printed fabric is usually printed straight along the lengthwise grain.

The crosswise grain runs across the width of the fabric between the two selvage edges. There is a little more stretch in this direction and printed fabric is rarely printed straight across the crosswise grain.

The bias grain is at any angle across the fabric other than lengthwise or crosswise. True bias runs at a 45° angle and has the greatest amount of stretch.

Selecting colors of fabric

Color is the most essential part of a quilt, even more than the precise piecing or the fine appliqué. We all see color differently, so color choice is intensely personal. A fabric that one person may find dull may be considered delicate by another. Fabric designers use different harmonies when creating fabric, and quilt makers can use the same harmonies to help select fabrics for a quilt.

When selecting the colors of fabric for a project, the choice may be determined by the room in which the quilt is to live, or simply by personal preference. Whatever the reason, colors need to be combined in an appealing way. Many quilt makers feel at a disadvantage at this stage if they have had no formal art training. While there is no right or wrong way to combine colors, some knowledge of color theory is useful.

Examining the way colors relate on a color wheel provides a view of how color

tones will work together as solids and with print fabrics in a quilt.

The center of the color wheel shows the three primary colors: red, blue, and yellow. They are pure colors and cannot be obtained by mixing other colors; however, mixing primary colors together creates all other colors. Mixing equal proportions of two primary colors creates a secondary color. Mixing a primary with a secondary color creates a tertiary color.

The central ring of the color wheel illustrated shows the hues that lie between the primary and secondary colors. As the ratio of its component colors can be varied, color can have an infinite number of hues. The colors in the inner ring are lighter than the hues, as they have been mixed with white; these are called tints. In the outer ring, the colors are darker, as they have been mixed with black; these are called shades.

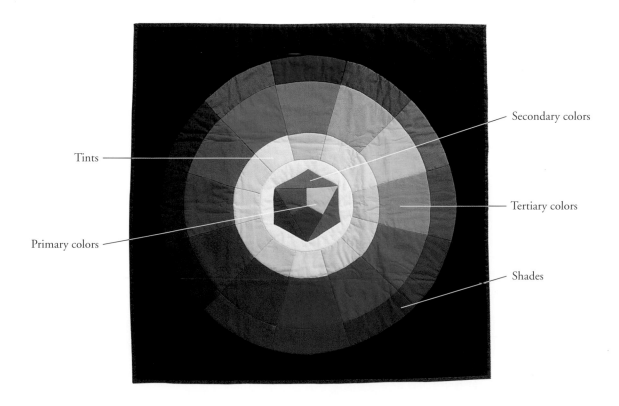

Tints

Primary colors

Secondary colors

Tertiary colors

Shades

Warm and cool colors

We accord different colors with qualities of warmth and coolness. Reds, yellows, and oranges are warm colors, and are associated with heat and light. Cool colors, such as blues, greens, and violets, are more subtle. Splashes of warm colors can enliven a cool quilt, while cool accents in a predominantly warm quilt can add depth and define shape.

The association between color and temperature can help us create quilts for particular places. A warm colored quilt gives the illusion of warmth in a cold room. A cool colored quilt introduces a note of calm in a busy setting.

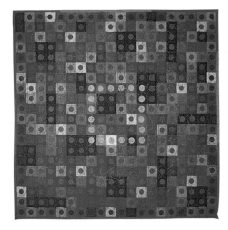

Monochromatic color schemes

Although the term "monochromatic" conjures up a vision of black and white, it more accurately refers to the combining of tints, shades, and tones from one color, and is one of the easiest color schemes to put together. However, monochromatic quilts can be dull unless an effort is made to select fabrics that differ in value and scale. Including some neutrals is a good way of providing variety without changing the character of a monochromatic scheme. A splash of bright fabric within such a scheme, or an accent in another color can enhance the combination.

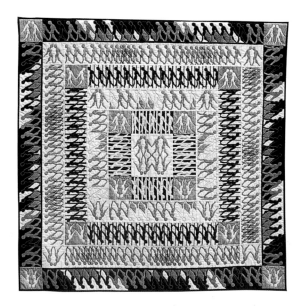

Rainbow colors

When we enjoy a child's painting, it will often feature a rainbow. The combination of all 12 colors from the color wheel appeals to everyone. If you use just the pure hues in a rainbow quilt, you produce an almost luminous effect. Combining them with white can allow the colors to be seen with their true tonal value, and combining them with black gives contrast.

continued on the next page...

Selecting colors of fabrics (continued)

Analogous colors

Colors that are next to each other on the color wheel are said to be analogous. They are easy to work with and, depending on their position on the color wheel, they can be either warm or cool in their effect.

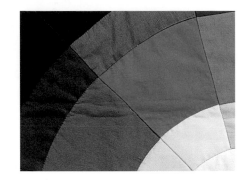

Complementary colors

Colors that are opposite each other on the color wheel are complementary; for example, red and green, or yellow and purple. Complementary colors harmonize well with each other but beware of using the colors in equal proportions. Two opposite colors will produce opposing warm and cool colors. Warm colors will dominate a quilt and attract the eye, so unless you want this effect, reduce the amount of warm color in the quilt, or use tints and shades to reduce the impact. The addition of neutrals to the color scheme will allow the eye to rest and the stronger colors will be prominent.

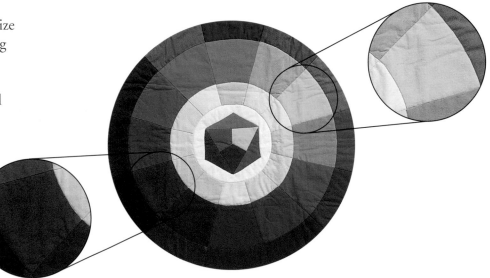

Triadic colors

This color scheme brings together three colors that lie in a triangle on the color wheel; for example, yellow, red, and blue, or orange, green, and purple. This selection is very popular with designers of multi-print fabrics.

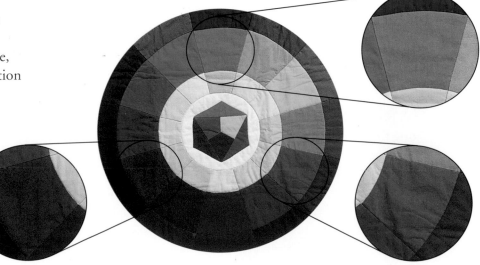

Arranging your fabric palette

Fabrics, of course, do not come only in solid colors. It is easy to identify the hue of a solid fabric. To determine the hue of a print is more difficult; stand back a little and squint at your fabric to see which colors dominate. The color you see in each fabric will determine its place in your personal palette.

Fabrics can be loosely divided into four categories:

- **Print fabrics**, which in turn can be subdivided into florals, foliage, novelty, abstract, and geometric prints.

- **Neutrals**, such as white, cream, black and gray.

- **Solids**, which will be hues, tints, or shades.

- **Tone-on-tone** fabrics, which read as solid from a distance but are actually made from a solid dyed or printed fabric with an overprint in a darker shade.

Using patterned fabrics

Patchwork made solely from solid fabrics can look stark, so unless this is the effect you want to create, avoid using too many solid fabrics. Wonderful choices of printed fabrics are now available, and using a mixture of these prints can create stunning effects.

At one time, quilt makers felt that they had to use small prints for their patchwork. However, mixing the scale of prints in a quilt adds variety and appeal. Small prints bring a soft, textured feel to patchwork without distracting the eye, and can be used to unify areas of color. Large-scale prints, on the other hand, create interest on a quilt when viewed from a distance. Novelty or conversational prints are fun to

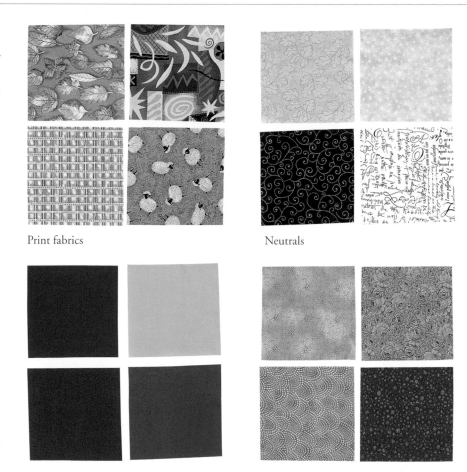

Print fabrics

Neutrals

Solids

Tone-on-tone

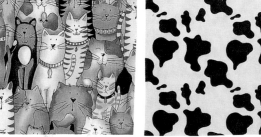

Novelty prints

Geometric fabrics

work with, and although usually associated with children's quilts, can also add an element of surprise to a more formal piece of patchwork.

Geometric or directional fabrics, whether woven or printed, create movement by encouraging the eye to move over the surface of a quilt. They lend themselves to a modern and dramatic effect or to the charm of a homespun quilt.

continued on the next page…

Tonal values

An attractive quilt will have a visual texture. This can be achieved by combining different scales and types of prints, and by introducing tones. Single color tones can be placed on a scale from light to dark; their relative position on the scale is known as their tonal value. To determine the tonal value of a selection of fabrics, lay them in a line and gradually close your eyes while staring at the fabrics; the darkest will disappear from your view first and the lightest last. It is easy to determine the tonal value of fabrics in the same color family, but more difficult with a mixture of colors, as sometimes light and bright can become confused. A black and white photocopy of the fabrics will more easily determine the tonal value of each one; you can also look through a value finder tool.

You may find you collect a range of fabrics all with medium tonal value. To expand your selection include dark and light fabrics. If you combine tones of equal value, you will produce a one-dimensional effect, but by including a variety of values you introduce contrasts and pick out shapes and forms within a design. The placement of different tonal values can give completely different effects when the blocks are combined.

 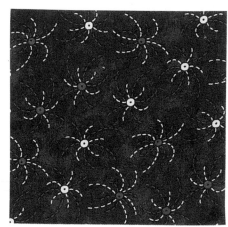

Using a focus fabric

Many quilters use a method of selecting fabric by first choosing one fabric they really love—the focus fabric—and then choosing other fabrics that pick out colors in the first fabric. By varying the nature of the prints—mixing large prints with small, flowery patterns with geometric, or light with dark—style, color, and textures start to come together. It is surprising how easy color selection becomes.

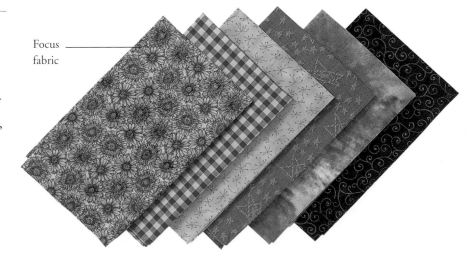

Focus fabric

Preparing fabric

Awareness of colorfastness and shrinkage in the choice of fabrics for quilting is essential. Whether to prewash or not lies in understanding fabric.

Colorfastness is the term used to describe whether color bleeds from fabric when it is washed. Color may transfer to another fabric if it comes in contact while wet. It is advisable not to leave fabric stacked together while wet, or to fold a wet quilt. Prewashing a fabric is not a guarantee against color loss but the temperature at which to wash cotton fabrics can affect their ability to retain color. Manufacturers recommend that cottons be washed at a temperature of 80 to 85°F (12 to 15°C); a higher temperature will affect colorfastness.

To test for colorfastness, cut small swatches from your chosen fabric and immerse them in a glass jar of lukewarm water. If the water remains clear, you do not need to wash them before using in a quilt. If color bleeds into the water, you may choose to wash the complete piece of fabric until the water is clear and then test again. If color continues to bleed, do not use the fabric for your quilt. Very few fabrics are problematic, but do beware of deep reds, blues, and purples.

Washing large pieces of fabric may cause shrinkage, but when cutting small pieces to join together, the noticeable shrinkage will be apparent only if the batting shrinks, as patchwork will shrink in line with the batting. Tumble-drying and ironing wet fabric will also cause shrinkage. If you tumble dry fabrics, remove them from the dryer while they are still damp.

Selecting backing

Once a great deal of time and effort has gone into the completion of a quilt top, you will want to choose a backing fabric to complement the design.

A multicolored print fabric will camouflage uneven or missed quilting stitches, whereas a solid fabric or muslin on the back can act as a showcase for excellent workmanship.

The backing fabric should be the same weight and fiber content as the top fabrics. The only exception to this rule is when working a wholecloth bed quilt. If you have chosen a silk or satin, or other slippery fabric for the top, it is advisable to choose a cotton fabric for the backing to help ensure the quilt stays on the bed.

Avoid using bed sheets, as they have a high thread count and will be difficult to quilt. A number of print fabrics and muslin are available in 90" (229 cm) and 108" (274 cm) widths. However, the majority of fabrics are 44" or 45" (112 cm to 114 cm) wide, and will therefore need to be joined.

Selecting batting

Batting is the filling that is placed between the quilt top and the backing to give loft and warmth to a quilt. Although this element of a quilt is unseen, it is perhaps the most important part as it provides not only the warmth and loft, but affects the ease of quilting and the drape of the quilt, whether it be a bed quilt or wall-hanging.

Batting is available in various fiber content: cotton, cotton and polyester blends, wool, silk, and 100 percent polyester. Each reacts differently to the quilting process, and has different characteristics regarding shrinkage, washability, and ease of quilting. Cotton is non-allergenic, while polyester and even wool may be a problem for people prone to allergies.

Cotton and cotton/polyester blend

Cotton and cotton/polyester blend battings are recommended for machine quilting as they stick to the fabric. Some cotton batting has been stabilized by having the fibers needled together or a scrim surface added. Although this is helpful for machine quilting, it makes hand quilting more difficult. For hand quilting, choose natural, unbleached cotton or cotton/polyester blends. The process of bleaching dries the fibers making bleached products unsuitable for hand work.

Cotton batting will soften with age, and it will shrink. If used with unwashed fabrics, the entire quilt will shrink with the first wash, producing a softly rumpled, antique look. If you do not want this effect, use cotton batting that can be prewashed. Always follow the manufacturer's instructions.

Wool

Wool is very warm and lofty, and is light to handle. It is extremely easy to hand quilt and is also a much favored batting for machine quilting.

Wool is washable, does not need prewashing, and little or no shrinkage will occur. As wool can absorb a large percentage of its own weight in moisture without feeling damp, it is the ideal choice for cooler climates.

Silk

Silk is the most costly natural fiber, but a lightweight and warm batting.

Polyester

Low-loft 100 percent polyester batting is the most commonly used batting for hand quilting. A good-quality, soft, even polyester batting makes it easier to achieve steady, even quilt stitches.

Polyester batting has a higher loft than natural fibers, such as cotton and wool, and it does not shrink. Its disadvantage is that it does not "breathe" so some people may find it uncomfortable to sleep under.

Wool

Cotton/polyester

100 percent polyester

Cotton

How much to buy

Determining the size of the finished quilt

Before making a quilt, you will need to know the finished size. If making a quilt for a bed, measure the mattress top and then add the length of drop you would like, plus allowances for the quilt going over pillows. If you would like the quilt to cover the mattress and be used with a dust ruffle, you will have a drop of approximately 13" (33 cm). If you wish the quilt to come down to the floor, you will need a drop of approximately 21" (53 cm).

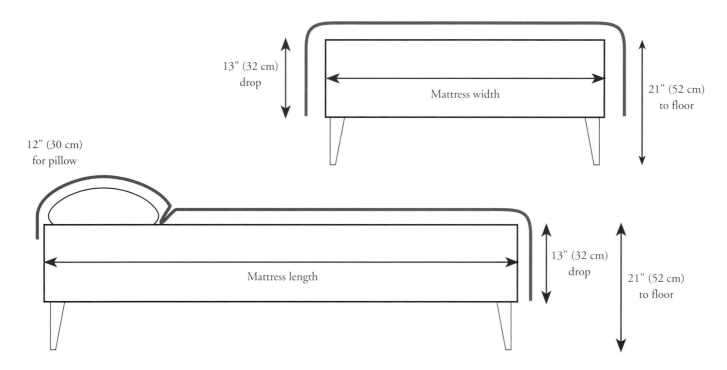

The following tables use some standard mattress sizes and make allowances for drop; the amount of quilt needed to tuck over the pillow is a guide only, so for different mattress sizes, you will need to create your own set of measurements, using the diagram to help you.

Standard measures

	Mattress	13" drop and 12" over pillow		21" drop and 12" over pillow	
		Width	Length	Width	Length
Crib	23" × 46"	40"	60"		
Twin	39" × 75"	65"	99"	84"	107"
Double	54" × 75"	84"	106"	100"	114"
Queen	60" × 80"	90"	112"	106"	120"
King	72" × 84"	102"	116"	118"	124"

Metric measures

	Mattress	32 cm drop and 30 cm over pillow		52 cm drop and 30 cm over pillow	
		Width	Length	Width	Length
Crib	57 × 115 cm	100 cm	150 cm		
Twin	98 × 187 cm	162 cm	247 cm	210 cm	267 cm
Double	135 × 187 cm	210 cm	265 cm	250 cm	285 cm
Queen	150 × 200 cm	225 cm	280 cm	265 cm	300 cm
King	180 × 210 cm	255 cm	290 cm	295 cm	310 cm

continued on the next page…

Once you have determined the size for your quilt, consider the setting you would like; for example, the number and size of blocks, the style of sashings, the width of borders. Each choice will determine how a setting fits into the finished dimensions. Careful planning at this stage is very important.

The charts below provide a guide to determine the final size of quilt, given the choice of different block settings. Two tables are given for each setting, for standard or metric measures. Work with one set of measurements, and remain with that set throughout.

Straight block setting

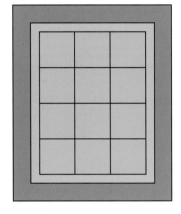

Standard measures

Quilt size	Crib 45" × 60"			Single 65" × 90"		Double 84" × 96"	Queen 90" × 112"	King 102" × 116"
Block size	6"	9"	12"	9"	12"	12"	12"	12"
Number of blocks across	6	4	3	6	5	6	7	7
Number of blocks down	8	5	4	9	7	7	8	8
Border width	4"	4"	4"	5"	4"	6"	6"	8"
Final size	44" × 56"	44" × 62"	44" × 56"	64" × 91"	68" × 92"	84" × 96"	96" × 108"	100" × 112"

Metric measures

Quilt size	Crib 110 × 150 cm			Single 160 × 225 cm		Double 210 × 240 cm	Queen 225 × 280 cm	King 255 × 290 cm
Block size	15 cm	22.5 cm	30 cm	22.5 cm	30 cm	30 cm	30 cm	30 cm
Number of blocks across	6	4	3	6	5	6	6	7
Number of blocks down	8	5	4	9	7	7	8	8
Border width	10 cm	10 cm	10 cm	12.5 cm	10 cm	15 cm	15 cm	20 cm
Final size	110 × 140 cm	110 × 132.5 cm	110 × 140 cm	160 × 227.5 cm	170 × 230 cm	210 × 240 cm	210 × 270 cm	250 × 280 cm

Straight block setting with sashing

Standard measures

Quilt size	Crib 45" × 60"			Single 65" × 90"		Double 84" × 96"	Queen 90" × 112"	King 102" × 116"
Block size	6"	9"	12"	9"	12"	12"	12"	12"
Width of sash	2"	2"	3"	2"	3"	3"	3"	3"
Number of blocks across	4	3	2	6	4	5	5	6
Number of blocks down	6	4	3	7	5	6	7	7
Border width	4"	4"	4"	4"	4"	4"	4"	4"
Final size	42" × 58"	43" × 54"	41" × 56"	72" × 89"	71" × 86"	86" × 101"	86" × 113"	101" × 113"

Metric measures

Quilt size	Crib 110 × 150 cm			Single 160 × 225 cm		Double 210 × 240 cm	Queen 225 × 280 cm	King 255 × 290 cm
Block size	15 cm	22.5 cm	30 cm	22.5 cm	30 cm	30 cm	30 cm	30 cm
Width of sash	5 cm	5 cm	7.5 cm	5 cm	7.5 cm	7.5 cm	7.5 cm	7.5 cm
Number of blocks across	4	3	2	5	4	5	5	6
Number of blocks down	6	4	3	6	5	6	7	7
Border width	10 cm	10 cm	10 cm	10 cm	10 cm	10 cm	10 cm	10 cm
Final size	110 × 145 cm	112.5 × 140 cm	102.5 × 140 cm	162.5 × 190 cm	177.5 × 215 cm	215 × 252.5 cm	215 × 290 cm	252.5 × 290 cm

Diagonal setting without sashing

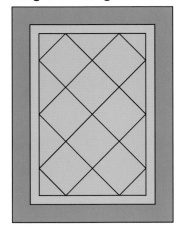

Standard measures

Quilt size	Crib 45" × 60"			Single 65" × 90"		Double 84" × 96"	Queen 90" × 112"	King 102" × 116"
Block size	6"	9"	12"	9"	12"	12"	12"	12"
Diagonal of block	8½"	12¾"	17"	12¾"	17"	17"	17"	17"
Number of blocks across	4	3	2	5	3	4	5	5
Number of blocks down	6	4	3	6	5	5	6	6
Border width	5"	4"	5"	6"	6"	6"	4"	8"
Final size	44" × 61"	46¼" × 59"	44" × 61"	63" × 88½"	63' × 97"	80" × 97"	93" × 114"	101" × 118"

Metric measures

Quilt size	Crib 110 × 150 cm			Single 160 × 225 cm		Double 210 × 240 cm	Queen 225 × 280 cm	King 255 × 290 cm
Block size	15 cm	22.5 cm	30 cm	22.5 cm	30 cm	30 cm	30 cm	30 cm
Diagonal of block	21.5 cm	32 cm	42.5 cm	32 cm	42.5 cm	42.5 cm	42.5 cm	42.5 cm
Number of blocks across	4	3	2	4	3	4	5	5
Number of blocks down	6	4	3	6	4	5	6	6
Border width	12.5 cm	10 cm	12.5 cm	15 cm	15 cm	15 cm	10 cm	20 cm
Final size	111 × 154 cm	116 × 148 cm	110 × 152.5 cm	158 × 222 cm	157.5 × 200 cm	200 × 242.5 cm	232.5 × 275 cm	252.5 × 295 cm

Diagonal setting with sashing

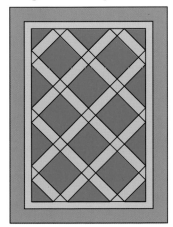

Standard measures

Quilt size	Crib 45" × 60"			Single 65" × 90"		Double 84" × 96"	Queen 90" × 112"	King 102" × 116"
Block size	6"	9"	12"	9"	12"	12"	12"	12"
Diagonal of block	8½"	12¾"	17"	12¾"	17"	17"	17"	17"
Width of sashing	2"	3"	2"	3"	3"	3"	3"	3"
Diagonal of sashing	2¾"	4¼"	2¾"	4¼"	4¼"	4¼"	4¼"	4¼"
Number of blocks across	3	2	2	3	2	3	4	5
Number of blocks down	4	3	2	4	3	4	5	5
Border width	4"	4"	4"	5"	8"	8"	3"	3"
Final size	45" × 56½"	46¾" × 63¾"	50½" × 50½"	65¼" × 82¼"	62¾" × 84"	84" × 105"	95" × 116⅕"	116½" × 116½"

Metric measures

Quilt size	Crib 110 × 150 cm			Single 160 × 225 cm		Double 210 × 240 cm	Queen 225 × 280 cm	King 255 × 290 cm
Block size	15 cm	22.5 cm	30 cm	22.5 cm	30 cm	30 cm	30 cm	30 cm
Diagonal of block	21.5 cm	32 cm	42.5 cm	32 cm	42.5 cm	42.5 cm	42.5 cm	42.5 cm
Width of sashing	5 cm	7.5 cm	5 cm	7.5 cm	7.5 cm	7.5 cm	7.5 cm	7.5 cm
Diagonal of sashing	7.25 cm	10.75 cm	7.25 cm	10.75 cm	10.75 cm	10.75 cm	10.75 cm	10.75 cm
Number of blocks across	3	2	2	3	2	3	4	5
Number of blocks down	4	3	2	4	3	4	5	5
Border width	10 cm	10 cm	10 cm	12.5 cm	20 cm	20 cm	7.5 cm	7.5 cm
Final size	113.5 × 142.5 cm	116.25 × 159 cm	126.75 × 126.75 cm	164 × 206.75 cm	157.75 × 210.5 cm	210.5 × 263.75 cm	238.75 × 292 cm	292 × 292 cm

continued on the next page...

Calculating yardage for blocks

Estimating how much fabric to buy is not as difficult as it may seem, but first it may help to draw out a sketch plan onto graph paper, noting measurements and drawing the shapes onto it.

If you are making a quilt with the same block throughout you will be able to count how many of each shape you will need, and it will then be possible to calculate how many will fit across the width of the fabric. Remember to include seam allowances on all shapes (see Seam allowances, page 40).

If you are making a sampler quilt, where every block is different, and where you may not know at the start exactly where you will use each fabric, a more approximate calculation needs to be made. For the blocks you will need to know the yardage needed to cover the bed, plus 25 percent to allow for the seam allowances. Then, divide this total yardage by the total number of fabrics you intend to use. The charts below give some examples.

Calculating yardage for sashing

Sashing is easy to calculate, as you are cutting strips across the usable width of the fabric, usually about 42" (107 cm) to the required width (to include seam allowance) of the sashing. You then sub-cut into the correct lengths. The charts below give basic measurements based on 3" (7.5 cm) wide sashing set with 3" (7.5 cm) setting squares

Calculating yardage for borders

To calculate the yardage for borders, once again a sketch plan is useful, especially if you want borders without joins, and longer than the width of the fabric. Cut border strips to the required widths, down the length of the fabric before cutting out the smaller pieces for the quilt. Remember that quilting may reduce the size of the quilt so it is always advisable to cut border strips generously as they can be trimmed to the desired size after quilting.

Standard measures

Quilt size	Number of 12" blocks	Total yardage	Amount each of 7 fabrics
Single	15	5½ yd.	¾ yd.
Double	20	5½ yd.	¾ yd.
Queen	24	7 yd.	1 yd.
King	30	10½ yd.	1½ yd.

Metric measures

Quilt size	Number of 30 cm blocks	Total meterage	Amount each of 7 fabrics
Single	15	5.1 m	70–75 cm
Double	20	5.1 m	70–75 cm
Queen	24	6.5 m	90–95 cm
King	30	9.7 m	1.4 m

Standard measures

Quilt size	Number of sashing strips cut 12½" × 3½"	Yardage for sashing	Number of setting squares cut 3½"	Yardage for setting squares
Single	38	1½ yd.	24	⅜ yd.
Double	49	1¾ yd.	25	⅜ yd.
Queen	58	2 yd.	35	⅜ yd.
King	71	2½ yd.	42	⅜ yd.

Metric measures

Quilt size	Number of sashing strips cut 31.5 × 9 cm	Amount of fabric for sashing	Number of setting squares cut 9 cm	Amount of fabric for setting squares
Single	38	1.2 m	24	20 cm
Double	49	1.6 m	25	30 cm
Queen	58	1.8 m	35	30 cm
King	71	2.2 m	42	40 cm

Equipment

One of the advantages of beginning patchwork and quilting is that you may already have the basic items necessary to begin so there is not a large initial outlay, and you can build up your equipment as your experience and skill develop. Remember when buying new tools to go for the best quality you can afford.

Keep your best scissors for cutting fabric only and have a separate pair for paper. A fine pair of embroidery scissors is useful for snipping threads and cutting seam allowances. There is a wide variety of different types of pins each useful for its own specialty, the glass-headed variety are easier to see and longer and finer than the regulation dressmaking pins. Have a mixture of needle sizes for general hand sewing; Sharps number 8 or 9 are a good standard to begin with. It is hard at first to get used to using a thimble but this will be essential, especially for hand quilting, so persevere and it will soon become second nature when hand sewing. Other items which make up a good sewing kit are tape measure, seam ripper, fabric markers, and a variety of colored threads.

A sewing machine will speed up the process of construction for many methods of patchwork, and the variety of makes and models can be confusing to the uninitiated. There are several models available with specially designed features for the quilter. When buying a new sewing machine, once again choose the best your budget will allow, and especially take advice from experienced quilters before buying.

A rotary cutting set, consisting of a cutter, ruler, and mat will speed up the cutting out process considerably. Look out for a short course, maybe run by your local quilting supply store or guild, on how to use this equipment safely and effectively. A few drafting tools to make templates, such as a basic geometry set, colored pencils, and graph paper, both isometric and squared, will be useful for the initial design stages.

A visit to a quilt supplier will demonstrate the huge number of gadgets available, but just remember that beautiful quilts were made before any of these items were manufactured with just fabrics, needle and thread and the most essential attribute for creating your own heirloom may be an enthusiasm for the color, texture, and pattern that is uniquely a quilt.

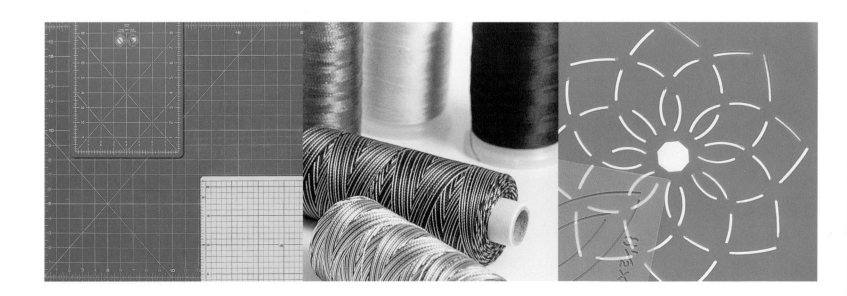

Cutting tools

Scissors

To successfully cut fabric for piecing and patchwork you need good-quality scissors which should be well balanced, move freely and unhindered by the screw, and close with even pressure right to the tip. If you are left-handed you can obtain left-handed scissors. Choose scissors that fulfill those criteria, but are also comfortable in your hand. Long blades give smooth cuts on long lines, while short-bladed scissors are for fine work. Finely serrated blades provide more control. Thread scissors or snips are invaluable for close work, whether hand or machine stitching.

Whichever scissors you choose for cutting fabric, keep them exclusively for that purpose and use a separate pair of utility or general-purpose scissors for cutting paper, card, and plastic.

Rotary cutters

Rotary cutters differ by the size of the blades, which can be 15 mm, 28 mm, 45 mm, or 60 mm set into both straight and curved handles. The most common size is 45 mm. Larger blades enable you to cut through several layers of fabric, while smaller cutters are ideal for trimming or cutting curves.

A straight-handled cutter should fit into the crease of your palm and your index finger should rest comfortably on the ridged area of the handle. Curved handle cutters are designed in order for the user to hold the ridged area with the thumb.

Before buying a cutter, try different sizes and different handles. Over time, it makes sense to build up a collection of rotary cutters.

Safety Note

Always keep the safety cover in place when not in use. Never leave the cutter open on the board.

Cutting mats

A cutting mat is essential when rotary cutting to provide the surface on which to cut and prevent dulling of the rotary cutter blade.

Mats are manufactured in a variety of sizes and in hard and soft, or layered plastic, and are designed with or without markings. Hard and soft mats can dull rotary cutter blades quicker than layered mats, and layered mats are sometimes referred to as self-healing, as the mat closes up again after each cut. Buy the largest board that you can afford. An 18" × 24" (46 × 61 cm) is the most convenient size if you need to transport it frequently.

Use the markings on the board, not to measure, as all measuring should be done with a special rotary cutting ruler, but to square up fabric or quilt blocks for cutting.

Store the board flat. If it is rolled or bent, it can become warped. Heat will also warp the board and the cold will make it brittle, so store it out of direct sunlight and at an ambient temperature.

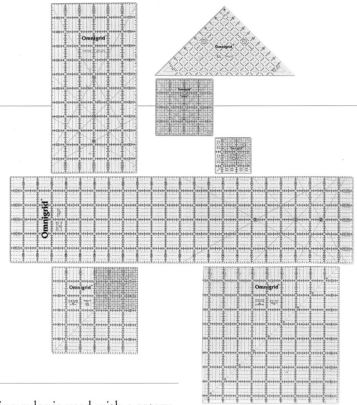

Rulers

A rotary cutting ruler is used with a rotary cutter and cutting mat to cut accurate shapes from multiple layers of fabric. The rulers are made of thick, clear acrylic, in a variety of sizes, with a variety of colored markings. The number, the spacing, and the thickness of the lines vary between brands. Some have few lines; some have lines every $\frac{1}{8}$" (0.3 cm); others have measures reading in both directions, making them easy to read whether you are right- or left-handed. Select a ruler with marked angles of 30°, 45° and 60°. The more lines the ruler has, the more useful you will find it as your quilting develops.

When buying your first ruler, purchase a good-quality 6" × 24" (15 cm × 61 cm) one that allows you to cut long strips from fabric with only one fold. Add a shorter length ruler for sub-cutting, and square rulers with a bias line for cutting across the diagonal. It is advisable to purchase rulers of the same brand, to ensure cutting accuracy, as there are slight variations in the markings by different manufacturers. Specialty rulers are available for specific shapes, including triangles, pineapple, kaleidoscope, and scrap savers. Rulers should be stored flat on a shelf or hung against a wall so that they do not "bow."

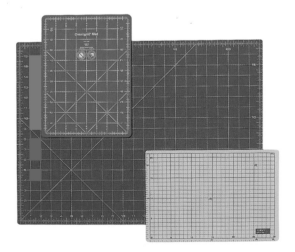

Marking tools

You will need a good selection of marking tools, including markers that can be used on card and plastic to make templates, and markers that can be used on fabrics to trace and outline patterns.

Marking templates

To ensure that you do not cut a larger template than is required, use a fine permanent marker to draw accurate template shapes. Always test markers to ensure they provide a fine permanent line on the chosen template material; the marks should not wipe off onto your hands or be transferred to the fabric.

Marking fabric

Marking tools will be needed to mark the cutting and sewing lines onto fabric. The marks are intended to be temporary so should wash out. Do not select permanent markers for this purpose.

Lead pencil marks are the most difficult to remove from fabric so use them lightly and with caution. A hard-leaded mechanical pencil gives a fine, light line that will often be hidden with your stitches. There are many washable, semi-hard, wax-based pencils available for marking on the right or the wrong side of fabric. Silver and white wax-based pencils are the most versatile as they show on both light and dark fabrics. Many art suppliers sell water-soluble pencils in a variety of colors. The colors allow you to choose shades that leave only very faint lines to quilt along. With all pencils, maintain a sharp point at all times, so keep a pencil sharpener in your sewing box.

Chalk-based marks are very easy to remove from the surface of fabric, but they are very temporary and can rub off too easily. If you use chalk to mark quilting lines, be aware that you will not be able to mark large areas at a time, as the marks will easily rub off. Chalk marks, however, are ideal for small areas or for those who prefer to mark their quilting lines as they go.

Water- and air-soluble pens, which look much like fiber-tip pens, can become permanent if exposed to heat, while others are removable by ironing. With all such pens, read the instructions first.

Test all marking tools on spare fabric before using them. Check for clarity of line, and that the marks can be washed out or rubbed off without putting undue stress on the fabric.

Threads

You will need threads for basting, piecing, quilting, and appliqué.

For both hand and machine piecing, match the fiber content of the sewing thread with that of the fabric; that is, natural fabrics need to be stitched with natural threads, and synthetic fabrics with synthetic threads. As a general rule, the thread used needs to be weaker than the fabric. For example, cotton fabric should be stitched with 100 percent cotton thread, and never be stitched with polyester thread, which is very strong thread and will wear at the fabric, eventually cutting through the seams. Better to replace broken thread than to have to replace damaged or worn fabric.

Threads come in different weights and thickness. The preferred thread for hand or machine pieced cotton quilts is 50/3. The 50 signifies weight and 3 signifies the number of ply twisted into the thread. The higher the weight number, the finer the thread; the more ply, the stronger the thread.

When piecing, by hand or machine, a neutral colored thread will be most appropriate for all the pieces, but when hand appliquéing, the thread should match the appliquéd fabric as closely as possible.

There are many decorative threads available, including rayon threads and fine metallic threads, which can be used with 50/3 on the bobbin. There are heavier decorative threads that can be wound onto the bobbin to quilt from the back, a technique that is often referred to as "bobbin drawing." Nylon monofilament can be used to machine quilt in the ditch or when the "hand quilting" stitch is chosen on a sewing machine, and for invisible hand or machine appliqué while using the blind stitch. When appliquéing by machine a 60/2 embroidery thread is good for satin stitch, or a heavier thread, like 30/3, or even a jeans thread, for blanket stitching.

Sewing equipment

Hand needles

Hand piecing, appliqué, quilting, and also basting require different types of needles.

"Sharps," which are long, thin needles (available in 5, 7, 8, 9, 10, and 12) vary in length from 1" to 1½" (2.5 cm to 3.75 cm). The larger the number, the shorter and finer the needle; for example, a size 12 is very fine and about 1" (2.5 cm) long. Although there will always be slight variations between different manufacturers, size 9 or 10 is ideal for piecing, while size 12 is good for fine appliqué (the latter are often sold as hand appliqué needles rather than sharps).

"Betweens" are the needles reserved for hand quilting. They are short, sturdy needles available in sizes 7, 8, 9, 10, and 12. They vary in length from 1" to 1¼" (2.5 cm to 3 cm); again, the higher the number, the shorter the needle. Use the shortest needle you can handle—short needles lead to short stitches. Start with size 9 and work toward size 12. Some manufacturers now produce size 11, which has the strength of a 10 and the length of a 12, which is helpful if you are prone to gripping needles tightly and bending them. "Big stitch" quilting or Sashiko uses the specialized Sashiko needles or embroidery needles, size 5 or 7. "Milliners" or "Darners" sizes 3 to 9 are good for the long simple stitches for basting as they range in length from 2" to 2½" (5 cm to 6.25 cm).

Machine needles

The choice of needle is critical to achieve a smooth stitch when machine sewing. Use a good-quality needle and start every new project with a new needle. A machine needle has a life of three to four sewing hours before it becomes blunt, resulting in poor quality or skipped stitches.

Sewing machine manufacturers will recommend a size and type of needle in the machine's manual and it is also often imprinted on the machine in the bobbin area. In the majority of cases, the needle recommended is 705N-universal, the most versatile needle. It has a slight ball end that allows the needle to part the yarns of the fabric rather than split them.

The smaller the size, the finer the needle. Choose a needle for piecing that is appropriate for the weight of the cloth. Quilting needles are sharp and strong while still being fine; a 75/11 is a good size. Fine jeans needles are also good for machine quilting, but again look for the finer needles.

When foundation piecing, where you are sewing through paper that is to be torn away from the back of the work, work with a larger needle and a small stitch; a size 90/14 is ideal.

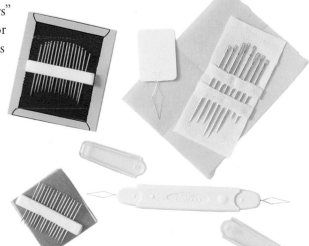

Pins

When hand piecing and hand appliquéing, pins are essential, although they are used less for machine piecing. Choose your pins carefully; those sold as quilting pins are often too large in diameter and will distort seams. Silk pins, fine patchwork pins, fine glass-headed pins, or long flower head pins, are best for hand and machine piecing. Small appliqué pins are available for positioning pieces to a background fabric. They are very short and fine so that threads do not become entangled in the pins.

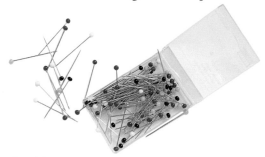

Thimbles

It is almost impossible to hand sew without a thimble, particularly when using the fine "betweens" needles for quilting. There are many types of thimble, from those made of metal with or without ridged tops, to plastic adjustable types that allow space for long finger nails, or leather thimbles, and those shaped especially for working with two thimbles for hand quilting (see page 231).

When choosing a thimble, it must feel comfortable on your longest finger. It may

be that you will need a smaller thimble to wear in cold conditions, and a large one for summer months when the temperature can affect the size of your fingers.

Pressing bars

Pressing bars are used to make large quantities of bias tubes for Celtic appliqué (see page 180). Strips of fabric are cut from the true bias of the fabric, and the strips are seamed, wrong sides together, using a pressing bar as an accurate stitching frame. The stitched "tube" is then rotated so the seam falls under the flat edge of the bias bar, and pressed with the bar inside. The bars are available in widths from $1/8$" (3 mm) through to $1/2$" (1.2 cm).

Freezer paper

Waxed paper for freezer storage use makes ideal template material for appliqué. It can be ironed to the front or the reverse of fabric and seals in place temporarily.

Paper-backed fusible web

Paper-backed fusible web is a fusible adhesive backed by detachable paper. It is a very soft webbed fabric onto which applique shapes can be traced, cut out, and then ironed onto the reverse side of the fabric to be appliquéd. The adhesive fuses the shape under the heat process. Ensure you read the manufacturer's instructions.

Stabilizer

Stabilizer is a white material used on the reverse of fabric when foundation piecing and appliquéing, where it lends support and prevents puckering. Once a piece is completed, the stabilizer is torn away.

Sewing machines

When choosing a sewing machine for quilting, there are considerations to take into account that go beyond whether a machine can give a smooth, straight stitch. A patchworker does not have the same needs as someone making appliqué or doing quilting. If you want a machine that does all three there may be compromises. Some sewers will have more than one machine for this reason. Talk to your quilt store as well as sewing machine suppliers, because your needs are different from a dressmaker or curtain maker.

When it comes to quilting, decorative stitches, or machine appliquéing, there are a number of key features to look for:

- a selection of feet designed for quilting—a ¼" (6 mm) foot, a walking foot, and a free-motion quilting foot or darning foot;
- a good machine light to illuminate the presser foot and stitching area;
- a good flat sewing surface to support growing areas of fabric, and a clear acrylic extension table;
- a two-speed motor with speed control, especially at slower speed;
- portability for classes.

A selection of standard feet will be included in most models. However, you will want some specialized feet in your collection for piecing, appliqué, and quilting.

An open-toe or a transparent plastic foot allows you a clear view of where you are as you sew and where you are going. Some quilters are happy to use the darning foot, but this gives a limited view of the work being stitched.

For applique, an even satin stitch and a blind hem stitch are required, both with variable width and length control. The bottom thread tension can be adjusted on a front-loading bobbin, which is essential for using invisible thread, whereas the tension is preset on a drop-in bobbin.

Some machines have a built-in even-feed facility—called differential feed—while other machines have a special walking foot that feeds the top and bottom layers through at the same pace, and maintains the even feeding of your work. Such a facility eliminates tucks on the reverse of the work or where lines of quilting cross and is excellent for matching plaids or for applying binding.

Many machines have the facility to allow the needle to swing in a zigzag motion and the throat plate (the flat plate that surrounds the feed dog) has to allow for such movement of the needle. The larger the hole in the throat plate the greater the tendency for the fabric to be pushed through the hole while you are

sewing, resulting in a less-than-perfect straight stitch. This can be overcome by purchasing a straight-stitch throat plate for your machine. It will also avoid the wandering effect that can happen when you start and finish stitching pieces. Take care to change the throat plate when changing your stitch style, to avoid broken needles.

With embroidery machines, the feed dogs are so widely spaced that the narrower presser foot does not come into contact with the feed dogs, resulting in poorly fed fabric.

Long arm quilting

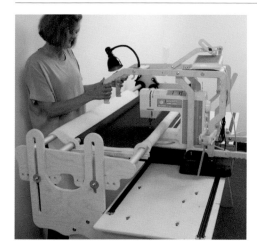

It is possible to have quilt tops professionally quilted. Long arm machines have made it possible for quilting to be completed rapidly with hundreds of options in the designs. You can choose edge-to-edge quilting; all-over quilting of one design, or select a number of patterns to complement each other, for example, medallions, feathers, cables, and cross-hatching all combined in one quilt.

Home-based long arm quilting machines are now available with the advantage of allowing the incorporation of your own home machine into the frame.

The machines effectively pre-baste your quilt and are certainly worth investigating if you plan to work large bed quilts or do not relish crawling around on the floor to baste your quilt.

Making a seam guide

An advantage is to have a regular presser foot designed for sewing an accurate $1/4$" (0.75 cm) seam. This positions the needle $1/4$" (0.75cm) from the edge of the foot and is marked along the edge of the foot for $1/4$" (0.75 cm) in front of the needle and $1/4$" (0.75 cm) behind the needle.

If you do not have a $1/4$" (6 mm) foot, it is possible to use a seam guide. These are available from needlecraft suppliers, or you can mark your machine with a piece of tape. To do this: trim a piece of $1/4$" (6 mm) graph paper along a straight line, place it under the presser foot. Lower the needle so that the needle punctures the paper the first line to the left of the cut edge (your $1/4$" or 0.75 cm seam allowance). Lower the presser foot. Stick layers of vinyl tape along the edge of the paper, on the machine bed, until you have a $1/8$" (3 mm) thick layer. Remove the graph paper and use the tape as a seam guide.

To check its accuracy, cut three strips $1^1/2$" (3.5 cm) wide and stitch them together. Press the seams toward the outer strips. The middle strip should now measure 1" (2 cm) between the seam lines.

Templates and stencils

Templates

Templates are master patterns and are used for marking fabric for cutting and for stitching. There are commercially available templates or you can make your own by drawing them to shape and size as desired. Thin card may be used for templates, although the edges will become worn through use. The best type of material for making templates is thin, rigid plastic which is accurate and long lasting. Templates can be drawn freehand, or traced from patterns. Seam allowance or turnings are added when the fabric is cut around the template, so the templates must be cut to the exact size of the chosen shape.

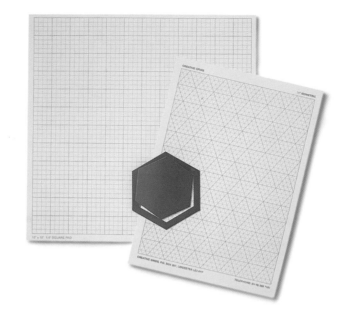

Stencils

Stencils are used to mark out a quilting pattern. In times past, quilters used household items such as cups, glasses, or cookie cutters to create a design. Today there is a host of ready-made stencils manufactured in semi-rigid plastic. They have slots in the surface through which to mark the design onto a quilt top. The designs are usually intended to be continuous, so the linking areas need to be drawn freehand to connect the design.

To create your own stencils, use semi-rigid plastic, which can be purchased in rolls, and cut the marked design with a craft knife—remember to leave some areas uncut so that the stencil does not fall apart.

When machine quilting, consider the ease with which a design can be sewn. The design needs to flow in continuous lines to avoid too much stopping and starting. Patterns can be purchased on fine, tearaway paper that is temporarily pinned to the quilt top, stitched through, and then is torn away (see Machine quilting, page 206).

Hoops and frames

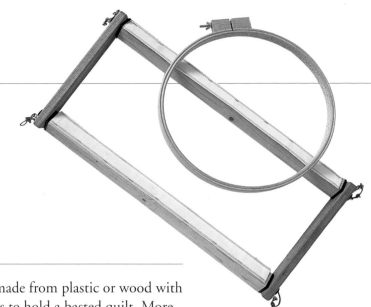

A quilting hoop or frame is useful for holding the work area open and flat. Working with a hand-held hoop or a rotating hoop on a stand allows you to move the work easily into comfortable positions for sewing in different directions.

Hoops

A 14" (35 cm) or larger hoop, made of good quality sturdy wood with a depth of at least ³/₄" to 1" (2 cm to 2.5 cm) is the best size to use, as anything bigger will put a strain on your arms. Embroidery hoops do not make suitable substitutes. If you elect for a hoop on a stand, select one that rotates on its central axis and tilts toward you.

Frames

Frames are made from plastic or wood with a pair of rods to hold a basted quilt. More elaborate floor frames, with three sets of rods, are designed to handle the quilt unbasted, with the central rod holding the batting. Frames are less maneuverable than hoops and can be difficult to work with.

Irons and pressing

A steam iron is an essential item for pressing seams. Travel irons are useful for small pieces of work, and are ideal for pressing appliqué shapes. When machine piecing or foundation piecing, finger pressing is sometimes sufficient as you work through a block. Small finger-irons are available, but a thumbnail is the best finger-pressing tool and is always at hand!

The ironing board needs to be firm and stable with sufficient padding that seam lines are not exposed when pressed.

Pressing is important to the success of a quilting project. Select the heat setting appropriate for your fabric and use steam. Lift and lower the iron in an overlapping pattern. Do not slide the iron down the seam as this can cause the fabric to stretch out of shape, especially on the crosswise grain or bias.

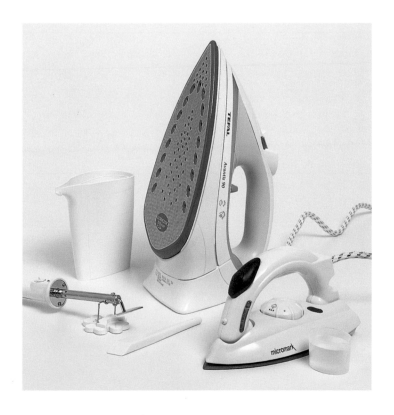

Work area

Quilters are collectors of fabric, tools, books, patterns, and magazines, and while not everyone has the space for a personal studio, a special quilting area where everything from sewing machine to fabric can be set aside, allows you to plan your work and storage to suit your needs. The area may be a bedroom that on occasion serves as a guest room.

Flooring in the room needs to be easy care; vinyl is good as it can be easily swept clear of pins and threads.

Ensure there is sufficient electrical supply for the equipment you intend to use and avoid long trailing extension cords. Fit your computer, iron, and sewing machine with surge protectors to maintain consistent power.

A cutting table or surface should be 6" (15 cm) below your bent elbow when standing upright. Custom-built tables are a luxury, so consider modifying an existing table with wooden blocks under each leg to bring it up to the correct height. If this is not possible, to avoid back strain, do not stand for too long over one task or position.

Have your sewing machine mounted into a sewing cabinet, where the machine drops into a hole in the table. Ensure you sit opposite the needle and not opposite the arch in the machine. If you use a machine on a regular table, raise your sitting position. Your bent elbow should be level with the flat bed of the machine and your hip joint on the same level as your bent knees. Patchwork and quilting are repetitive tasks, so ensure you are comfortable and move around and change tasks to alter the position of the body.

Always use strong, clear light in your sewing area. Good overhead light is important and this can be supplemented

A design wall provides an area on which to pin inspirational images and swatches for your quilt designs.

with task lighting using daylight bulbs. Wherever possible use natural lighting.

Fabrics need to be stored on shelves or in boxes or drawers, filed by color or type. Some quilters like to store them on open shelves so they can see everything at a glance. Fabrics need to breathe, so avoid storing them in plastic bags or boxes with fitted lids. Take care of the tools such as cutting boards and rulers, which need to be stored flat or hung up. Store equipment in easily accessible places.

Shelving is useful to store books and magazines that you will use for reference. These need to be accessible if they are to provide the inspiration they are designed for. Many magazine publishers provide a filing and index system to aid your storage, or you can use magazine files available from stationery suppliers.

A design wall is a wonderful asset allowing you to play with pattern and work out block arrangements. Cork or fiberboard, covered with batting or flannel, makes an ideal surface. If you do not have wall space, consider using a portable pinboard that can be propped up in front of shelving when required.

Cutting and stitching techniques

Patchwork and quilting techniques seem to advance in diversity with ingenious quilters continually inventing more and more methods of working, and manufacturers adding to the available tools and equipment to speed up the processes. This can be confusing for the new student and it's always best to keep a sense of proportion and remember that the best place to start is at the beginning.

Accurately made templates will ensure that patches will fit together, so use a sharp pencil when drawing them out and always make a sample block before embarking on a major project. That way mistakes will come to light before time and effort has been spent unnecessarily.

Once you are familiar with the processes involved in the traditional methods of cutting patches, using templates and scissors, you will want to try out the rotary cutting set. Once mastered, this equipment will speed up the processes involved in cutting out a quilt considerably. If your local shop or guild arranges short courses in the use of the rotary cutting set, this will help you to get started. Then for more specialized projects, such as a Pineapple Log Cabin, you can add to the basics.

As with cutting, there are a number of different ways to stitch the fabrics together and these all have their own specific advantage. Hand sewing has the advantage of being portable, making it a good "carry along" project for times spent waiting for your child in the dancing or swimming lesson, delays at airports, or as a vacation project. With just a little preparation you could achieve quite a lot during such times.

For the quilter with limited time, the sewing machine makes it possible to work quilts relatively quickly, and used in conjunction with the rotary cutting set, it's possible to make simple quilt tops in a matter of hours.

Learning the different processes involved in making patchwork quilts is often about finding which method works best for you; there are no right and wrong ways to work. The sheer variety of tasks and possibilities will keep up your interest and will certainly result in something to be proud of.

Seam allowances

Quilting, almost universally, uses standard measures for seam allowances, and you will find this is the case in books, magazines, and in patterns and equipment.

A $1/4$" seam allowance is used throughout this book unless otherwise stipulated. Some quilters, however, prefer to work with metric measures, and rotary cutting equipment is available with both standard and metric markings. It is now recognized that the $1/4$" seam allowance converts to 0.75 cm for metric work.

As $1/4$" and 0.75 cm are not equal, it is crucial that quilters choose to work either in standard or metric and never mix the two measurements.

Sewing machines have a $1/4$" foot available for accurate machine stitching of seam allowances. If this is not available on your machine, or you wish to work in metric measurements, it is a good idea to mark your own guide onto your machine (see page 35), or purchase one from a needlecraft supplier.

When making templates for hand-piecing you create them to the exact size of the finished piece, *without* seam allowances, which are added as you cut out the fabric. For machine piecing, however, you make templates *with* seam allowances included into the finished size, and then cut to the template marks.

Making templates

Patchwork and piecing blocks must be exact, and so it is important that templates are made accurately. Ready-made templates are available in a range of shapes and sizes, however, it is more satisfactory to make your own, especially as it will enable you to copy and create original designs. Templates can be made out of cardboard, although card will eventually wear at the edges and template plastic is more hard-wearing.

Every shape of the block will need a template. Mark grain lines on the template parallel to the edge of blocks to match against the straight of grain on the fabric. This will ensure the correct positioning for cutting.

Some blocks have shapes that are used in mirror images of each other; for these, make one template, and simply turn it over to mark the reverse shapes.

Hand-piecing templates are made without seam allowances and machine-

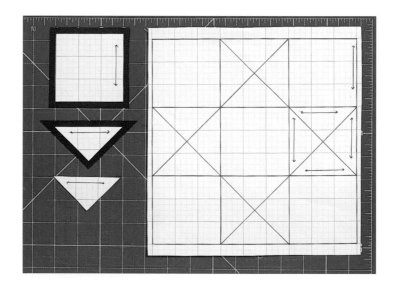

piecing templates are made incorporating seam allowances. Start by drafting the shape or pattern onto graph paper. Use standard graph paper marked in $1/4$" or $1/8$" intervals, not $1/10$" intervals, or if working in metric use metric graph paper marked in 1 mm intervals.

Without seam allowances

Mark the graph paper so that the edge is the sewing line. Cut the shapes from the graph paper and mount them onto card. Cut around the edge (the sewing line) to create the finished templates. Some plastic is transparent, in which case lay the plastic over the graph paper shape and trace it onto the plastic using a craft knife and ruler. Cut out with a craft knife.

With seam allowances

A second method of making templates incorporates the seam allowance into the template. Cut the shapes out of graph paper, and mount them on card. Add the appropriate seam allowance by measuring with a ruler along the edge (sewing line) of the shape, and marking a cutting line $^1/_4$" (or 0.75 cm if working in metric) outside the sewing line. Cut out the shape along the outer marked line. If you use plastic to make the template, lay it over the graph paper shape and trace it onto the plastic using a craft knife and ruler. Cut out with a craft knife.

Cutting fabrics

When cutting your fabric the accuracy of your templates and the cutting of seam allowances will affect the size of the finished quilt, which may be too small or too large if you have not cut exactly to the templates.

Make sure that the straight of grain of your fabric is square and position the template so that the marked grain line is parallel with the fabric grain.

Mark the shapes on the wrong side of the fabric, using a sharp color pencil. Mark a dot at each corner of the template, and draw along each of the edges of the template between these dots. To prevent dragging the pencil along the fabric, hold it at a slight angle.

To prevent fabric slipping while you mark, you can stick fine sandpaper to the back of the template.

With templates that do not include the seam allowance, remove the template and add the seam allowance by aligning the $^1/_4$" (0.75 cm) line on the ruler against the drawn line and draw the cutting line $^1/_4$" (0.75 cm) outside the sewing lines.

In order to avoid wasting fabric, always abut shapes like triangles, as shown in the diagram.

Cut the fabric along the marked cutting line if seam allowances are incorporated. Cut along the outer of the two lines if a seam allowance has been added to the template shape.

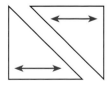 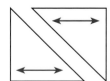

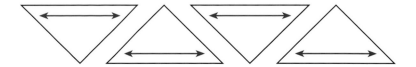

Rotary cutting

Rotary cutting will liberate you from tracing around templates and cutting fabric with scissors. You simply need to know the finished size of your pieces, based on your block pattern, add the appropriate seam allowances and you can quickly cut almost all shapes used in patchwork.

Safe practice is paramount. The cutter blade is dangerously sharp, and it is essential you close it the moment you lay it down after use. Never leave it unattended and store away from children. Dispose of used blades in a clearly marked protective container.

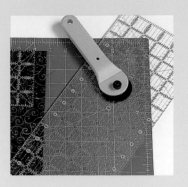

Cutting strips and shapes

Rotary cutting of squares, rectangles, diamonds, and hexagons begins with the cutting of strips of fabric. These shapes can be cut on the crosswise or lengthwise grain of fabric to the required dimensions. There is no need to prepare templates and all measurements include a $^1/_4$" (0.75 cm) seam allowance, unless otherwise stated.

Strips

In order to ensure that any strips cut are straight, the fabric needs to be set square. This is the only time an expanse of fabric is cut. Other cuts are made through four layers of fabric.

1

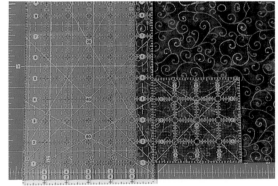

Right handed

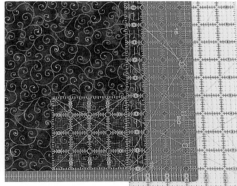

Left handed

1 Fold the fabric, with selvages together aligning the crosswise and lengthwise grains. Position on the cutting mat with the edge to be cut directly in front of you and the spare fabric away toward the right if you are right-handed,

to the left if you are left-handed.

Place the square on the folded edge, and slide toward the edge to be cut. Place the long ruler against the square, matching a horizontal line with the base of the square.

2 Hold the long ruler firmly near the bottom and slide the square out of the way. Open the cutter and start cutting on the board. Cut firmly until level with the top of your fingers. Stop, hold the cutter in place, and walk your hand up the ruler away from you, moving first the thumb and then the fingers. Cut again, until level with the fingertips and continue in this way to the top of the fabric. Discard the thin strip of fabric—you now have a straight edge from which to begin cutting strips to the required width.

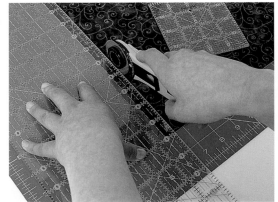

Right handed

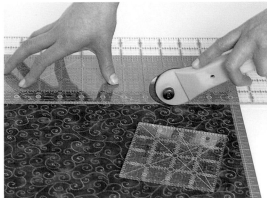

Left handed

Squares and rectangles

To cut fabric strips into squares or rectangles, position the folded strip horizontal on the board, with the selvage on the left and the fold on the right, if you are right-handed. If you are left-handed, position the folded strip horizontal on the board with the selvage on the right and the double fold on the left.

1 Using a horizontal line on the ruler, square up the top and bottom edges of the strip and cut the fabric into squares the width of the strip plus ½" (1.5 cm) for seam allowances.

2 For rectangles, cut the length of the required rectangle plus ½" (1.5 cm) for seam allowances.

1

Right handed

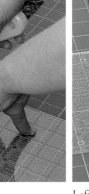

Left handed

2

Right handed

Left handed

continued on the next page…

Cutting strips and shapes (continued)

Half-square triangles

1 Cut a square from the folded fabric that is $7/8$" (2.5 cm) larger than the finished size of the short edge of triangle, for seam allowance. Rotate the square.

2 Place the ruler across the square from corner to corner, being absolutely sure that the ruler is on the corner points. Cut the square in half diagonally.

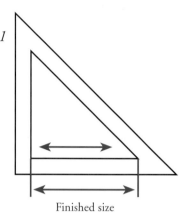

Finished size

Right handed

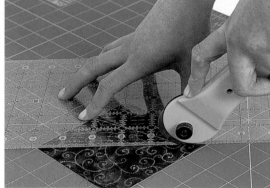

Left handed

Quarter-square triangles

1 Cut a square from the folded fabric that is $1^1/4$" (3.5 cm) larger than the finished size of the long edge of the triangle.

2 Place the ruler across the square from corner to corner being absolutely sure that the ruler is on the corner points. Cut the square in half diagonally. Reposition the ruler across the opposite corners and cut.

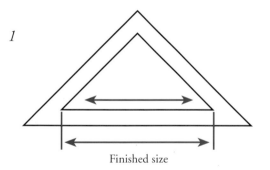

Finished size

Equilateral triangles

1 Cut a strip from the folded fabric ³/₄" (2.25 cm) wider than the finished height of the triangle, for seam allowances.

2 Cut the strip at a 60° angle. Right-handed—align the 60° line on the lower right edge of the ruler with the bottom edge of the strip. Left-handed—align the 60° line on the lower left edge of the ruler with the bottom edge of the strip.

 Cut along the edge of the ruler.

3 To cut the second side of the triangle: Right-handed— rotate the ruler so that the 60° line is on the bottom edge of the strip and the right-hand edge of the ruler is lined up at the top edge of the first cut. Left-handed—rotate the ruler so that the 60° line is on the bottom edge of the strip and the left-hand edge of the ruler is lined up at the top edge of the first cut.

4 Continue cutting equilateral triangles from the strip, alternately rotating the ruler between the two 60° lines.

1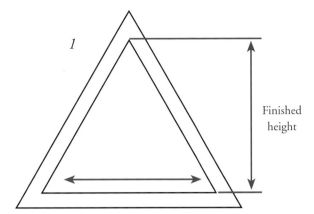

2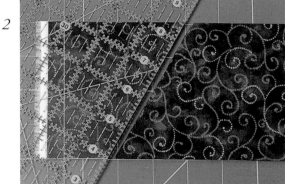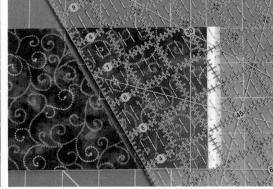

Right handed   Left handed

3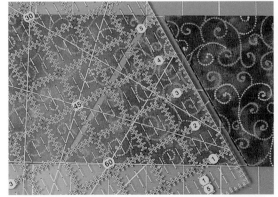

Right handed   Left handed

4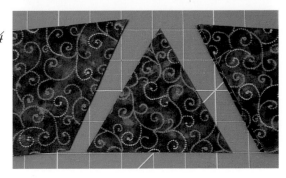

continued on the next page...

Diamonds and parallelograms

The method for cutting diamonds and parallelograms is exactly the same for 45° diamonds and 60° diamonds. By aligning either the 45° line on the ruler or the 60° line, you can simply alter the shapes. Seam allowances remain the same.

1 Cut a strip from the folded fabric ½" (1.5 cm) wider than the finished distance between the first set of parallel lines, for seam allowances.

2 Cut the strip at a 45° or 60° angle: Right-handed—align the 45° or 60° line on the lower right edge of the ruler with the bottom edge of the strip. Left-handed—align the 45° or 60° line on the lower left edge of the ruler with the bottom edge of the strip.
  Cut along the edge of the ruler.

3 To make the second cut, find the measurement on the ruler that corresponds with the finished distance between the second set of parallel lines, plus ½" (1.5 cm). Keep the 45° or 60° line on the bottom edge of the strip, slide the ruler along the strip until the required measurement lies on the cut edge.

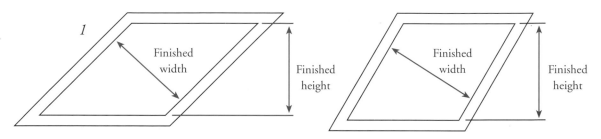

1

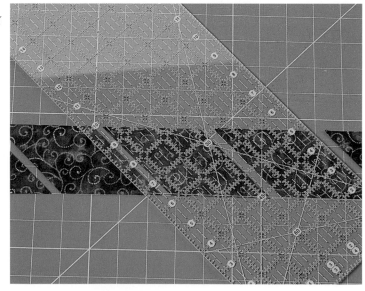

2

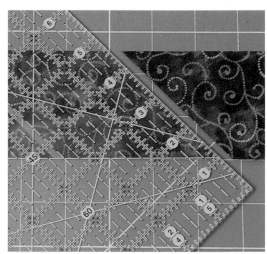

3

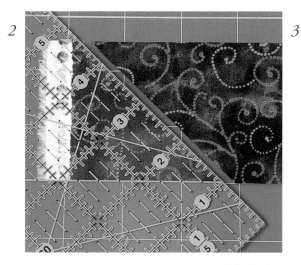

4 Cut from the strip until the required number of pieces are cut.

Hexagons

Hexagons are cut from 60°
diamonds (see page 46).

1 Place the diamond on
the cutting mat with the
long diagonal running along
a horizontal line on the mat
and the short diagonal
running along a vertical line
on the mat.

Find the measurement on
the ruler that is half of the
cutting measurement used
when cutting the diamond.
Place this measurement line
onto the short diagonal of the
diamond. Cut away the
surplus.

2 Turn the piece around and
repeat the process to remove
the second diamond tip,
creating a hexagon.

3 You can discard the offcuts
or use them for smaller
piecing elsewhere.

1
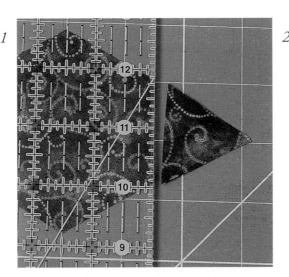

2
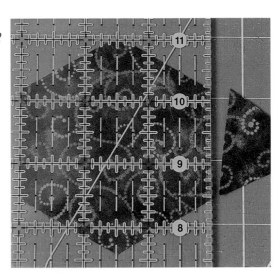

3
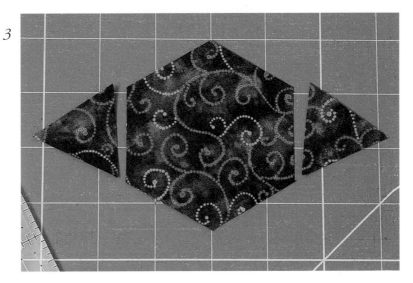

continued on the next page...

Trapezoids

The method for cutting trapezoids and half-trapezoids is exactly the same for 45° diamonds and 60° diamonds. By aligning either the 45° line on the ruler or the 60° line, you can simply alter the shapes. Seam allowances remain the same.

1 From folded fabric, cut a strip ½" (1.5 cm) wider than the finished height of the trapezoid.

2 Cut the end of the strip at 45°, as for cutting for diamonds.

3 Measure from the 45° angle along the bottom edge of the strip 1¼" (3.5 cm) longer than the finished base length of the trapezoid. Mark the point with a pencil.

4 Rotate the ruler so that the 45° line lies along the bottom of the trapezoid and the edge of the ruler passes through the pencil mark. Cut along the edge of the ruler.

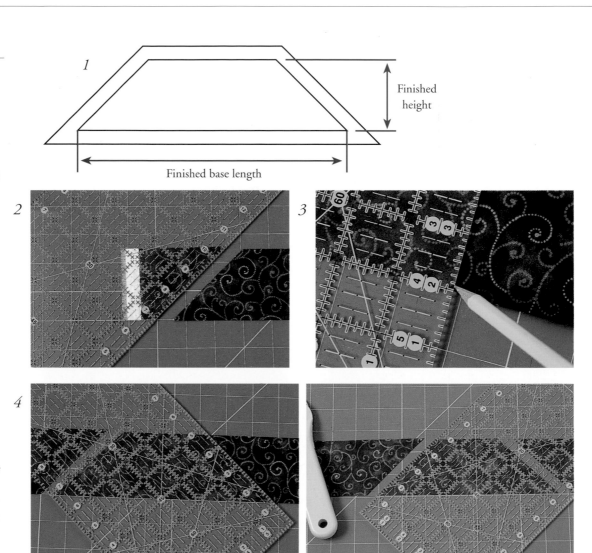

Finished height

Finished base length

Right handed

Left handed

5 At the top edge, there is now a 45° angle, which forms the bottom of another trapezoid. Measure the same base measurement along the top of the strip and mark with a pencil. Rotate the ruler so that the 45° line lies along the top edge and the edge of the ruler passes through the pencil mark. Before cutting, check that there is a trapezoid lying under the ruler.

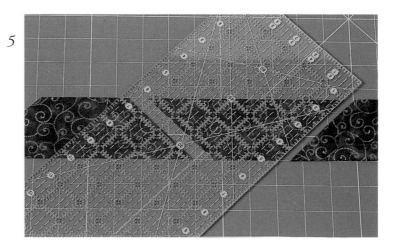

Half-trapezoids

1 To cut half-trapezoids measure along the bottom edge of the strip $^7/_8$" (2.5 cm) longer than the finished base length of the half-trapezoid. Mark with a pencil.

2 Rotate the ruler so that the 45° line lies along the bottom of the half-trapezoid and the edge of the ruler passes through the pencil mark. Cut along the edge of the ruler.

3 At the top edge, there is now a 45° angle, which forms the bottom of another half-trapezoid. Measure the same base measurement along the top of the strip and cut.

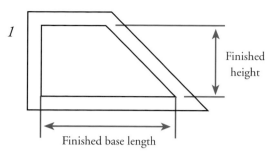

Finished height

Finished base length

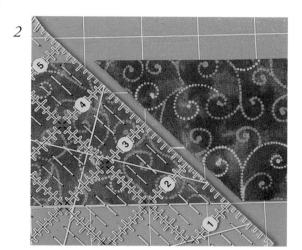

Piecing

Once you have cut your patches, you will want to decide whether to hand- or machine-piece them into the block patterns. You may choose to hand-piece to make your work portable. It will be slower but it is easier to make seams meet where they should. Piecing by machine is faster, but accuracy with seam allowances is all-important so you will want to be comfortable with your machine. Once you have mastered rotary cutting, easy-piecing is an efficient way to speed things up and make sewing easier.

Straight seams

Hand-stitched

1 Pin two pieces, right sides together, along the marked sewing line, or ¼" (0.75 cm) seam allowance.

2 Use a Sharp needle and about 18" (45 cm) of cotton thread. Thread the needle and tie a small knot in the end. Backstitch at one corner, and then sew forward with small straight running stitches. Aim for about 8 stitches to the inch (3 to 4 stitches to the centimeter).

3 Check the stitching is on the seam lines. Stitch to the end corner, removing the pins as you go, and secure with backstitch.

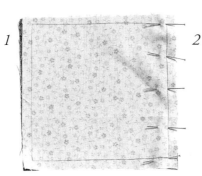
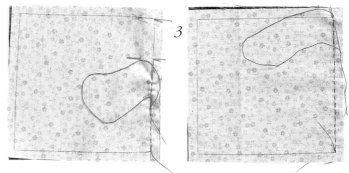

Machine-stitched

1 Pin two pieces, right sides together, with fine pins, points facing either outward or inward from the edge, rather than along the seam line, making them easier to remove as you stitch.

2 Machine stitch a ¼" (0.75 cm) seam allowance from edge to edge.

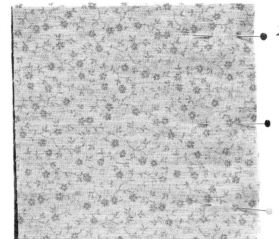
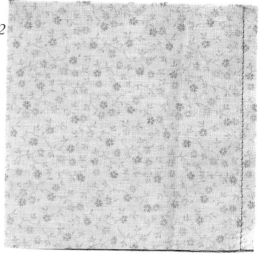

Butted seams

Hand-stitched

1 Pin together pairs of sewn pieces, right sides together, along the marked sewing line, or at the ¼" (0.75 cm) seam allowance. Pin vertically, on the seam line. Begin with a backstitch at a corner, and, with a small running stitch sew toward the center seam, checking all the time that the stitching is on line on both sides.

2 Push the straight seam allowances back toward the line that has been sewn. Backstitch to secure and continue with small running stitches to the end corner. Finish with a backstitch. Cut the thread. Press the seams in a radiating fashion.

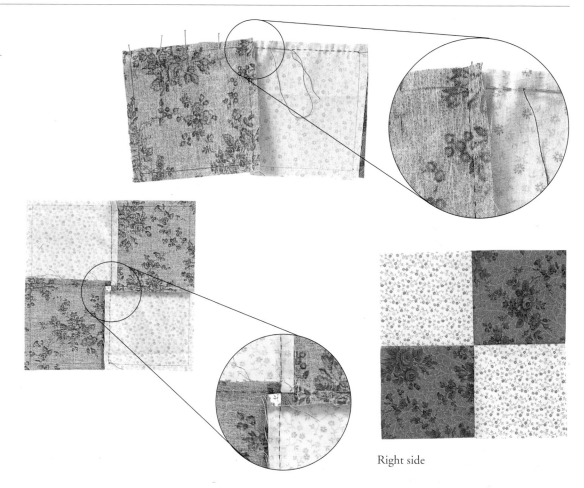

Right side

Machine-stitched

1 Pin blocks, right sides together, matching seams, with pins perpendicular to the seam line.

2 Stitch with a ¼" (0.75 cm) seam allowance. Stop at needle-down position when reaching the butted seams, check they are aligned, and continue to the end.

3 Press the seams flat toward the darker fabric.

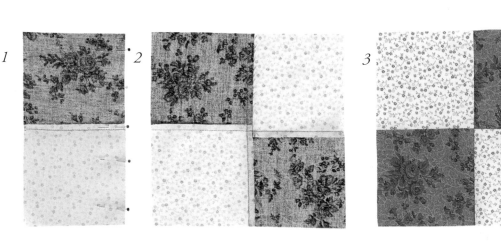

Set in seams

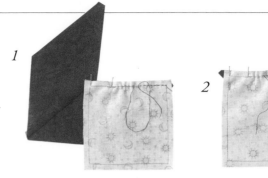

Hand-stitched

1 Pin two pieces, right sides together, along the ¼" (0.75 cm) seam allowance.

Stitch the seam, checking that the sewing is on line on both sides. Remove the pins, and backstitch at the corner. Do not cut the thread.

2 Pivot the square at the seam and pin the second side corner to corner. Start with a backstitch, and sew a running stitch to the end corner. Remove the pins, finish with a backstitch, and cut the thread.

3 Press both seams flat.

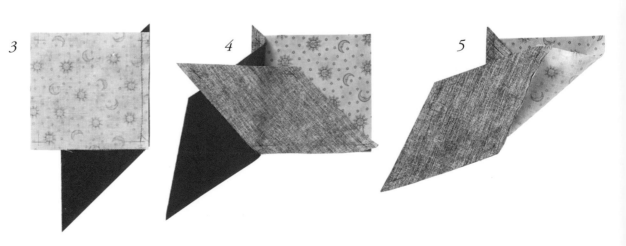

Machine-stitched

1 Mark ¼" (0.75 cm) seam allowance with crossed lines.

2 Pin a square to a diamond with pins perpendicular to the seam line, making them easy to remove as you stitch.

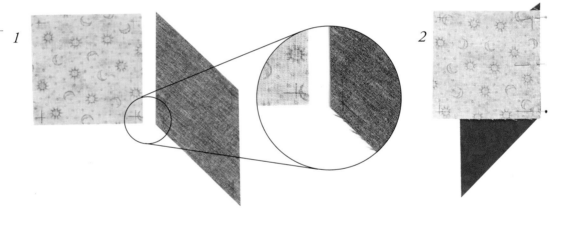

3 Stitch from one marked point to the other, and backstitch to secure. Finger press away from the square.

4 Position another diamond right sides together, on the square, and pin. Stitch from mark to mark but not beyond. Finger press away from the square.

5 Bring two points of the diamonds together, and pin the edges. Stitch, but again not beyond the marks. Then backstitch at the outer mark and stitch off the end to secure. Press this seam to one side, and the seams with the square away from the square to give a "Y" finish.

Points

1 When many pieces come together at a central point it is possible to avoid a bulk in the center, by stitching with the needle lying along the inner side of the drawn sewing line, instead of exactly on the sewing line. Stitch to the center in this manner, turn the work at the center dot, and stitch back for about ½" (1 cm). Finish with a backstitch at this point.

2 To avoid a hole where all the seams come together, thread a needle with a double strand of thread, knot the end, and, pass the needle through each of the central points. Pull up tight, stitch to secure the thread, and cut the thread.

Press the seams in a radiating manner.

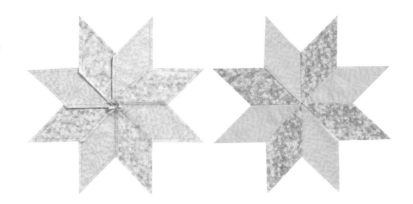

Curved seams

1 When making templates with curved edges, marks need to be made on the fabric to help when matching seams between concave and convex shapes.

2 Pin two pieces, right sides together, along the marked sewing line, or ¼" (0.75 cm) seam allowance, matching the marks. Pin down into the work perpendicular to the seam line.

3 Stitch the two pieces together. Start with a backstitch at one corner, and with a small running stitch sew to the next corner, removing the pins as you go and checking the stitching is on the seam line front and back.

4 Press the seams toward the concave shape; if necessary clip the curves to allow the seam allowance to lie flat.

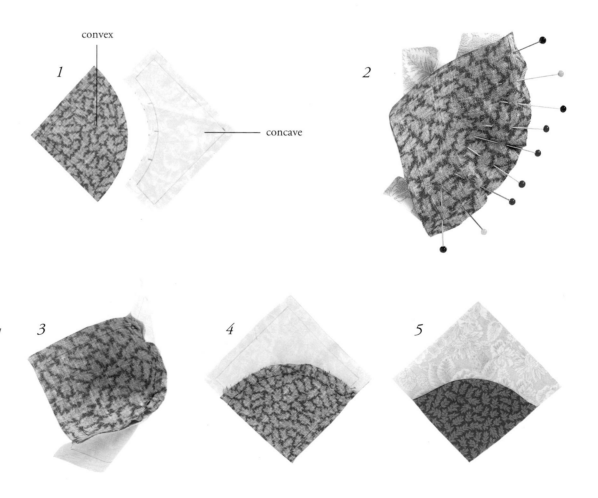

Easy-piecing

Quick four-patch

1 Cut one strip each from two contrasting fabrics. The width of the strip needs to be the finished size of the squares in the four-patch block, plus ½" (1.5 cm) for seam allowances. Stitch the strips, right sides together, along one long edge. Press toward the darker fabric.

Cut the strip section into units measuring the same width as the initial strips. To ensure that these units are cut accurately, square off one end first.

2 Pin pairs of these units, right sides together, alternating the light and dark fabrics. Stitch.

3 Press the seams flat toward the darker fabric.

1

2
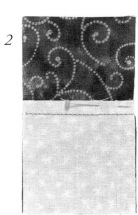 

3
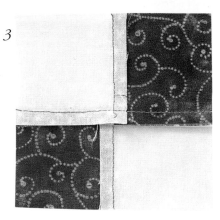

Quick nine-patch

1 Cut three strips each from two contrasting fabrics. The width of the strips needs to be the width of the finished squares plus ½" (1.5 cm) for seam allowances.

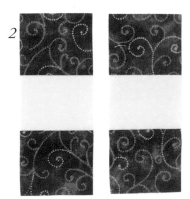

2 Stitch the strips together in two sets: one set dark–light–dark and another set light–dark–light. Press seams toward the dark fabric. Cut the strip sections into three units the same width as the initial strips, this time cutting across all three colors.

3 Each nine-patch is made from two units from one set and one unit from the second set. Stitch a unit one and a unit two together, matching the seams as you go, alternating the contrasting fabrics.

Press the seams flat toward the darker fabric.

4 Add a second unit, alternating the contrasting fabrics.

5 Press the seams flat toward the darker fabric.

continued on the next page…

Easy-piecing (continued)

Quick half-square triangles

1 Cut a rectangle from each of two contrasting fabrics. On the wrong side of the lighter rectangle, draw a grid of squares. Each square needs to measure the finished size of the half-square triangle plus ⁷⁄₈" (2.5 cm) for seam allowances. Draw diagonal lines.

Draw a scant ¼" (0.75 cm) line either side of the diagonals.

2 Pin the light rectangle on top of the dark rectangle, right sides together. Stitch on the lines either side of the original diagonal lines.

3 Cut apart on all the vertical and horizontal lines of the grid to make squares. Cut the squares in two along the diagonal line.

4 Open these triangles to make squares ready sewn. Press toward the darker triangle.

5 Before using these units in a quilt, trim off the ears to make a neat and tidy square.

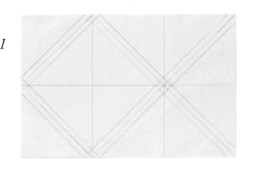

1

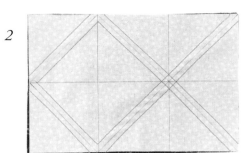

2

3

4

5

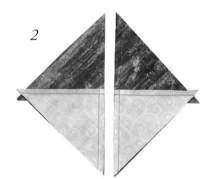

Quick quarter-square triangles

1 Cut light and dark squares that measure 1¼" (3.5 cm) larger than the finished size of the quarter-square triangles needed. On the reverse of the light squares, mark a diagonal line. Mark a scant ¼" (0.75 cm) either side of this diagonal line. Stitch on these lines to give make a half-square triangle (see page 44). Press.

2 Pin two units, opposite fabrics and right sides together. Mark a diagonal line across the top unit. Mark a scant ¼" (0.75 cm)

either side of the diagonal, and stitch on these lines. Cut in two along the diagonal.

3 Press the seams flat toward the darker fabric. Trim the ears to finish.

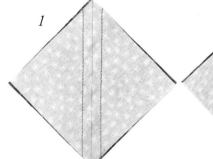

1

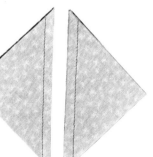

2

3

Quick square within a square

1 Cut a large square from a focus fabric, the size of the finished block plus ½" (1.5 cm) for seam allowance.

Cut four smaller squares from contrasting fabric, half the size of the finished block plus ½" (1.5 cm) for seam allowance. Mark a diagonal on each of these smaller squares.

Place a small square on the corner of the large square, right sides together. Sew across the marked line. Repeat on the opposite corner.

2 Trim off the corner triangles, leaving ¼" (0.75 cm) seam allowance.

3 Press toward the triangles.

4 Place the remaining two small squares on the remaining corners of the large square and stitch across the diagonals. Trim as before and press toward the triangles.

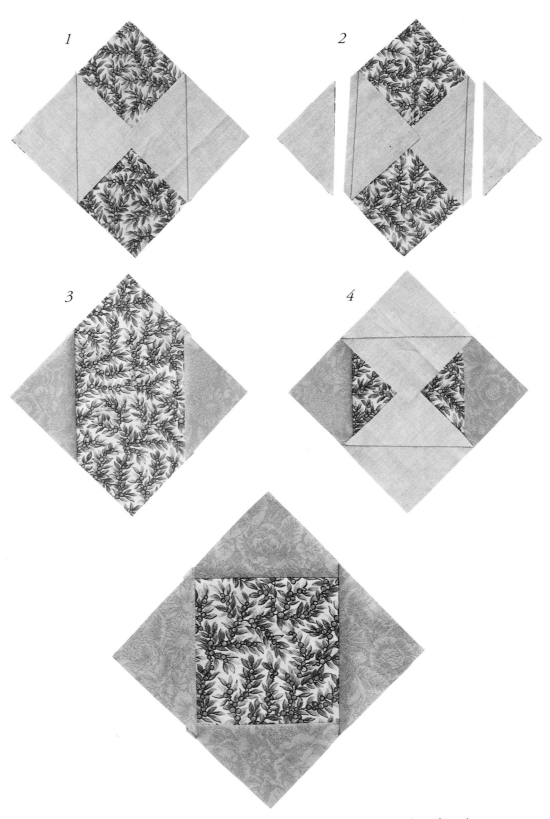

continued on the next page...

Easy-piecing *(continued)*

Quick Flying Geese

1 Cut one square measuring the finished width of the "goose" plus 1¼" (3.5 cm) for seam allowance, from the chosen "goose" fabric. Cut four background squares measuring the finished height of the "goose" plus ⅞" (2.5 cm) for seam allowance.

Pin two background squares, right sides down on opposite corners of the goose square, right side up. Mark the overlap.

2 Trim the corners of the squares at the overlap. Mark a diagonal line across the squares and stitch a scant ¼" (0.75 cm) either side of this diagonal.

3 Cut in half on the diagonal.

4 Press toward the small triangles.

5 Place one of the remaining squares on the top corner of the goose fabric, right sides together. Mark a diagonal, and stitch a scant ¼" (0.75 cm) either side of this diagonal.

6 Cut on the diagonal. Press toward the background triangle. Repeat for the other units to make four Flying Geese.

Hand and machine appliqué

Appliqué is the term used to apply fabric shapes onto the surface of a background or foundation fabric. Appliqué can be as forgiving—allowing shapes to take on a form that nods toward realism—or as exacting as one would wish.

There are several ways to prepare the shapes to be appliquéd, using templates or fusible adhesive. Applique stitching by hand may achieve invisibility, while machine applique stitches capitalize on covering raw edges with decorative satin and zigzag stitches.

Preparing the shapes

1 Templates are used to prepare individual shapes. Mark each shape from a design onto template material indicating those edges that tuck under another shape, so that you know not to turn those edges under.

2 Mark around the shape on the wrong side of the fabric. When cutting out the shapes, allow a ¼" (0.75 cm) turning or seam allowance.

3 Turn under and baste.

1

1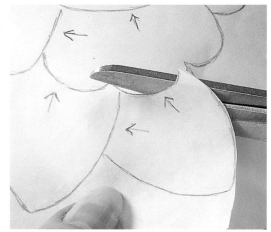

2

3

continued on the next page…

4 Place the shape on the background fabric, using the traced design as a guide, and pin or baste in position, ready to be stitched.

5 An alternative method is to use freezer paper as a template material. Place the template shape, shiny side down onto the right side of the fabric and press with a dry iron. The paper shape will temporarily stick to the fabric. Cut the fabric around the paper shape allowing ¼" (0.75 cm) seam allowance. Remove the paper from the fabric. Place the fabric shape on an ironing surface wrong side up. Position the paper shape, shiny side up, on top of the fabric. Fold the seam allowance over onto the paper and press again with a dry iron. The fabric will temporarily stick to the freezer paper holding the seam allowance in place, and giving a crisp edge to the shape, which is then ready for stitching to foundation fabric.

6 Once the shape is stitched into position the paper is removed. Here one edge of the shape is open—because it will tuck under another shape—and the paper is removed through that opening.

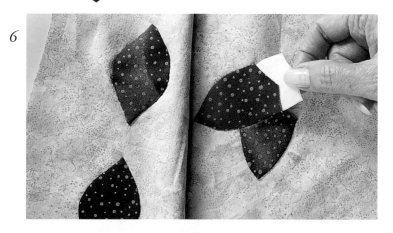

7 When a shape is completely enclosed, remove the paper by slitting the background fabric behind the shape, or trim the background fabric away (leaving a seam allowance) to remove the paper.

Circular shapes

1 To achieve a perfect circle use lightweight card and cut out a template circle to the finished size. Cut out the fabric with a ¼" (0.75 cm) seam allowance. With matching thread, sew a running stitch around the outside edge. Do not tie off the thread, but leave it threaded in the needle. Retain the template in the circle.

2 Pull the thread, drawing up the outside edge of the fabric. Stitch to secure the gathers and to fasten off the thread.

3 Position the circle on the appliqué design. Secure with pins at the back. Hold the work so that the foundation fabric falls away from the circle. This makes the stitching easier and the card guides the needle into the correct position.

4 Once the circle is appliquéd, slit or cut away the background fabric behind to remove the card.
  For small circles, a medium to heavyweight interfacing can be used and left in place.

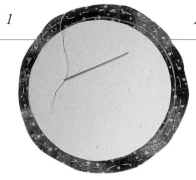
1

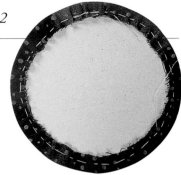
2

3

4

Machine-stitched shapes

1 Mark the design onto the wrong side of the foundation fabric. Select which shape to add first. Cut a piece of chosen fabric large enough to cover the area of that shape, pin it right side up on the right side of the foundation fabric, over the position on the design.

2 Turn over and on the wrong side, machine a short straight stitch on the lines for the selected shape.

3 Turn the work over and carefully trim away the excess fabric from the shape, cutting close to the stitching. Continue adding fabrics in this manner until the whole design has been fulfilled. It is then ready for decorative stitching.

1

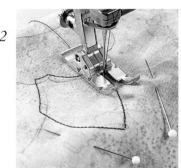
2

3

continued on the next page...

Using fusible adhesive

1 Fusible adhesive can be used to position shapes ready for final stitching. The shapes are traced onto the paper side. The design must be marked in reverse. Cut out the paper shape, slightly larger than the drawn lines. With paper side right side up, use a steam iron to press it onto the wrong side of the chosen fabric. Cut out the fabric on the drawn line, leaving an allowance for tucking under a neighboring portion of the design.

2 Peel off the paper and place the shape right side up on the right side of the foundation fabric in the correct location. Press with a steam iron to fuse in place. Continue until all portions of the design are in place.

3 To avoid a build up of fused areas creating stiffness, cut the fusible web so that only the outside edges of the shape will be bonded to the foundation fabric.

1

2

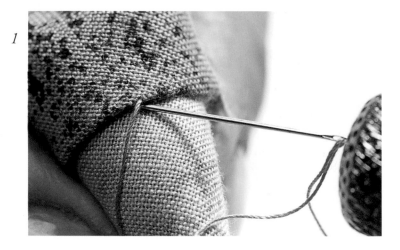
3

Appliqué stitches

Blind stitch

1 To achieve an invisible stitch, use a fine needle and match the color of the thread used to the fabric of the shape being appliquéd.

Thread the needle and knot the end. Place the needle so that it enters the fabric shape from the wrong side and will exit in the fold of the seam allowance. Pull the thread so that the knot lodges in the fold. Place the needle into the foundation fabric immediately under the shape at the point where the thread exits the fold. The needle will exit again in the fold of the seam allowance on the shape, slightly in front of the point where it entered the background. When the thread is pulled through, it should pull the edge of the appliqué under slightly and the stitch will disappear.

1

Needle turn stitch

1 This method combines the turning under of the seam allowance with securing the shapes. Turn the raw edge of the shape under with the needle. The amount turned under at one time should only be enough for the next few stitches. The stitches should be small and close together for durability.

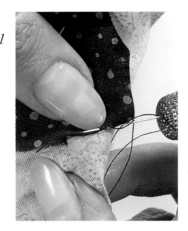

Blanket stitch

1 For a decorative (visible) effect, using contrasting thread. Take the needle and thread down through the appliqué shape and to the background fabric and exit outward beneath the shape edge to form a loop over the following thread. Work toward yourself.

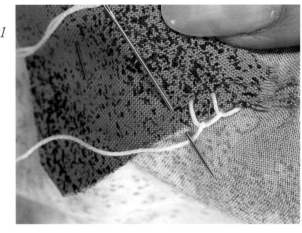

Machine stitching

The open-toed foot is essential for machine appliquéing, and for riding over several fabrics. The thread used for stitching can match or contrast the fabric of the shape.

1 Shapes can be finished with a straight stitch placed along the edge.

2 Shapes that have been stitched through from the wrong side and trimmed, are best finished in short wide zigzag stitch, called a satin stitch.
  Shapes that have been fused into position can be finished with a narrow open zigzag stitch, blanket stitch, or decorative embroidery stitch.

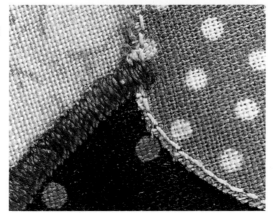

3 Start the first two or three satin stitches on the shape that it is tucked under. Stitch around the selected shape, finishing with two or three stitches into the neighboring shape so that they will cover the starting and stopping stitches on the one just completed.

Basting

Before a quilt top is quilted, it is sandwiched together with the batting and the backing fabric. The sandwich is basted through all three layers to prevent the layers from moving around while quilting.

Basting for hand quilting

It is preferable to hand baste if you intend to hand quilt. The basting stitch is a long running stitch. Long milliners needles are useful to stitch these long stitches, and the thread used must be light in color, to prevent the possibility of any residue of color on the surface of the quilt. Select a lightweight thread which will break easily, rather than pull and damage the surface of the quilt when the threads are pulled out after quilting.

Basting is worked in horizontal and vertical rows at intervals of 3" to 4" (7.5 to 10 cm). Start each row from a center line and work toward the outside edge.

Basting for machine quilting

Basting is not advised for machine quilting as it is difficult to remove the basting without possibly damaging the machine stitches. Instead there are alternative methods to secure the quilt sandwich, in the same grid format but using safety pins, Quiltaks™, or adhesive spray (see Machine quilting, page 209).

Design

Quilts are made for a number of different reasons and inspiration for quilt design can come from many sources. Even traditional patterns that have endured for a long time can be rich sources of innovation in quilt design. Patterns have continually developed, from the use of simple folded squares of paper for designing blocks to more sophisticated designs being created with straight, then curved seams. Makers have always looked for original ways to interpret the medium and set themselves new challenges.

If you want to create your own original quilt designs, there are sources of inspiration everywhere. Obvious sources are the geometric patterns that occur in other forms of decorative art. Floor tiles, wrought ironwork, architectural forms in domestic, commercial, and industrial building will all provide starting points for the design process. Look at forms in doors, windows, and skylines. Look at items in the domestic interior; for example, look at the decorative details on furniture such as marquetry, carving, and turned wood. Silverwork often has areas of decoration that can be translated into designs for quilts. A day out with a camera, taking random shots in your local environment, may give you ideas. Focus on detail to reveal the patterns in nature.

Other textiles are worth investigating. Look at weaving from Peru and Guatemala, African "Kuba" raffia work, Navaho and Oriental rugs; they all contain rich patterns and colors ready to be translated into quilt designs. Look for repeated patterns in both the natural and built environment: avenues of trees, bark patterns, furrows in ploughed fields, and the waves breaking on a sandy beach. A visit to a museum or art gallery can be useful when looking for shapes and color combinations. Color, in particular, is often a source of anxiety to quilters. Try arranging groups of fabric together in harmonizing and contrasting groups, bearing in mind the importance of value, as well as color, in quilt making.

Styles of design can be exploited to create a particular atmosphere. Art Nouveau, with its organic swirls and curves, lends itself to quilting and appliqué designs, while Art Deco, a more geometric and angular style, is reminiscent of the geometry of pieced quilts.

The study of traditional quilt patterns reveals that early quilt makers used to interpret and depict familiar objects in their quilts with much ingenuity: Baskets, Bear's Paw, Bow Tie, and Log Cabin for example. By observing our environment, we, as quilt makers, are simply continuing and developing this tradition.

Copying a design

To copy a pattern from a book or a magazine, or create a design from any source of inspiration, you will need a few simple drafting tools: graph paper, card, an accurate ruler, a sharp pencil, glue stick, a craft knife, and a cutting board. To try out different colorways, colored pencils are a useful addition.

First, you need to establish the finished size of the quilt. Decide how the blocks are arranged across the surface and how many there are both across and down. Look at other details, such as the sashing strips and borders. Now draw a scale diagram to establish what size to make the blocks in order to make a quilt to your required size (see Settings and assembly, page 72).

If the blocks are pieced, then categorize them by whatever grid they will fit into—four-patch, nine-patch, and so on. Select a measurement that will divide easily into the grid. For a nine-patch block a 9" or 12" square is suitable. If you work in

metric measures, calculate an equivalent length that is divisible by three, such as 24 cm or 30 cm.

Use a sharp pencil to draw the block onto graph paper at full size and identify how many different shapes there are in the block pattern. Draw arrows parallel to the sides of the block to indicate the direction of the straight grain of the fabric.

Some of the shapes may be asymmetrical, in which case they will only fit into the block one way. Cut out one sample of each shape and mount these onto card. Now trace them onto template material or card and cut around these shapes again, adding $1/4$" (0.75 cm) all around the edges for the seam allowance.

Many blocks can be made without using templates, such as squares, triangles, and diamonds, with a rotary cutting set. If, however, you are a beginner, it is a useful exercise to begin with templates, then graduate to template-free construction.

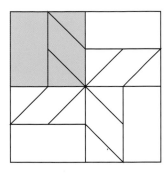

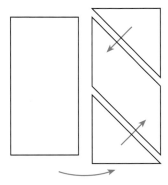

In the Clay's Choice block, the windmill blade shape is asymmetrical so the template must be used the right way up in order for it to fit into the block.

In Day Lily and Fruit Basket blocks the piecing is done first, and the appliqué shapes are added later.

Always make a sample block to try out a design and to reveal any pitfalls in the construction. If you can arrange a vertical surface onto which blocks can be pinned to view them from a distance this helps in the overall composition.

To reproduce an appliqué block, the shapes may either be traced or drawn freehand. Study traditional appliqué blocks and, for a first attempt, try one without too many overlapping shapes and sharp curves. To get them to the desired size, take them to a copy shop and have them enlarged, or square up the design and reproduce it on an enlarged grid.

Seam allowances are sometimes added to templates, depending on how the appliqué is to be done. Some blocks have a combination of both patchwork and appliqué.

When selecting a quilt pattern, it is tempting to start cutting fabrics straightaway, but remember that the project will take some time, and that planning the design and carefully choosing the colors are important stages in the making of a quilt. These stages will help you to maintain interest during the process of construction, build on your skills, and result in a piece of work to be proud of.

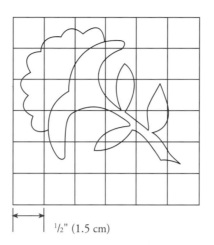

½" (1.5 cm)

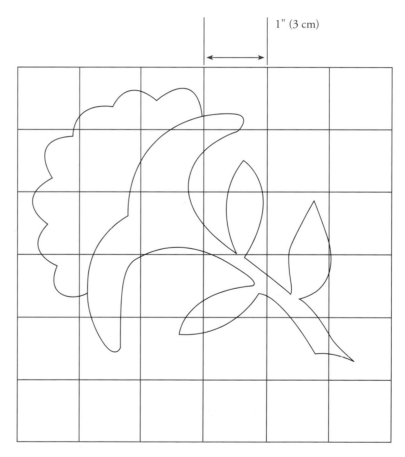

1" (3 cm)

To enlarge a design, impose a grid over the tracing, then redraw it into a larger grid, copying the lines carefully into each square.

Creating a design

There are several ways to create your own original quilt design. One way is to introduce innovation into a traditional quilt design by altering the accepted arrangement of tonal value by the specific placement of dark, medium, and light values. In Snail Trail variation (below), the values have merged in some parts of the quilt so that the Snail Trail block becomes hidden, creating the illusion of interlocking shapes spinning around. The viewer has to work to recognize that it is still there. The effect created over the surface of the quilt by the contrast between the "hidden" blocks and the more obvious ones breaks with the traditional interpretation of this pattern.

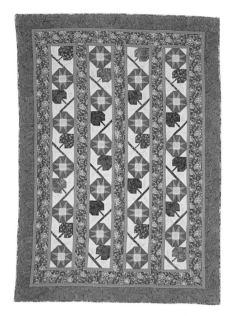

Morning Glory by Nancy Breland.

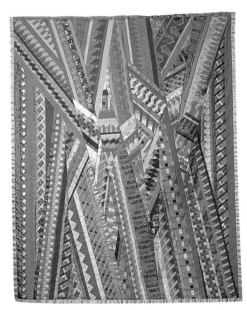

Arvieto by Sally-Anne Boyd.

Snail Trail variation by Katharine Guerrier.

Blocks can also be more radically altered to create contemporary designs. Nancy Breland introduced her own flower block design into the traditional format of the strippy quilt in Morning Glory (right). The decorative pieced strips are arranged in vertical lines between channels of border fabric. In creating Arvieto (right), Sally-Anne Boyd based the design on letter shapes. It was made using an innovative interpretation of the technique of Seminole patchwork. The change in direction of the strip sections exploits the qualities of the silks used in the construction, subtly changing the colors and textures by the direction of the weave.

New ideas for original designs often stem from a work in progress, and lead to a series of quilts worked on the same theme, forming a development of ideas. This might be based on the geometry of the pieced quilt or a pictorial approach more suited to the techniques of appliqué.

The patterns and templates necessary will depend on the techniques to be used. Template making, rotary cutting, and appliqué techniques are all possibilities; the key when creating patterns for yourself is to try out whatever technique seems appropriate. With a practical subject like patchwork, which is wide ranging both in techniques and interpretations, the common-sense approach is often the best. With a basic knowledge of techniques at your fingertips, all you need is the imagination to follow your inspiration and create something original.

QUILT TOPS

Patchwork and piecing

One of the original reasons for quilt making was the need for thrift and economy when fabrics were scarce and the construction of patchwork, whether from recycled worn garments or scraps from dressmaking was necessary to provide warm bedding. From the purely practical motives for the creation of pieced quilts grew the aesthetic traditions of a picturesque folk art. Although no longer a necessity, quilt making remains not only hugely popular, but continues to be an important artistic tradition at the heart of American needlecraft.

There are many reasons for this. The basic equipment for quilt making is widely available and relatively inexpensive, and with the potential for experimenting with color and design, the interest in the piecing construction process is maintained. Even simple shapes such as squares, triangles, diamonds and rectangles can be made into spectacular quilts with a little ingenuity in the arrangement of tonal value and color combinations. In addition to this, the level of expertise necessary can vary from absolute beginner to the highly skilled, giving the maker the opportunity to build on experience, and providing new challenges with each new project.

Many quilters enjoy the social aspect of the craft. Joining a quilt guild and working with a group on individual or cooperative projects is an important aspect of the patchwork tradition. Strong bonds are made within such groups which often have a beneficial effect on the community.

Quilts now have a significance beyond their original function serving as a link between generations, families and societies. Antique quilts have been used by students of textile design as a source of inspiration. Quilts can also be a valuable reference for the social historian, providing, as they often do, the stories of the everyday lives of their makers, documented in letters, diaries and by oral history.

Although the reasons for making a quilt today are very different from those which originally motivated the early quilt makers, the popularity of this enduring craft is unending.

About blocks

Pieced patchwork squares, or patched blocks, are the key design units from which patchwork quilts are constructed.

The early recorded blocks used every available scrap of fabric, reflecting the need to conserve and recycle precious fabric. Crazy quilts, haphazard designs of fabric scraps stitched together to make utilitarian bedcovers, were some of the first recorded patterns. Despite their limited resources, early quiltmakers devised designed patterns. One-patch blocks, such as a checkerboard arrangement of dark and light rectangles, created repeat patterns, making use of available scraps of fabric.

Simple repeat designs were being developed by folding squares of paper into three, four, then nine, equal parts. These were then subdivided into simple geometric shapes: triangles, rectangles, and diamonds, and were the very beginnings of block designs, that became ever more sophisticated.

Each category of geometric blocks is categorized by the grid that can be imposed over the design, either a four-, five-, seven-, or nine-patch. For example, the four-patch will always be divisible by four, even though the working grid may be sixteen or more squares. To determine which category a block falls into, impose a grid of equal squares over the design, as shown below. This will help when deciding on the desired finished size of a block and for making the templates or using rotary cutting tools. The order of piecing is to start with the smallest pieces and work in straight lines where possible.

Established designs for pieced blocks have names, many of which reflect the lives of the quiltmakers who devised them. Names such as Flying Geese, Lincoln's Platform, and Walls of Jericho record their preoccupations with everyday tasks and religion, and the names endure today.

The application of the geometric units is diverse. Placed edge to edge, secondary designs appear, adding complexity to even the simplest blocks. When separated by strips of fabric called sashing strips, each block is given a frame, isolating it as a separate block. This is used on sampler quilts, where each block has a different pattern. Placing them edge to edge would result in a confusion of different shapes. Set "on point," square blocks are presented as diamonds. The edges of the quilts are filled with triangles to make up the square or rectangular shape. Two or more block designs can be used together to create intriguing secondary patterns, and alternating a pieced block with a solid one provides a showcase for elaborate quilting stitching.

The concept of the repeat block provides a versatile way to approach quilt design. Variation and individuality can be introduced, even to a straightforward, traditional pattern, by fabric choices, use of borders, and different settings of the blocks.

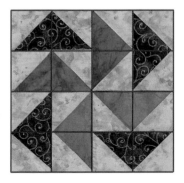

Four-patch blocks
A four-patch block is always recognizable by its 4 × 4 grid. Count four squares across and four down.

Five-patch blocks
Here five squares run across and five down, identifying the 5 × 5 grid.

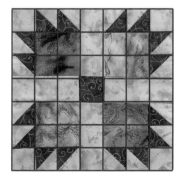

Seven-patch blocks
If an equal grid of 7 × 7 can be placed over a block, it is a seven-patch block.

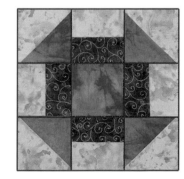

Nine-patch blocks
Unlike the four-, five-, and seven-patch blocks, the nine-patch block comprises a grid of 3 × 3.

Setting and assembly

Patch blocks, once they are prepared, and whether they are pieced or appliquéd, can be set together in a number of different settings. Straight sets, that is, the setting of the blocks edge to edge, will create secondary designs, the shapes linking and blending together to create more complex patterns than is evident when a single block is separated by sashing. The individual design of each block appears to be lost in an overall pattern.

1 Nine-patch blocks set edge to edge show the potential of a pieced block to create secondary designs.

2 Two different block patterns set together alternately increase the possibilities further.

3 When separated by sashing strips, the blocks appear more clearly as a single pattern. This is the best way to showcase block designs.

4 The sashing can be made of straight strips or with small contrasting squares called cornerstones stitched at the intersections.

5 Alternatively, blocks are set together "on point." The blocks are turned on their corners so they appear as diamonds. Given this treatment, the blocks look completely different. The sides and corners of the quilt have to be squared up with triangles and the blocks joined in diagonal lines. When stitching blocks together on point, it is best to work from a diagram of the quilt to establish how many blocks are needed in each line and how to position the triangles. When planning a quilt with on point blocks, it is useful to know that the diagonal measurement of a square can be calculated by multiplying the measurement of the side by 1.141.

6 Another effective way of setting blocks on point is to alternate them with solid blocks. For appliquéd blocks, this will separate the motifs and provide a plain space for fancy quilting. If you give pieced blocks this treatment and use the same fabric for the solid squares as for the background shapes of the block, the background and setting squares will merge to give the impression that the blocks are floating.

1
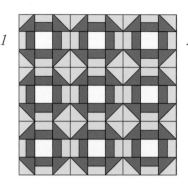

2
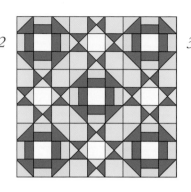

3
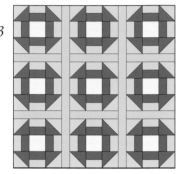

4
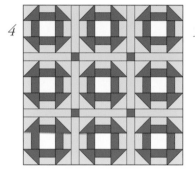

5
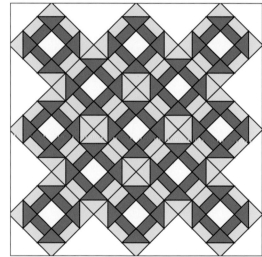

6
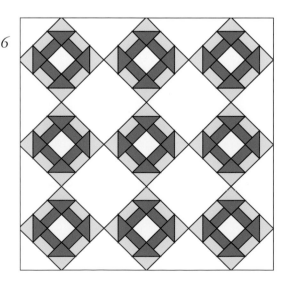

7 Sashing can also be used to separate blocks set on point.

8 Quilts do not necessarily have to be made from blocks. This pattern uses just one shape repeated all over the quilt top. This can be a square, rectangle, triangle, hexagon, or diamond—in fact, any shape that will fit together without leaving gaps. A popular interpretation of the one-patch in the nineteenth century was the charm quilt in which every patch was a different fabric.

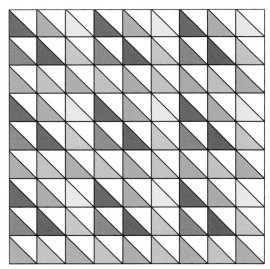

9 A single block quilt is one in which the whole quilt top is taken up with one large motif such as the Lone Star, or a Hawaiian appliqué in which a large cut-out shape is applied to a background, then quilted.

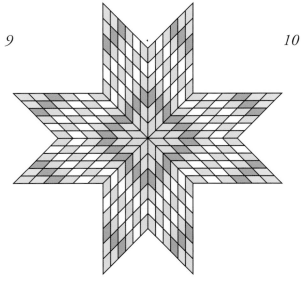

10 Strip or strippy quilts have a pattern of columns down the quilt. There are specific, named patterns associated with these, such as Flying Geese and Stacked Bricks. These pieced or appliquéd columns are separated by solid strips.

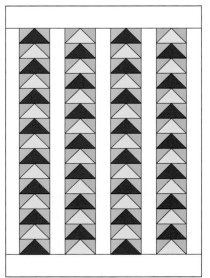

11 A medallion quilt always has a large central motif. This can be pieced, appliquéd, or even be a printed panel framed by a series of borders, which may also be pieced, appliquéd or created with a combination of techniques.

12 A four-block quilt is composed of four large blocks, each of which forms a quarter of the quilt top.

Four-patch blocks

Four-patch blocks are enormously popular, and they are the simplest form to understand. As their title suggests, four-patch blocks are made up of four equal squares that are then pieced together to make a whole block. The more complex four-patch blocks are made of 16 squares (4×4) and even 64 squares (8×8). As a basic rule, if a 2×2 grid can be placed over the design, it is a four-patch block. The treatment that each of these squares receives is what determines the overall pattern of the block. Four patterns are demonstrated in detail, with further diagrams for four-patch blocks shown on page 79.

Windmill

The finished Windmill block gives the impression of the sails of a windmill, hence its name. It is made up from a repeated patch turned through 90° each time. Three colors of fabric should be used for best effect in this block: one light, one medium, and one dark.

1 Draw a 9" (24 cm) square on graph paper. Divide this into four quarters. Using the diagram as a guide, draw the Windmill pattern within the grid. Mark the grain lines on each shape with arrows parallel to the outer edges of the block. Cut out one of each shape and mount onto card. Cut the card around each shape, adding a 1/4" (0.75 cm) seam allowance all around. Label the templates with the relevant letters. (See Making templates, page 40.)

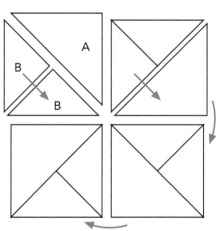

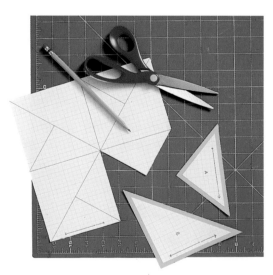

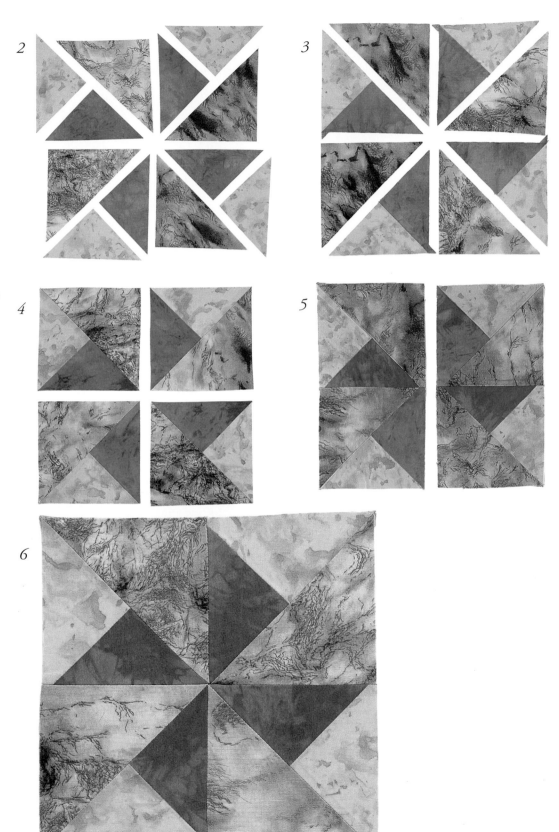

2 Cut the fabric patches using the templates, as follows: four mauve A triangles, four blue B triangles, and four gray B triangles. On a flat surface, lay out the patches in the correct order, following the block pattern.

3 Stitch the B triangles in blue and gray pairs along their shorter edges, right sides together, taking a ¹⁄₄" (0.75 cm) seam allowance.

4 Stitch the B/B triangles to the A triangles to make four pieced squares, each of which is a quarter of the finished block.

5 Stitch the squares together in pairs, ensuring that they are correctly oriented, to create two vertical strips.

6 Stitch the two strips together and press all the seams to finish the block.

Indian Star

A combination of squares and triangles is used to create the Indian Star. It is a variation of the Eight-pointed Star that is used in the Sampler quilt (see page 98), which has one single square center instead of the four-patch center square here. Three fabrics are used for this block.

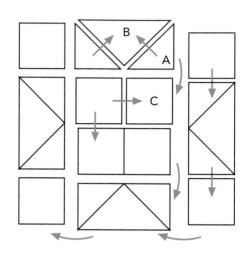

1 Draw a 9" (24 cm) square on graph paper. Divide this into an equal 4 × 4 grid. Using the diagram as a guide, draw the Indian Star pattern within the grid. Label each piece that will be made into a template. Mark the grain lines on each shape parallel to the outer edges of the block. Cut out one of each shape and mount onto card. Cut the card around each shape, adding a ¼" (0.75 cm) seam allowance all around. Label the templates with the relevant letters. (See Making templates, page 40.)

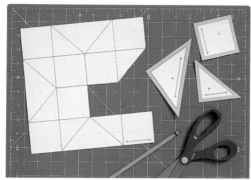

2 Cut the fabric patches using the templates, as follows: eight turquoise A triangles, four gray B triangles, two gray C squares, six mauve C squares.

To make the star points, stitch an A triangle to one side of each B triangle, right sides together. Press seams, then stitch another A triangle to the opposite side of each B triangle to make four rectangles. Stitch two gray C squares to two mauve C squares, right sides together, to make two rectangles.

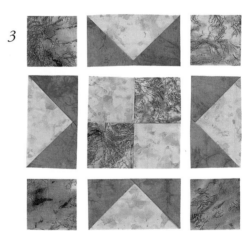

3 Stitch the two C/C rectangles together to create the center square.

4 Lay out the pieces on a flat surface to check positioning. Stitch pieces together to make three vertical strips.

5 Seam the three pieced sections together and press all the seams flat to complete the Indian Star block.

Dutchman's Puzzle

As with the Windmill block, Dutchman's Puzzle is made from a repeated patch turned through 90° each time. Here, three fabrics have been used, but it works equally well with just two.

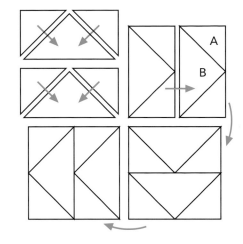

1 Draw a 9" (24 cm) square on graph paper. Divide this into a 4 × 4 grid. Using the diagram as a guide, draw the Dutchman's Puzzle block within the grid. Label each piece that will be made into a template. Mark the grain lines on each shape parallel to the outer edges of the block. Cut out one of each shape and mount onto card. Cut the card around each shape, adding a ¼" (0.75 cm) seam allowance all around. Label the templates with the relevant letter. (See Making template cuttings, page 40.)

2 Cut the fabric patches, using the templates, as follows: 16 gray A triangles, four turquoise B triangles, and four blue B triangles.

To make each rectangular unit, stitch right sides together, an A triangle to each side of each B triangle. Press the seams. Lay out the rectangles on a flat surface in the correct pattern.

3 Stitch the rectangles in pairs, right sides together, to make four equal squares, each of which is a quarter of the finished block.

4 Stitch the squares in pairs to create two vertical strips.

5 Stitch the two strips together and press all seams to complete the block.

1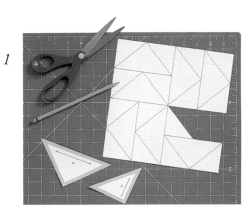

2

3

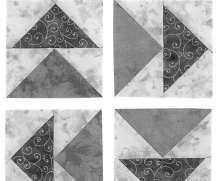

4

5

Double X

Four fabrics are used here to make this four-patch block of squares and triangles. Alternatively, using just two contrasting colors can create a wonderful geometric pattern, especially if used in a straight set quilt.

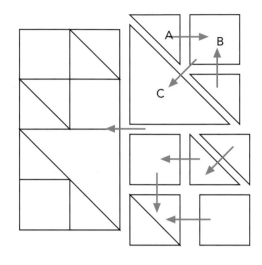

1 Draw a 9" (24 cm) square on graph paper. Divide this into an equal grid of 4 × 4. Using the diagram as a guide, draw the Double X pattern within the grid. Label each piece that will be made into a template. Mark the grain lines on each shape parallel to the outer edges of the block. Cut out one of each shape and mount onto card. Cut the card around each shape, adding a ¼" (0.75 cm) seam allowance all around. Label the templates with the relevant letters. (See Making templates, page 40.)

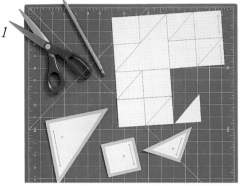

2 Cut the fabric patches using the templates, as follows: four blue A triangles, eight gray A triangles, four yellow B squares, two blue B squares, and two mauve C triangles.

Stitch four pairs of blue/gray A triangles, right sides together, to make four pieced squares. Stitch one gray A triangle to one blue B square, right sides together. Press the seams to one side. Add a second A triangle to make a larger pieced triangle. Repeat to make the second one.

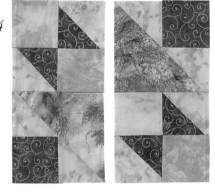

3 Stitch two C triangles to the larger pieced triangles to make two squares, each of which is a quarter of the block. Stitch the AA squares to the B squares in pairs. Stitch the pairs together to make two more squares the size of a quarter of the finished block.

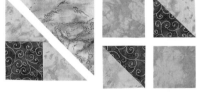

4 Arrange the four squares in the correct order and stitch the quarter squares of the block together in pairs to make two vertical strips.

5 Stitch these two strips together and press all seams to complete the block.

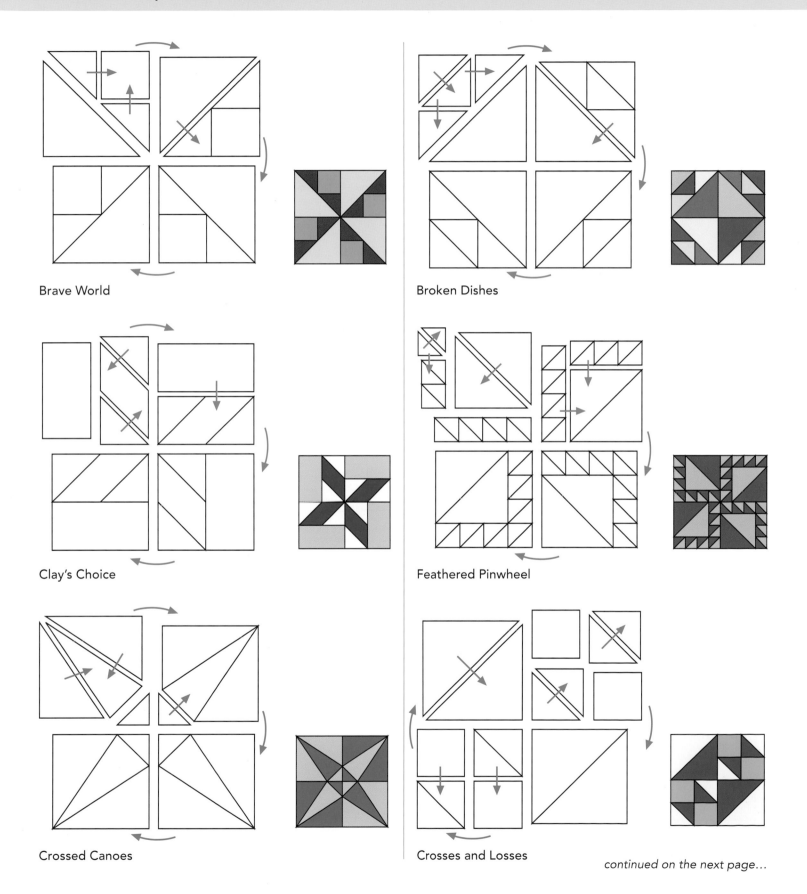

Brave World

Broken Dishes

Clay's Choice

Feathered Pinwheel

Crossed Canoes

Crosses and Losses

continued on the next page...

More four-patch blocks (continued)

Flock

Snail Trail

Rose Bud

Squares and Arrows

Seesaw

Stars and Diamonds

Five-patch blocks

Five-patch blocks are always designed on a grid of 5 × 5, totalling 25 squares. The variety of ways in which each of the pieces within this grid is treated is what determines the overall pattern of the block. Here, two such blocks—Fruit Basket and Jack-in-a-box—are demonstrated, along with diagrams for six alternative five-patch blocks.

Fruit Basket

The Fruit Basket is an asymmetrical block, which can create some interesting patterns if set without sashing, either straight set or diagonally. It is built up of three different sizes of triangles and one size of rectangle. Here, three colors have been used.

1 Draw a 9" (24 cm) square on graph paper. Divide this into an equal grid of 5 × 5.

In order for the five-patch block to fit into a 9" (24 cm) square, one of the divisions is ¼" (0.75 cm) wider than the others. It is therefore advisable to make separate triangle templates for the two patches that form the base of the basket.

Use the diagram as a guide to make the Fruit Basket pattern within the grid. Label each piece that will be made into a template. Mark the grain lines on each shape parallel to the outer edges of the block. Cut out one of each shape and mount onto card. Cut the card around each shape, adding a ¼" (0.75 cm) seam allowance all around. Label the templates with the relevant letters. *(See Making templates, page 40)*

1

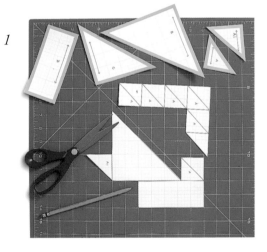

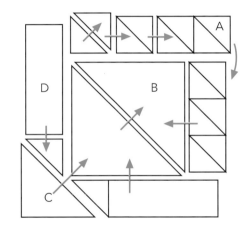

2

2 Cut the fabric patches, using the templates, as follows: nine blue and seven gray A triangles, one blue and one turquoise B triangles, one gray C triangle, and two gray D rectangles. Lay out the patches in the correct positions on a flat surface.

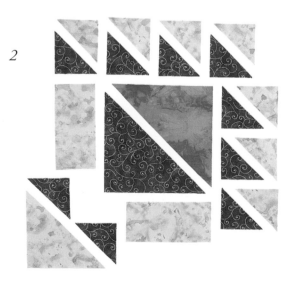

continued on the next page...

Fruit Basket (continued)

3 Make seven bi-colored squares by stitching together blue and gray A triangles. Stitch the large B triangles together to make one large square. Add the two remaining blue A triangles to one end of each D rectangle.

4 Stitch the small A/A squares into one set of three and one set of four.

5 Stitch these rectangles to the top and right-hand side of the large B/B square, also joining the two strips where they meet at the corner.

6 Stitch the D/A pieces to the remaining two sides of the large B/B square.

7 Stitch the C triangle to the remaining corner of the whole block. Press to complete the block.

3

4

5

6

7

Jack-in-a-box

With careful selection of fabrics, the Jack-in-a-box provides a block pattern with a 3-D, folded appearance. Five colors of fabric are needed to achieve the effect.

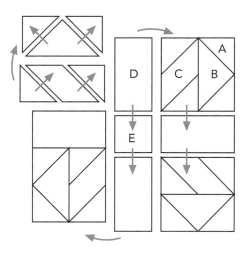

1 Draw a 9" (24 cm) square on graph paper. Divide this into an equal grid of 5 × 5. In order for the five-patch to fit into a 9" (24 cm) block format, the center cross is ¼" (0.75 cm) wider than the other grid sections. Using the diagram as a guide, draw out the Jack-in-a-box pattern within the grid. Label each piece that will be made into a template. Mark the grain lines on each shape with arrows parallel to the outer edges of the block. Cut out one of each shape and mount onto card. Cut around each shape, adding a ¼" (0.75 cm) seam allowance all around. Label the templates with the relevant letters. (See Making templates, page 40.)

2 Cut the fabric patches, using the templates, as follows: 16 gray A triangles, four turquoise B triangles, four mauve C rhomboids, four blue D rectangles, and one yellow E square. Lay out the patches in the correct order.

   Taking a ¼" (0.75 cm) seam allowance, stitch two A triangles and one B triangle together to create a rectangle; make four of these. Stitch two A triangles and one C rhomboid together to make another rectangle; repeat to create four.

3 Stitch the A/B/A and A/C/A units together to create four equal squares, ensuring that the orientation of the pieces is correct.

1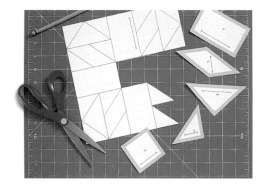

2

3

4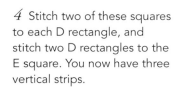

5

4 Stitch two of these squares to each D rectangle, and stitch two D rectangles to the E square. You now have three vertical strips.

5 Complete the block by stitching together the three strips and pressing the seams.

More five-patch blocks

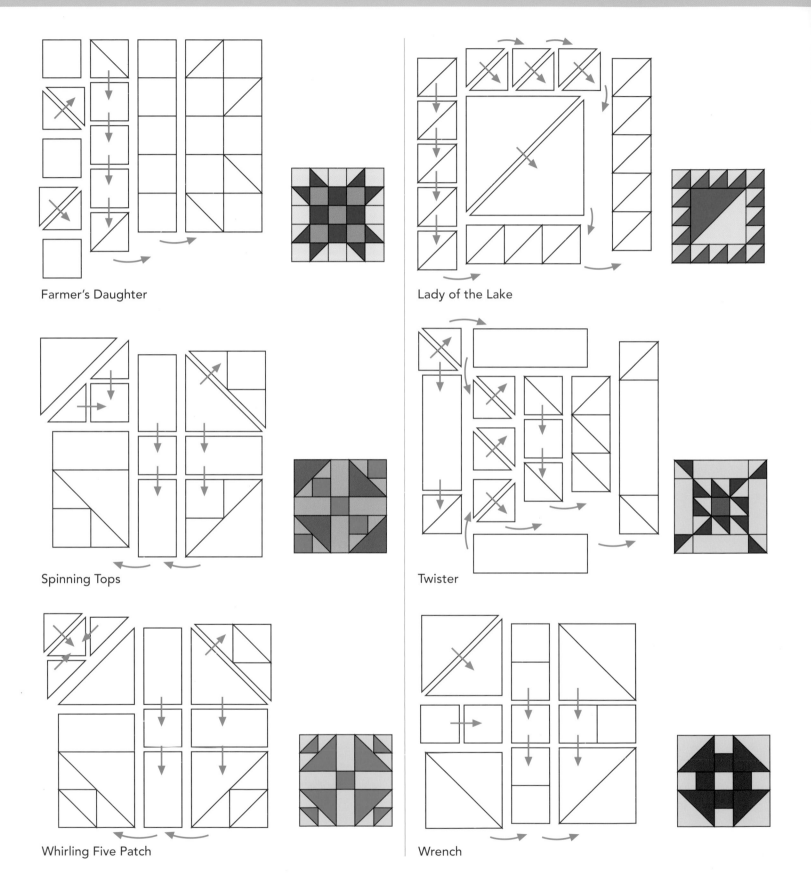

Farmer's Daughter

Lady of the Lake

Spinning Tops

Twister

Whirling Five Patch

Wrench

Seven-patch blocks

Seven-patch blocks are block patterns that are constructed on a 7 × 7 grid, totalling 49 squares. Seven-patch blocks are more challenging than others because of the increased number of smaller pieces required to construct the designs.

Bear's Paw

The Bear's Paw can look quite complicated, because of the number of pieces of fabric to cut, but it is actually a fairly simple construction. One way to reduce the time it takes to piece the initial stages of this block is to use the quick-sewn, half-square triangles technique (see page 56). Here, three fabrics have been used to create the block, although more can be used, if desired.

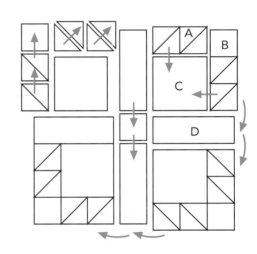

1 Draw a 9" (24 cm) square on graph paper. Divide this into an equal grid of 7 × 7. For the seven-patch to fit into the 9" (24 cm) block, the pieces that make up the center cross (D template and the center square) are ¼" (0.75 cm) wider than the other squares. Therefore, make a separate square template for the center.

Use the diagram as a guide to mark out the Bear's paw pattern within the grid. Label each piece that will be made into a template. Mark the grain lines on each shape parallel to the outer edges of the block. Cut out one of each shape and mount onto card. Cut the card around each shape, adding a ¼" seam allowance (0.75 cm) all around. Label the templates with the relevant letters.

1

2 Cut the fabric patches, using the templates, as follows: 16 gray and 16 blue A triangles, four gray B squares, one blue center square, four mauve C squares, and four gray D rectangles. Lay out the patches in the correct order.

2

continued on the next page…

3 Make 16 bi-colored squares by stitching together one of each of the A triangles.

4 Stitch these squares into eight rectangles, then stitch a corner B square onto the end of four of these rectangles. Be careful to keep the orientation of the seams and the position of the fabrics correct.

5 Stitch the remaining A/A rectangles to the C squares first, then add the A/A/B rectangles to make the four large squares, the "paws."

6 Link two of the four paws together with a D rectangle to make the left column, and repeat for the right column; ensure that the A triangles point outward from the center. Stitch the center square between the remaining D rectangles.

7 Seam the three pieces together and press to complete the block.

Note

Accuracy when making templates, cutting out patches, and keeping a $1/4$" (0.75 cm) seam allowance is essential, especially when working with smaller patches, such as the A triangles and the B squares in this block.

Prickly Pear

This block looks daunting, but as with the Bear's Paw (see previous pages), it is a simple construction that can be made speedier by using the quick-sewn, half-square triangles technique (see page 56).

1 Draw a 9" (24 cm) square on graph paper. Divide this into an equal grid of 7 × 7. (As it is difficult to divide nine by seven, the simplest way is to draw the grid squares 1¼" (3 cm) and use a scant seam allowance when sewing the seams.)

Use the diagram as a guide to mark the Prickly Pear pattern within the grid. Label the pieces to be made into templates. Mark the grain lines on each shape with arrows parallel to the outer edges of the block. Cut out one of each shape and mount onto card. Cut around each shape, adding a ¼" (0.75 cm) seam allowance all around. Label the templates with the relevant letters. (See Making templates, page 40.)

2 Cut the fabric patches, using the templates, as follows: 20 turquoise and 20 yellow A triangles, four yellow and one blue B squares, four blue and four mauve C triangles, and four yellow D rectangles.

Stitch the turquoise and yellow A triangles together to create 20 bi-colored squares. Stitch 16 of these squares together in pairs, checking their orientation. Stitch a yellow B square to the end of four of the pairs. Stitch the remaining four A/A squares to the D rectangles. Join the C triangles into mauve and blue pairs to create four squares.

3 Stitch the remaining A/A squares to one side of each of the C/C squares first, then add the A/A/B rectangles to the other sides, again checking their orientation. Press the seams as you go.

4 Stitch the center blue B square between two of the A/A/D rectangles, making sure that the small triangles face outward from the center. Stitch the three pieces on either side together until you have three columns.

5 Stitch the three columns together and press the seams to finish the block.

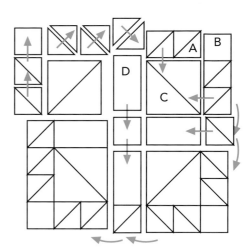

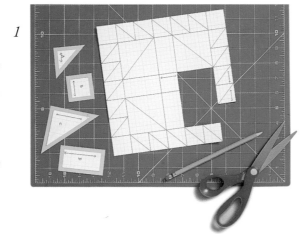

More seven-patch blocks

KEY The arrows indicate the sequence in which each piece is stitched to its neighbor, to create the block patterns.

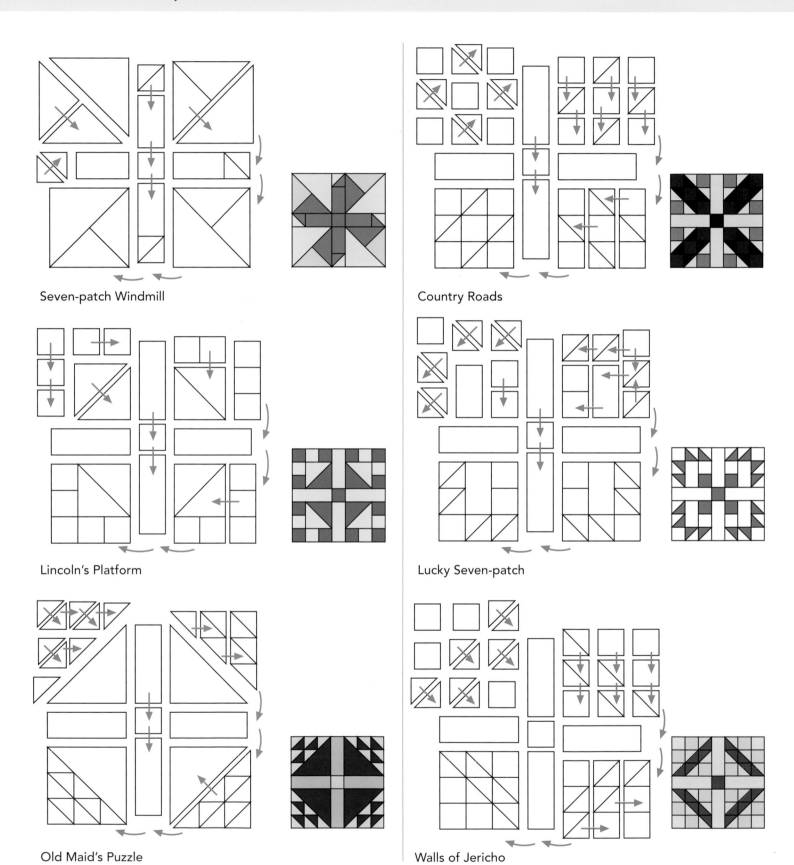

Seven-patch Windmill

Country Roads

Lincoln's Platform

Lucky Seven-patch

Old Maid's Puzzle

Walls of Jericho

Nine-patch blocks

Nine-patch blocks can cause confusion for piecemakers. Whereas the other categories of blocks are made up of a divisible grid, the nine-patch is made up of nine squares *in total*, with a grid of 3 × 3. Think of the term nine-patch as simply a name rather than a description. Some of the most popular blocks around are nine-patches, because they are relatively easy to make and the grids allows for some very interesting and unusual designs.

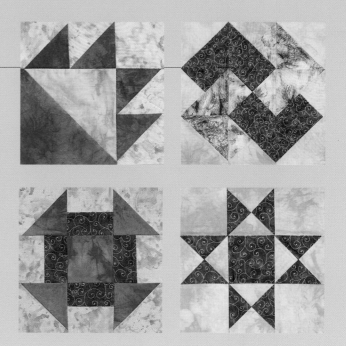

Ohio Star

The Ohio Star is a traditional pattern, and often appears in other decorative art forms, such as floor tiles. The design is older than the American state and one theory explains that the name was adopted as exploration of the continent progressed. In the example here two colors have been used, one of light value and one of dark value, and if desired a third can be introduced by adding another fabric as the center square.

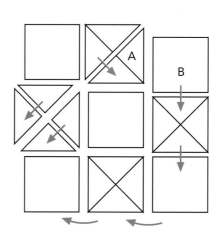

1 Draw a 9" (24 cm) square on graph paper. Divide this into an equal grid of 3 × 3. Using the diagram as a guide, draw out the Ohio Star pattern within the grid. Label each piece that will be made into a template. Mark the grain lines on each shape parallel to the outer edges of the block. Cut out one of each shape and mount onto card. Cut around each shape, adding a ¼" (0.75 cm) seam allowance all around. Label the templates with the relevant letters.

continued on the next page…

2 Cut the fabric patches, using the templates, as follows: eight blue and eight yellow A triangles, and four yellow and one blue B squares.

Make bi-colored triangles from pairs of A triangles, checking the position of the fabric to make the star points.

3 Stitch these triangle units into pairs to make squares that will form the star points.

4 Stitch three squares together to form three columns.

5 Stitch two vertical seams to complete the block. Press.

Churn Dash

Many popular traditional blocks—of which Churn Dash is one—have names that relate to the everyday lives of early quiltmakers. The blocks would have been devised by folding paper to create new patterns.

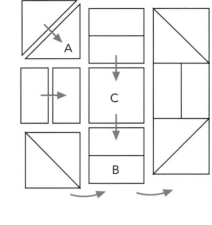

1 Draw a 9" (24 cm) square on graph paper. Divide this into an equal grid of 3 × 3. Using the diagram as a guide, draw the Churn dash block within the grid. Mark the grain lines on each shape parallel to the outer edges of the block. Cut out one sample of each shape and mount onto card. Cut the card around each shape, adding ¼" (0.75 cm) seam allowance all around. Label the templates with the relevant letters. (See Making templates, page 40.)

1

2 Cut the fabric patches, using the templates, as follows: four gray and four turquoise A triangles, four gray and four blue B rectangles, and one turquoise C square. On a flat surface, lay out the patches in their correct positions.

2

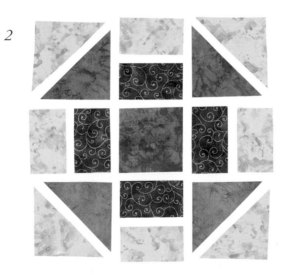

3 Stitch the gray and turquoise A triangles together to make four bi-colored, corner squares. Stitch the gray and blue rectangles together on the long edge to make the four side squares.

3

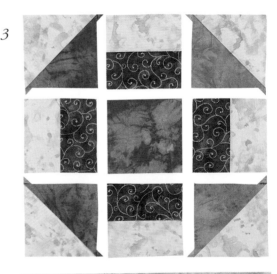

4 Stitch the squares into three columns of three, ensuring that they are correctly oriented.

4

5 Stitch the three columns together. Press the seams to complete the block.

5

Card Trick

By using a combination of dark, medium, and light fabrics, an illusion of folded shapes is created. It is a challenge to get the fabrics in the correct sequence to achieve the overlapping effect, but the results can be stunning.

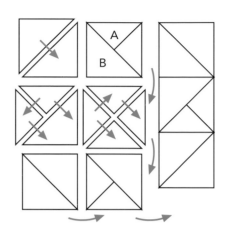

1 Draw a 9" (24 cm) square on graph paper. Divide this into an equal 3 × 3 grid. Follow the diagram to mark the Card Trick pattern within the grid. Label each piece that will be made into a template. Mark the grain lines on each shape parallel to the outer edges of the block. Cut out one of each shape and mount onto card. Cut the card around each shape, adding a ¹/₄" (0.75 cm) seam allowance all around. Label the templates with the relevant letters. *(See Making templates, page 40.)*

2 Cut the fabric patches, using the templates, as follows: four yellow, four mauve, four blue A triangles; and four yellow, four mauve, four blue B triangles.

Make six bi-colored triangles by stitching together two blue and mauve A triangles ; two blue and yellow A triangles; and two yellow and mauve A triangles.

3 Arrange the A/A triangles and the B triangles in the correct order on a flat surface and stitch them into nine squares.

4 Stitch the squares into three vertical columns.

5 Stitch the three columns together. Press the seams to complete the block.

1

2
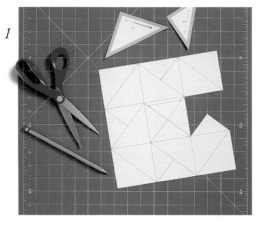

3

4

5
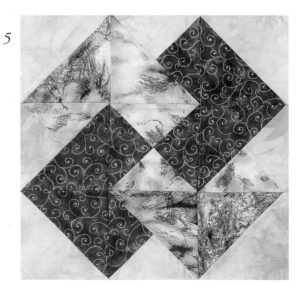

Sawtooth

As with many pieced blocks, the Sawtooth is named after a familiar everyday object; the triangles set as they are here representing the cutting edges of a saw. Triangles set like this in a line are also often used as a border motif to frame the center panel of a quilt. High contrast between the dark and light triangles gives a strong graphic effect.

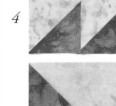

1 Draw a 9" (24 cm) square on graph paper. Divide this into an equal 3 × 3 grid. Use the diagram as a guide to draw the Sawtooth pattern within the grid. Label each piece that will be made into a template. Mark the grain lines on each shape parallel to the outer edges of the block. Cut out one of each shape and mount onto card. Cut the card around each shape, adding a ¹⁄₄" (0.75 cm) seam allowance all around. Label the templates with the relevant letters. (See Making templates, page 40.)

1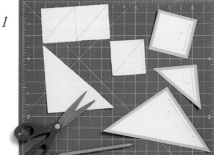

2 Many blocks, including the Sawtooth, use pieced squares made from half-square or right-angled triangles. Quick-sewn half-square triangles are the simplest and quickest way to create many of these . To determine the size of the squares to cut for quick-sewn half-square triangles, measure one of the shorter sides of the relevant triangle (see Easy-piecing, page 56).

3 Cut the fabric patches, using the templates, as follows: four gray and four turquoise A triangles, one yellow and one turquoise B triangle, and one gray C square.

2
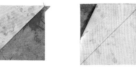

Stitch together the gray and turquoise A triangles to make small bi-colored squares; stitch the B triangles together to make one large square.

3

4 Stitch the bi-colored A/A squares together. Add the C square to the end of one rectangle, maintaining the orientation of the seams and the positions of the fabrics.

4

5 Stitch the shorter of the rectangles to the large square first, then add the longer rectangle. Press the seams to complete the block.

5

More nine-patch blocks

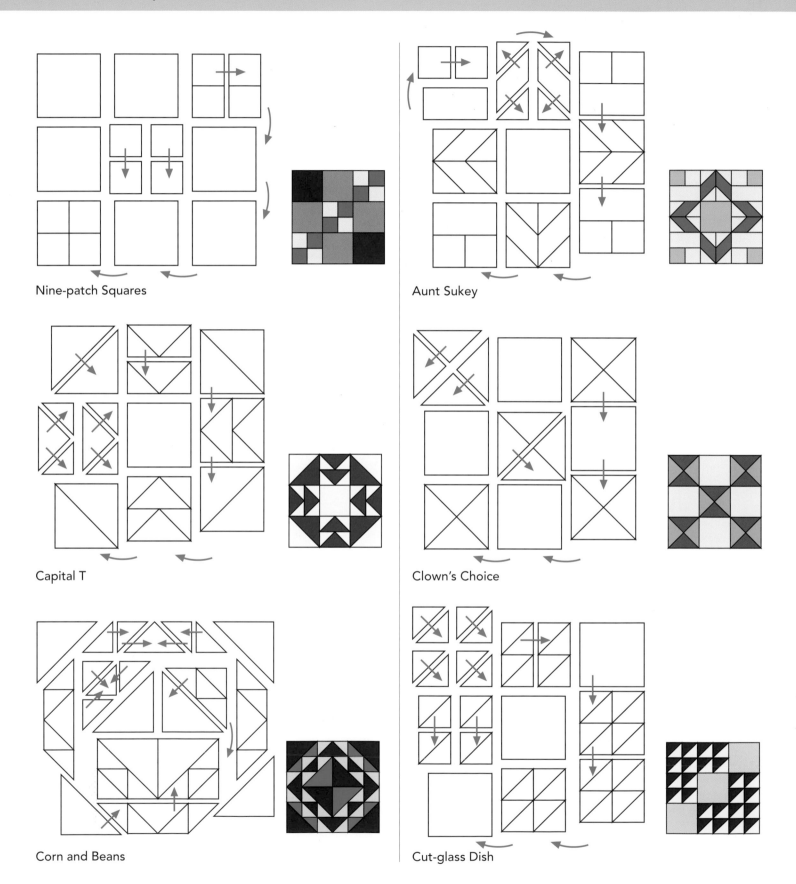

Nine-patch Squares

Aunt Sukey

Capital T

Clown's Choice

Corn and Beans

Cut-glass Dish

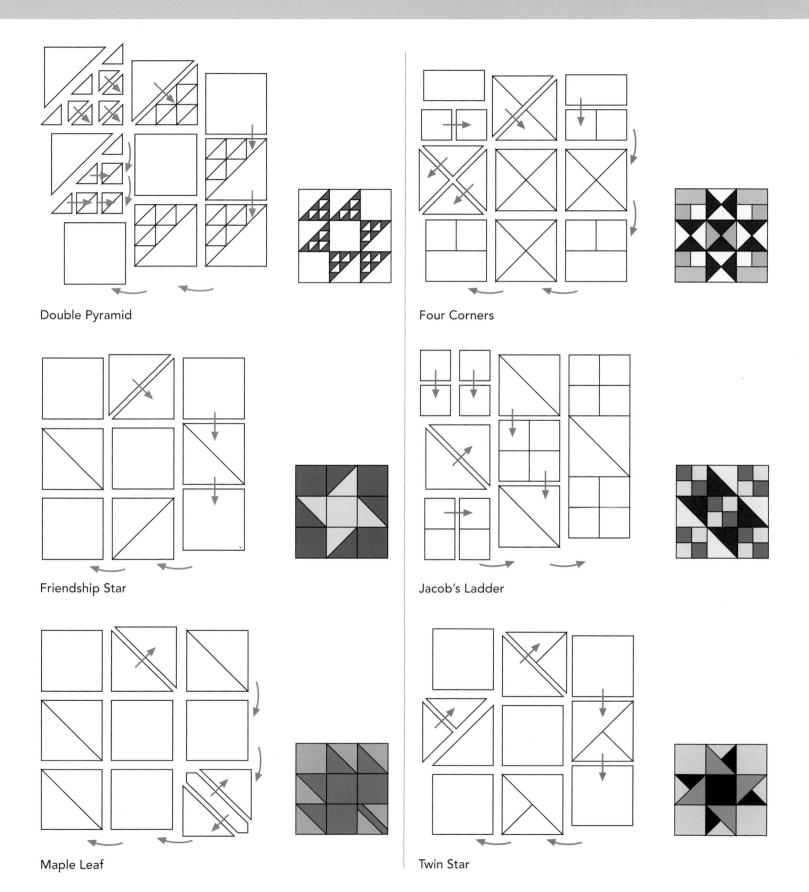

Double Pyramid

Four Corners

Friendship Star

Jacob's Ladder

Maple Leaf

Twin Star

Hexagon blocks

Hexagon and related shapes are often associated with "English patchwork," the method of construction in which each patch is basted around a paper template (see page 126). The patches are whip stitched together by hand.

To construct these patterns is a challenge as there are many inset corners. Isometric graph paper can be used to plot out the designs below.

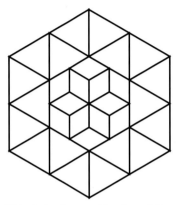

This design is a combination of diamonds, triangles, and stars.

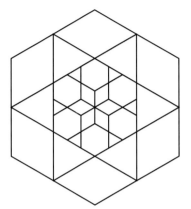

A combination of diamonds, hexagons and triangles.

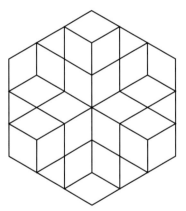

Repeated diamonds are set to form a star pattern.

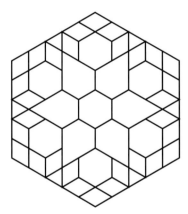

A complicated pattern to provide a challenge.

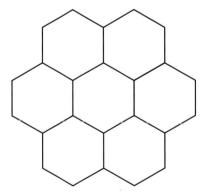

Hexagons in rosettes; the traditional pattern known as Grandmother's Flower Garden.

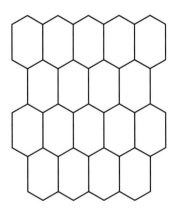

The long hexagon is sometimes referred to as "Church Window," not to be confused with "Cathedral Window."

Pictorial blocks

Pictorial blocks are often a whimsical interpretation of common objects, translating geometric shapes into picture form. The six illustrated are simple patterns, ideal for children's quilts. The addition to the blocks of novelty fabrics adds to their appeal.

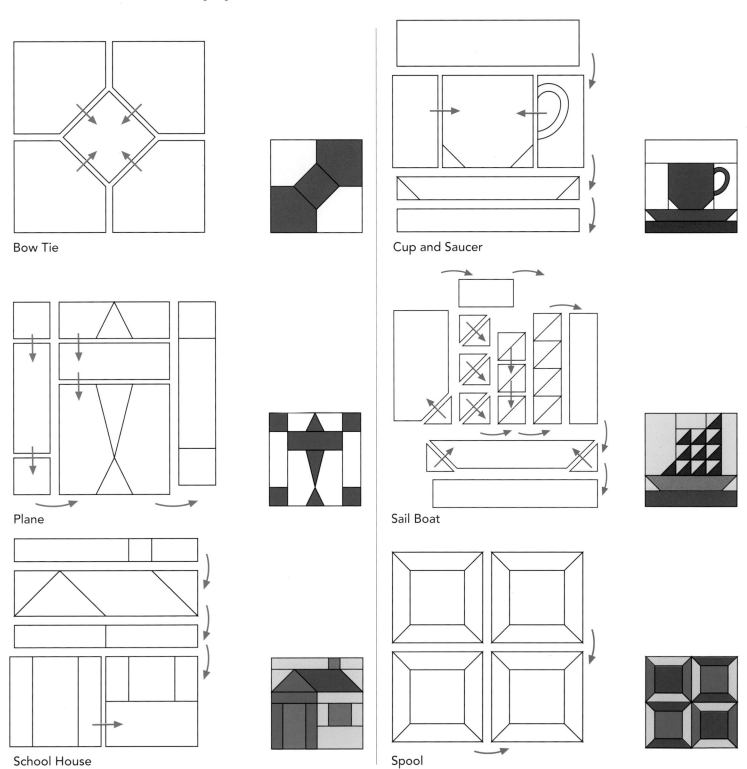

Bow Tie

Cup and Saucer

Plane

Sail Boat

School House

Spool

Patchwork project: Sampler quilt

Making a sampler quilt is an ideal way to learn the first techniques of patchwork. All the blocks in this quilt are pieced from basic shapes: squares, rectangles, and triangles. For detailed instructions on how to make each of the 12 blocks featured in the Sampler quilt, see pages 74 to 93. The Indian Star pattern (see page 76) has been slightly simplified in this quilt, and instead has an Eight-pointed Star in the center column with a single square at its heart. Each finished block dimension is 9" square (24 cm). The blocks can all be easily scaled up to 12" square (30.5 cm) for a larger format quilt. All the fabrics used in the quilt top are cut from 45" (115 cm) widths.

Finished size

52" × 40" (131 × 102 cm)

Fabric

½ yd. (½ m) each of purple, lavender, burgundy, and white
1 yd. (1 m) of pink, to include binding
1½ yd. (1½ m) of pale green, for the sashing and borders
53½" × 45½" (137 × 120 cm) batting
53½" × 45½" (137 × 120 cm) backing

---

1 First make the 12 blocks to be used in the sampler quilt—Fruit Basket (see page 81), Indian Star/Eight-pointed Star (see page 76), Windmill (see page 74), Bear's Paw (see page 85), Jack-in-a-box (see page 83), Churn Dash (see page 91), Ohio Star (see page 89), Sawtooth (see page 93), Prickly Pear (see page 87), Card Trick (see page 92), Dutchman's Puzzle (see page 77), and Double X (see page 78). There are dozens of possibilities for fabric choice and placement. All fabrics used in the quilt top are 45" (115 cm) wide. When stitching all pieces together, use a ¼" (0.75 cm) seam allowance.

2 Arrange the blocks three across by four down on a flat surface.

Sashing strips

1 Cut nine short sashing strips 3½" (9 cm) wide. All sashing should be cut to the width of the narrowest block in order to square up the quilt. Stitch each short sashing strip between each of four blocks to create three columns.

2 Cut two sashing strips 45½" × 3½" (120 × 9 cm). Trim the strips to the length of the shortest column in order to square up the quilt. Stitch the two long sashing strips between the three columns of blocks, taking care to line up the seams across the width of the quilt. (See Sashing and Borders, page 200.)

Borders

1 Measure across the center of the quilt. Cut two border strips 4½" (10 cm) wide by this measurement. Stitch these to the top and bottom edges.

2 Measure the quilt top to bottom. Cut two strips 4½" (10 cm) wide by this measurement. Stitch these to the left and right sides of the quilt. (See Sashing and Borders, page 200.)

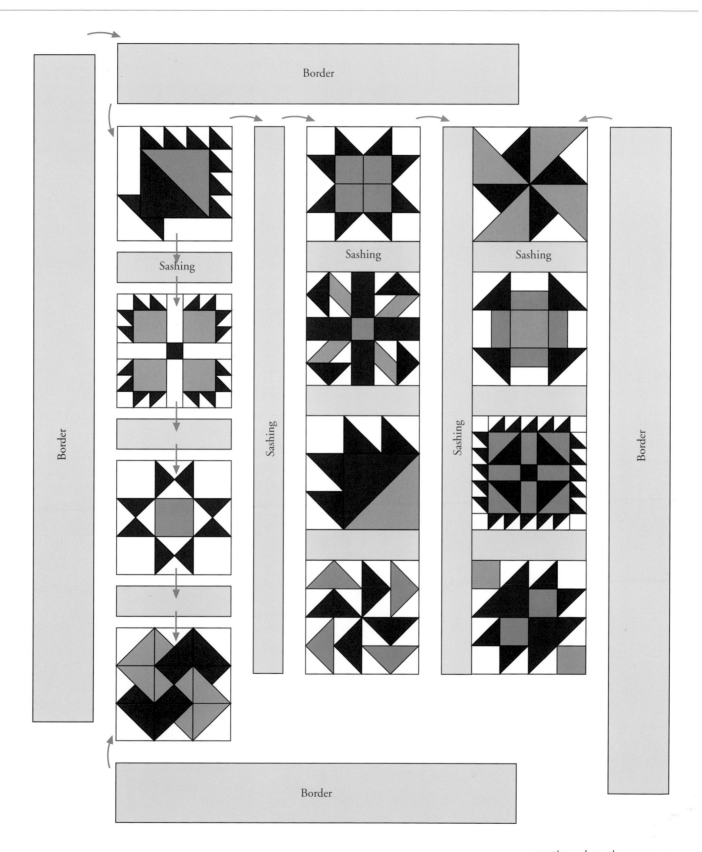

continued on the next page...

Quilting and finishing

1 Lay out the backing, right side down, and smooth out any wrinkles; press if necessary. Center the batting on top of the backing, and then the pieced top, right side up, leaving a margin of batting and backing showing all around.

2 Pin and baste the fabric sandwich together.

3 Quilt by hand or machine in your desired quilting pattern (see pages 213 to 217 for the possibilities).

Binding

1 Cut five binding strips 2³/₈" (6 cm) wide, across the width of the fabric.

2 Join strips to make a piece long enough to go around the quilt edges, with 4" to 6" (10 to 15 cm) extra for the corner miters.

3 Fold the full length of strip in half lengthwise, wrong sides together, and press.

4 Trim the batting and backing of the quilt sandwich so that all the layers are evenly sized to the quilt top.

5 Align the folded binding to the right side of the quilt, stitching through all the layers by machine.

6 Fold the binding over and hand stitch to the back of the quilt to finish the project.

Specialty piecing

The construction of regular blocks can be varied in a number of ways to create a host of design possibilities. Many of these following examples, although based on traditional patterns, can be pieced more quickly when using the tools and equipment available today—a rotary cutting set and a sewing machine with an accurate ¼" (0.75 cm) foot.

Irish Chain

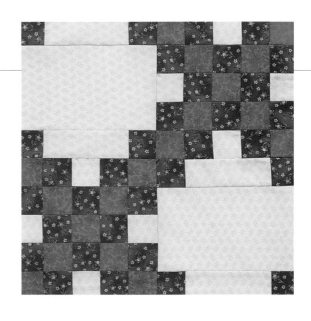

Many traditional quilt designs were brought to America by the pioneers. Settlers from particular communities, influenced by an existing folk heritage, made quilts that adapted American quilting ideas. The Irish Chain is one such design. Rather than just a single four- or nine-patch of squares, the pattern alternates two different block patterns which, when set together present a seemingly complex pattern. One block of squares provides opportunity to use small scraps of fabric and the second block of rectangles makes a showcase for decorative quilting motifs. With modern tools and techniques. it is possible to create Irish Chain quickly with strip piecing. Here, three fabrics are required, two patterned and one solid.

1 Both of the blocks that make up the Irish Chain fit into a 5 × 5 grid. Decide on the size of block you wish to create. Choose a measurement divisible by five, for example 10" or 15" (25 or 40 cm).

1

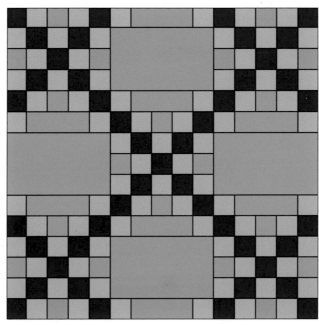

continued on the next page…

All-squares blocks

1 The first block construction begins with three sequences of strips. Divide the finished block size by five, add ¹/₂" (1.5 cm), and cut this measurement across the width of the fabric. For example, for a 10" (25 cm) block, cut several strips 2¹/₂" (6.5 cm) wide of each color. Stitch the strips together, along the long edges, in the following sequences: cream, red, green, red, cream; red, green, red, green, red; red, green, cream, red, green. Press the seams of the first and third set away from the center. Press the seams of the second set toward the center.

2 Cut sections across the strips to the same width as the strips, 2¹/₂" (6.5 cm). Arrange these in the order shown, with the first strip section in the center, the second strip section either side of the center column, and the third strip sections on the outer two sides.

3 Stitch the columns together matching the seams. Press the seams toward the center.

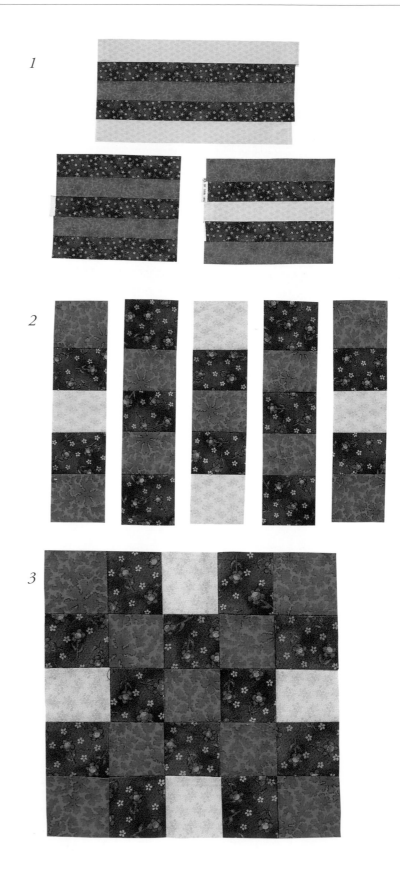

Rectangle blocks

1 For the second block, you need two pieced strips plus one cream rectangle. Cut a center rectangle in cream fabric, $10^{1}/_{2}$" × $6^{1}/_{2}$" (26.5 × 16 cm). Cut two red strips $2^{1}/_{2}$" × $10^{1}/_{2}$" (6.5 × 26.5 cm) and another cream rectangle, $6^{1}/_{2}$" × $10^{1}/_{2}$" (16 × 26.5 cm). Stitch together these three pieces in the sequence: red strip, cream rectangle, red strip. Press seams toward the outer strips.

2 Cut sections from the strip sequence and with the remaining cream center rectangle, arrange in the order shown, taking care to correctly orientate the center cream rectangle. Press seams toward the center.

3 Stitch the three pieces. together to complete the second block.

4 Stitch the first and second blocks together alternately to form the Irish Chain pattern.

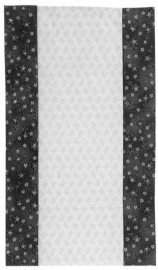

1

2

3

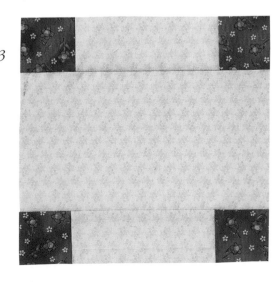

4

Pineapple

The Pineapple block is a variation of the Log Cabin pattern (see page 107), in which the strips appear to cut across the corners of the center. Traditionally, a separate template had to be made for each round, making the whole construction process rather laborious. Using rotary cutting tools, you can speed up the operation by stitching straight strips around the center and trimming them as you progress. As with basic Log Cabin blocks, the sizes can be changed by altering the dimensions of the centers, the width of the strips, and the number of rounds used. This design provides an ideal showcase for many fabrics, which when sorted into dark/light value groups make a strongly graphic quilt.

1 Cut a 3$\frac{1}{2}$" (9 cm) square of red fabric. From a light fabric, cut four strips 2" (5 cm) wide × 3$\frac{1}{2}$" (9 cm) long. Stitch two strips to opposite sides of the red square, and press seams toward the strips. Stitch two more strips to the remaining two sides, and press.

2 Place the block wrong side up on the cutting board. Line up the 45° angle on the rotary ruler with a seam and ruler edge $\frac{1}{4}$" (0.75 cm) from the stitched corner. Trim off the fabric triangles that project beyond the ruler. Rotate the block and repeat on the other three sides.

3 Take a dark fabric and cut strips 2" (5 cm) wide and slightly longer than the trimmed edges of the block. Stitch these strips to all four sides, as for Step 1.

4 Place the block face down on the cutting board. Line up the 45° markings on the ruler with a seam of the outer square and the ruler edge

1

2

3

4
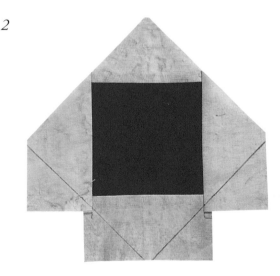

¹/₄" (0.75 cm) from the stitched corner. Use the horizontal markings on the ruler to line up with the inner square (first seam attaching round 1). Trim the strips off along the side of the ruler. Rotate the block and repeat on the other three sides.

5 Cut strips of a second light fabric 2" (5 cm) wide and once again slightly longer than the trimmed edges. Stitch these to all four sides of the block.

6 Place the block face down on the cutting board. At this stage, the sewing lines no longer make a complete square. Place the ruler edge along the small straight edge of round 2 and trim away the strips of round 3 parallel with this edge. Keep the block square by checking that this cut is parallel with the seams attaching round 1 by using the lines on the ruler.

7 Continue to add four more rounds of strips, alternating between dark and light fabrics, trimming each round as you work.

8 The final round is made of four dark triangles that square up the block. Cut two squares of fabric 3¹/₂" (9 cm) and divide these across one diagonal to make four triangles. Stitch these to the corners on the last light round. When the blocks are joined in a quilt, these triangles will create small dark diamonds.

5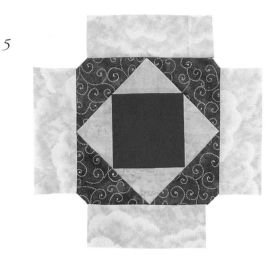

6

7

8

This Pineapple quilt, right, is made with fabrics in two highly contrasting tonal groups and a variety of scrap fabrics. The repeated red centers unify the different fabrics used in each block.

Rail Fence

Rail Fence is one of the simplest of the strip pieced patterns to achieve. Fabric strips of equal width are stitched together, then cut and reassembled to form the quilt top. By turning the blocks, a stepped pattern is created. It is an ideal project for a beginner to learn rotary cutting skills and straight seaming. Once the strips are assembled and the blocks cut, there are few points to match when stitching them together. Four boldly colored fabrics are used in this sample. The strips can be cut any width between 2" and 4" (5 and 10 cm), depending on the desired finished size of the quilt.

1

2

1 Cut four strips across the width of the fabric, adding $^1/_2$" (1.5 cm) for seam allowance to the desired finished width of each strip. Stitch along the long edges, right sides together, placing the strongest colored strips at the edges. Press all seam allowances in one direction. Trim one end of the strip section straight by lining up one of the horizontal lines on the ruler with one of the seams, then cutting at a 90° angle. Cut across the strip section to make the square blocks. If, for example, the four strips are 2$^1/_2$" (6 cm) wide, cut the squares to a width of 8$^1/_2$" (19.5 cm).

2 Arrange as many blocks as desired, and stitch them together in columns. Press all seam allowances away from the pieced edge.

3 Stitch the columns together to complete the quilt top.

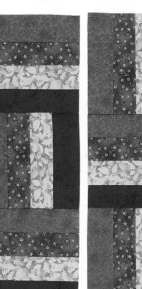

3

Log Cabin

The Log Cabin is one of the quintessential scrap quilt patterns. It is an ideal block for beginners as there are no points to match up, and yet the end result always gives a dramatically graphic effect. The block is based on the principle of contrasting dark fabrics against light ones, and it does not matter if you run out of a particular fabric when cutting the strips, you can simply substitute fabrics with similar color values. The technique is very simple: strips are stitched to center squares in rotation, beginning with a light fabric on the first two sides then a dark fabric on the third and fourth sides to establish the pattern. Two more rounds of strips are added in the same way.

1 Cut a center square of fabric 3" × 3" (7.5 × 7.5 cm). Cut two strips of light fabric 1³/₄" × 3" (4.5 × 7.5 cm) and 1³/₄" × 4¹/₄" (4.5 × 11 cm). Place the shorter strip and the center square right sides and raw edges together. Stitch, taking a ¹/₄" (0.75 cm) seam. Press the seam allowances toward the strip.

2 Hold the block with the light strip at the top and place the second light strip along the right-hand edge, right sides together. Stitch and press as before.

3 Cut two strips of dark fabric 4¹/₄" and 5¹/₂" × 1³/₄" wide (11 and 14 × 4.5 cm). Turn the block so that the second light strip is at the top. Position the shorter dark strip, right side down on the right-hand edge, and stitch.

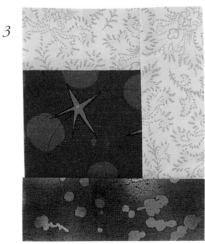

4 Add the second dark strip along the final edge. The first round of strips is now complete, establishing the light/dark sequence.

5 Add another round of strips, increasing the length of every alternate strip by 1¹/₂"

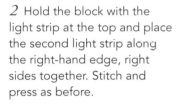

(4 cm) to accommodate the growing size of the block.

6 Add one final round of strips, again increasing the length of every other strip.

Specialty piecing project: Log Cabin quilt

This quilt has been prepared to the traditional Straight Furrow pattern of Log Cabin. See page 111 for other possibilities in Log Cabin settings. This quilt has 48 blocks, each block a finished size of 10" (25 cm) square, with three rounds of strips in each block. You can alter the dimensions of the block centers and the width of the strips, or you can add one or more rounds to the block to change the size of your finished quilt.

Finished size

60" × 80" (152 × 203 cm)

Fabric

1 yd. (1 m) red, for center squares
2 yd. (2 m) each in light and dark prints,
    for 1¾" (4.5 cm) wide strips:
65" × 85" (165 × 216 cm) batting
65" × 85" (165 × 216 cm) backing
1 yd. (1 m) binding

1 Mark out the block to scale on a piece of graph paper, with sizes indicated.

2 When cutting out the centers and strips, add a seam allowance of ½" (1.5 cm) to both the horizontal and vertical. This will give a stitched seam of ¼" (0.75 cm) on all sides.

3 Prepare and stitch 48 Log Cabin blocks (see page 107).

Stitching the blocks together

1 Use the diagram as a guide to arrange the blocks into the Straight Furrow design, using six blocks for the width and eight for the length.

2 Stitch them together by placing blocks in rows horizontally or vertically, right sides together and stitching with a ¼" (0.75 cm) seam allowance. Press seam allowances of each row in alternating directions so they will mesh neatly when the rows are stitched together.

continued on the next page…

Quilting and finishing

1 Once the quilt top is complete, lay out the backing, right side down, and smooth out any wrinkles. Press if necessary. Center the batting on top of the backing, then layer the quilt top, right side up, on top of these, leaving a margin of batting and backing showing all around.

2 Baste or pin the quilt sandwich together (see page 209).

3 Quilt in the desired quilting pattern, by hand or machine.

Binding

1 Cut binding strips 4³/4" (12 cm) wide. Join strips to make a long enough piece to go all around the quilt edges, with 4" to 6" (10 to 15 cm) extra for the corner miters.

2 Fold in half lengthwise, with wrong sides together, and press.

3 Trim the batting and backing fabric, leaving ³/4" (2 cm) beyond the quilt top all around.

4 Apply the double-fold binding to the right side of the quilt by machine, making a folded miter at the corners (see page 204), and hand-stitch to the back of the quilt to finish the piece.

Alternative setting options

The Log Cabin blocks can be set together in a wide variety of designs, making it a most versatile pattern. Just by altering the orientation of the dark/light diagonal lines, a range of different effects is possible.

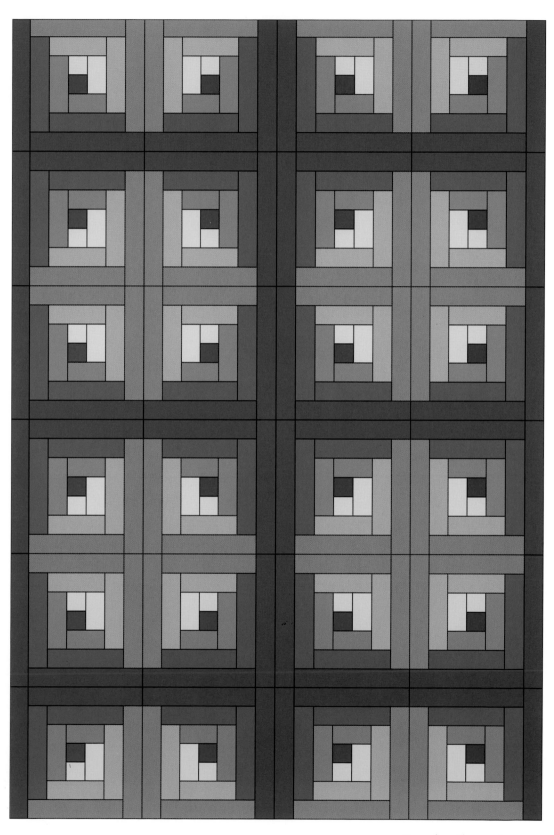

In Sunshine and Shadow, or Light and Dark, diamonds are formed by putting the dark and light sides of the blocks together in groups of four.

continued on the next page…

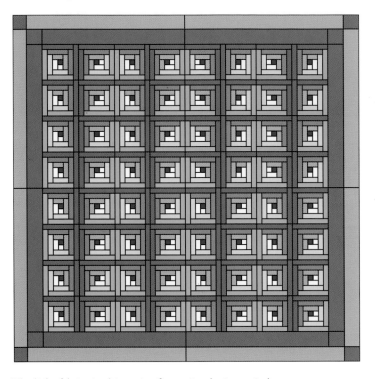

The light fabrics in this setting form triangles in vertical rows.

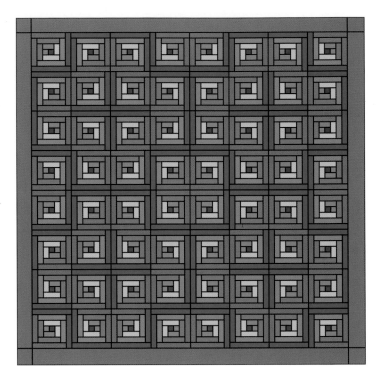

Four diamonds make up the overall design in this version.

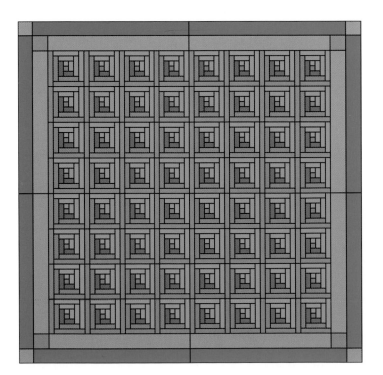

By setting the blocks together in a straight set, strong diagonal lines become apparent.

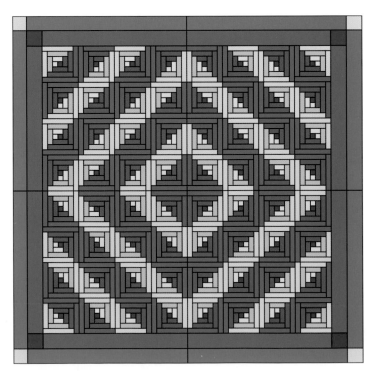

The Barn Raising pattern is made by creating concentric dark and light diamonds radiating from the center of the quilt.

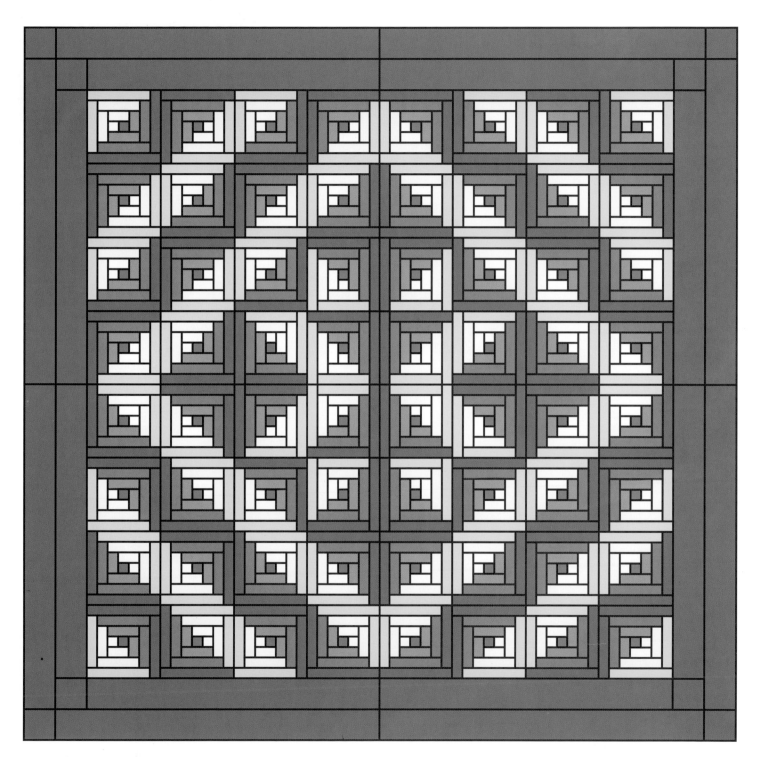

A large star in the center of the Barn Raising pattern is another option when setting blocks together.

Lone Star

One of the most spectacular quilt designs, but also one of the most technically challenging, the Lone Star is made from a single diamond that is repeated until a star of the desired size is reached—often a single large star filling the whole quilt. In the Star of Bethlehem, a similar but smaller star is repeated on the quilt top four or more times. The design was often chosen for a special quilt and the fact that many of them survive from the past (the oldest Lone Star quilt dates from 1835) suggests they were brought out only on special occasions to honor a special guest or showcase the quilter's talent.

Strip piecing is the shortcut method of construction of the diamonds. A star block can be made any size by adding more strips or increasing their width to make the diamonds larger. This finished block measures 22" (56 cm).

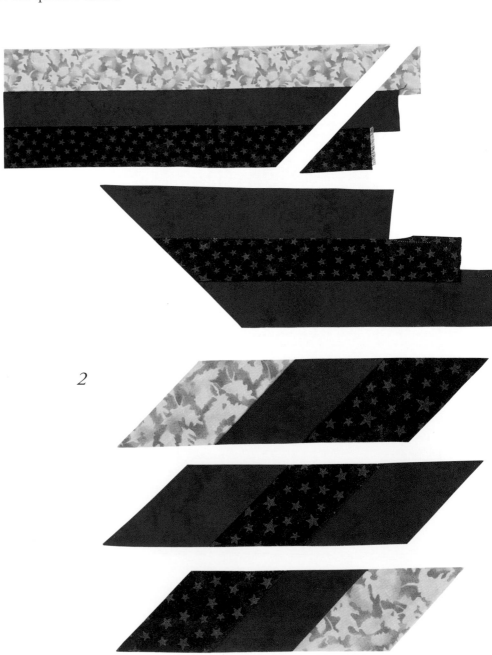

1 Each star point has nine diamonds, and these are prepared first. Cut strips across the width of the fabric 2" (5 cm) wide. Stitch two rows of strips, taking a ¼" (0.75 cm) seam allowance, in the yellow/red/blue sequence and one in the red/blue/red sequence. Offset the ends by the width of the strips, 2" (5 cm). Press seam allowances to one side. Trim one end of the rows to a 45° angle by positioning the 45° line on the ruler along one of the seams and cut.

2 Cut sections from the pieced strips of the same width as the strips were cut, 2" (5 cm). You will need three sections for each of the star points, which are composed of two yellow/red/blue sections and one red/blue/red section.

3 Arrange these in the order shown and stitch the three sections together to make one star point. Repeat seven more times to make eight diamonds altogether.

4 For the background, choose a densely patterned fabric so that the seams will be less visible.

To avoid having to stitch the background squares and triangles along the pieced bias edges of the star points, the background square and triangle shapes are divided into two. This allows all joining seams to be straight.

Cut four 7$\frac{1}{2}$" (19 cm) squares and four 5$\frac{3}{4}$" (14.5 cm) squares. Cut each of these across one diagonal to make eight triangles in each of the two sizes.

First, stitch one of the larger triangles to one edge of each diamond and one of the smaller triangles to the opposite edge.

Stitch two diamond sections together to make one quarter of the block. Make three more.

5 Stitch the quarter blocks into two halves. Stitch one final seam across the two halves to complete the block. Trim the outer edge, if necessary, and press the block to finish.

3

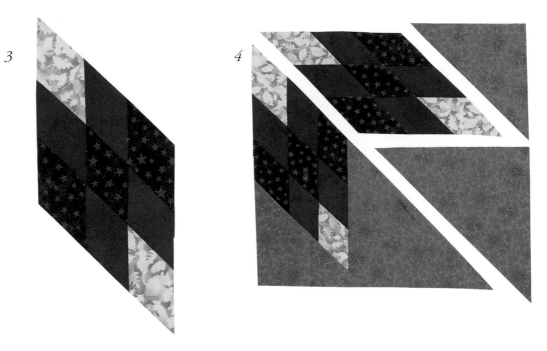

4

5

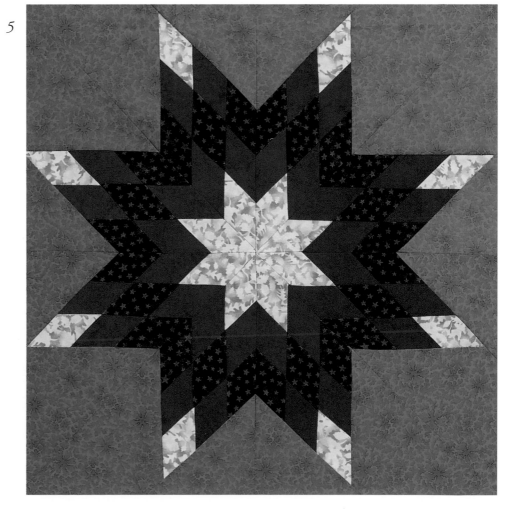

Drunkard's Path

The Drunkard's Path block is comprised of a quarter circle set into its corresponding curve. It uses three fabrics with dark/light contrast. A 4" (10 cm) square is a good size for each unit, as the units are combined in a 4 × 4 grid, to make a 16" (40.5 cm) finished block. In this setting of 16 units, called Sunshine and Shadow, three fabrics have been used. Two different darks are combined with the same light in two sets of four each.

1 Draw a 4" (10 cm) square on graph paper. Using a drawing compass, mark a curve two-thirds into the square. Label the two pieces of the block A (convex) and B (concave), and mark the grain lines with arrows parallel to the outer edges of the block. Cut out each shape and mount onto card. Cut each shape, adding a ¹⁄₄" (0.75 cm) all around for the seam allowance.

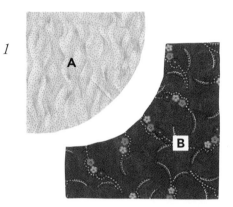

2 Cut the pieces from the selected fabrics. Fold a crease in the center of the curved edge on both the A and B pieces. Snip into the curve of the B piece within the ¹⁄₄" (0.75 cm) of seam allowance.

3 Place the A and B pieces right sides together, matching the creases at point X and easing the curves to fit. Pin and stitch together. Press the seam allowances toward the B piece.

For each set of four squares, reverse the fabrics in pairs—concave pieces: two light, two dark and convex pieces: two light, two dark.

4 Stitch the units together into groups of four. Stitch first into pairs and then join these pairs across the center.

5 When you have made four groups of four, they can be stitched together to make the block.

Alternative setting options

With 16 squares, there are a number of alternative ways to set them together.

Around the World—resembles a stylized floral motif and looks effective set with alternate solid blocks.

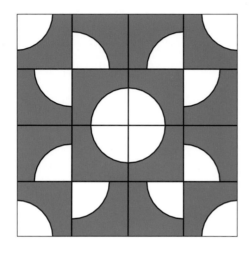

This arrangement is known by a number of names, among them Vine of Friendship, Dove, and Snake Trail.

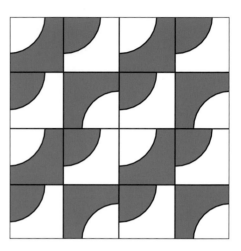

This version was designed by Ruby McKim in the 1930s and first appeared as a pattern in the *Kansas City Star* newspaper.

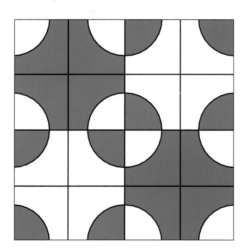

Mill Wheel—an overall design that is effective with many fabrics sorted into dark and light values.

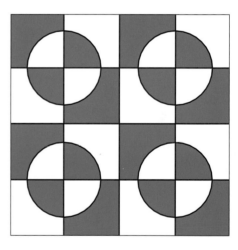

Tumbleweed—a variation that originated in Canada.

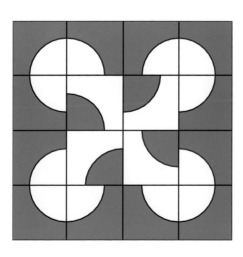

Falling Timbers—interesting secondary designs are created when the full blocks are set edge to edge.

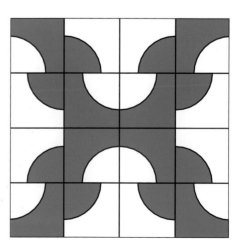

Dresden Plate

This design provides an ideal showcase for a number of different fabrics used together. It was popular in the 1920s and 1930s when new dyes became available, aiding the production of a wide variety of colorful, printed fabrics. The circular motif, made up of wedge-shaped segments, can be rearranged into fans or half plates, as were popular in the Art Deco era. The fan in particular was a favorite

motif in crazy quilts, often made up in exotic fabrics such as silk, satin, and taffeta.

There is variation in the outline of the wedges (see opposite); they can be pointed, rounded, or made with a smooth curve around the outer edge (Grandmother's Fan). The size of the motif can be altered by reducing the length of the wedge from the wider end.

1 Use template A (at 3 times the size shown here) to cut 20 wedges—four in each of five different fabrics.

2 To create pointed wedges for Dresden Plate, fold each wedge A lengthwise, right sides together and stitch a ¹/₄" (0.75 cm) seam along the top edge. Clip the folded corner at an angle.

Turn the point right side out and press, with the seam centered on the wedge. Repeat for all 20 wedges.

3 Arrange the colors in your desired sequence. Stitch the wedges, right sides together, beginning ¹/₄" (0.75 cm) from the top edge, backstitch to the top edge, then continue stitching the length of the wedge. This will keep the thread ends out of sight.

Stitch into four sets of five, to make four quarters of the "plate." Stitch the quarter plates together in pairs and finally stitch the two halves together to join the circle.

4 Use the B template to cut a circle of fabric for the center, adding ¹/₂" (1.5 cm) extra all around. Sew a running stitch around the edge of the fabric circle. Center the card circle on the wrong side of the fabric circle and gather up the stitches. Press the gathered fabric over the card to form a smooth crease around the outer edges of the circle. Remove the card.

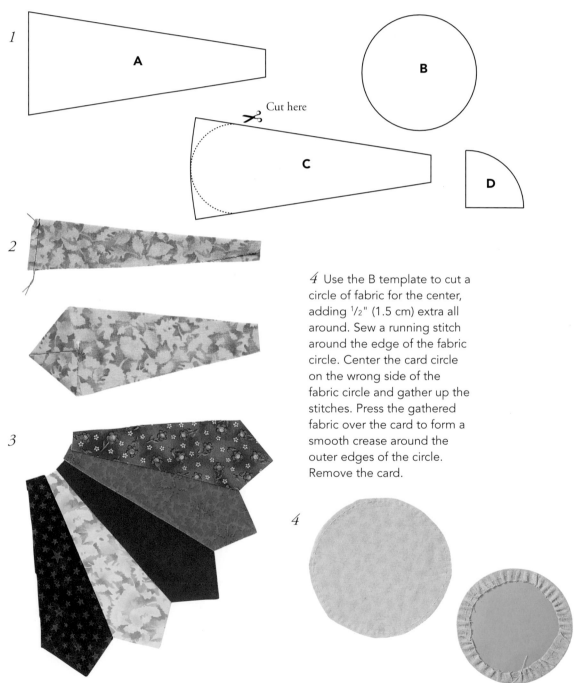

Cut here

5 Cut a 24" (61 cm) square of background fabric. Fold into quarters and crease lightly, for positioning guidelines. Place the circle of wedges onto it, smoothing the layers together and lining up the points of the wedges with the creases. Pin to the background.

Position the circle of fabric in the middle of the wedges. Pin, then appliqué the whole Dresden Plate motif to a background fabric by hand or machine. Stitch the circle first, then around the outside of the wedges.

5

Variation on Dresden Plate

To make wedges with rounded or curved tops, use template C (at 3 times the size shown here). Cut out the wedges and shape the ends by gathering stitches along the top edges of the fabric and pulling them over the card, and pressing—as for the center circle in Step 4. Stitch the wedges together as directed in Step 3.

Grandmother's Fan

Use template C to cut five wedges and stitch them together along the long seams. Press, then position the fan shape onto a square of fabric. Appliqué the fan to the background fabric along the outer curved edge, turning in ¹/₄" (0.75 cm) to neaten.

Use Template D to make a quarter circle, adding a ¹/₄"

(0.75 cm) seam allowance on only the curved edge. Gather the curved edge and press over the template to create a smooth curve, then position this over the corner of the fan, and stitch down. When the block is stitched into the quilt, the outer raw edges of the fan and quarter circle will be contained in the seams.

Tumbling Blocks

With careful manipulation of tonal value and shape, it is possible to create a 3-D appearance. A number of traditional quilt designs exploit this; Tumbling Blocks, or Baby Blocks as it is sometimes known, is one of the most graphic. It is composed of differently angled diamonds, fitted together into hexagons, each of which uses dark, medium, and light fabrics. It is possible to speed up the construction with an ingenious method of strip piecing, cross-cutting, and reassembly. This method creates a seam across the medium diamond, so choose a densely patterned fabric for this to mask the seam line.

1 Cut two strips of each fabric: the dark and light 2³/₄" (7 cm) wide and the medium a scant 3¹/₄" (8.25 cm) wide. The extra width on the medium fabric is to allow for the cross-cutting and rejoining. Stitch strips in the following sequences: one dark/medium/dark and one light/medium/light. Press the seams toward the center.

Trim one end of the first strip sequence to a 60° angle by positioning the 60° line on the ruler along one of the seams near the end of the strip sequence. Repeat with the second strip, reversing the direction of the 60° angle.

2 Cut sections across the strips, 2³/₄" (7 cm) wide, parallel to the angled edges.

3 Cut each section diagonally across the medium center diamond.

1

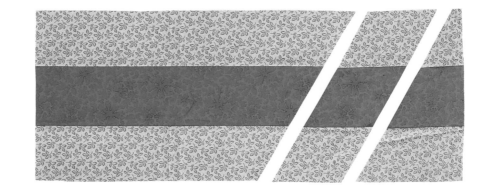

2

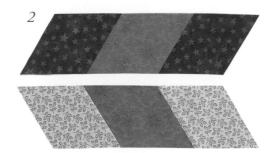

3

4

5

4 Reposition these pieces to form a line composed of medium triangles which alternate with dark and light rhomboids. Stitch in strips of sufficient length for the required size of your panel/quilt and press.

5 Stitch the lines together, matching the points at the seams between all patches.

6 Stitch sufficient lines together for the required size of your panel. Handle the pieces carefully so as not to stretch or pull the bias edges out of shape. When the panel is complete, either turn in the outer edges and appliqué it to a background, or trim the top and bottom edges straight, then add borders.

6

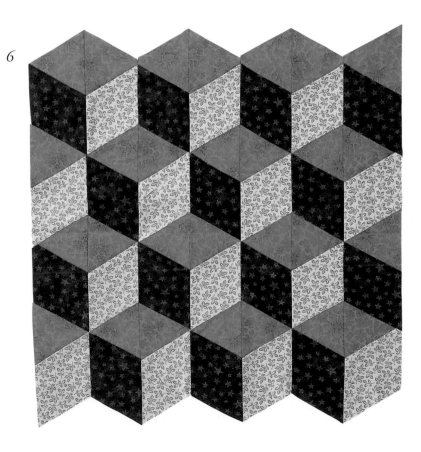

Streak of Lightning

Streak of Lightning creates a zigzag effect by arranging scraps of fabrics into dark and light sections of a block, split diagonally. It is a creative solution to the use of many fabrics in one quilt and separates the tonal values into groups. If you run out of one particular fabric, you simply replace it with another from the same tonal group to continue making the quilt.

The sample here demonstrates the effect with a simple four-patch of squares and triangles. All can be made using quick piecing and rotary cutting techniques, without the necessity to make templates.

1 Sort your fabrics into two sets—dark in one set and light in the other. There should be a distinct difference between the two sets, although there will be variations in value between the fabrics in each set.

2 To make the triangle units, cut squares to the finished size of the unit, adding 7/8" (2.5 cm). For example, for a finished 3" (7.5 cm) square cut 37/8" (10 cm) squares.

Place one dark and one light square, right sides together. Draw a diagonal line from one corner to the other of the light square and stitch lines 1/4" (0.75 cm) either side of the line. Cut along the center line and press the seam allowance toward the dark triangle. Each pair of squares will yield two triangle units.

1

2

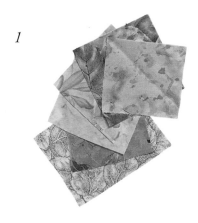

3

3 The block requires two triangle units, one dark square, and one light square. Cut out all of the squares, adding a 1/2" (1.5 cm) to the finished size. Therefore, for 3" (7.5 cm) squares, cut them to a size of 31/2" (9 cm). Place these squares and the triangle units on a flat surface in the order shown and stitch into two pairs.

4 Stitch the pairs together to complete one block.

5 When you have made enough blocks to make the required size of quilt, stitch them together, ensuring that you turn the blocks to position the fabric tones into the zigzag design.

Alternative setting options

The Streak of Lightning effect can be easily created with a simple square made of one dark and one light triangle.

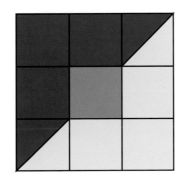

A center square in the same fabric for every block will give a similar impression to the Log Cabin block in the quilt.

The reversal of a dark and light triangle in the center patch will create a break in the straight line of the zigzag.

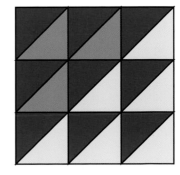

A block composed entirely of triangles and using a medium value as well as dark and light creates a lot of movement and visual texture.

Trip Around the World

Trip Around the World is a one-patch block composed of squares set in concentric diamonds over a whole quilt. The colors can be set to contrast with each other as illustrated here, or blended together to create a softer, more homogeneous effect. An ingenious form of strip piecing is used, which means that the squares do not need to be cut or worked individually. Five solid colors are used. To make a larger panel, add more strips to the initial set or cut them wider. The sections will always be cut the same width as the strips.

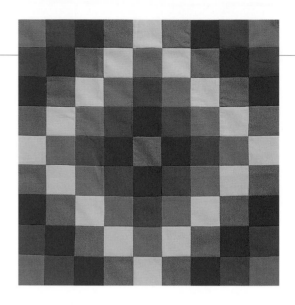

1 Cut five strips 2½" (6.5 cm) wide across the width of the fabric. Arrange strips in your chosen color sequence and stitch them together along the long sides. When all the strips are stitched together, place the top and bottom strips right sides together. Pin and stitch so that the strips now form a tube. Place the tube flat and trim one edge off at a 90° angle to the seams, then cut sections from the tube 2½" (6.5 cm) wide. For the complete Trip Around the World panel illustrated, cut 18 sections.

1

2 The panel is made up from four sections (refer to the diagrams). Start with section A, which includes the larger center square of the panel. Work from the center line out toward the left-hand side. Identify which is the key fabric (marked)—in this case the yellow. Take one of the strip sections, open the short seam next to the key fabric, and lay the strip flat with the key fabric corresponding in position to section A in the diagram.

Take a second strip section, open the seam that is second

2

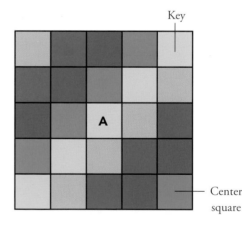

Key

A

Center square

along from the key fabric. Place this next to the first strip, with the key fabric one square on a diagonal away from the first.

Continue to open seams, moving down a square from the key fabric until five strips are prepared.

Stitch these strips together. Press the seams in opposing directions as you work. This will help you to match the points and reduce bulk.

3 Section B requires only four strips. Referring to section B in the diagram, work from the center out toward the right-hand side and note that the key fabric begins one down from the top. Open the seams, lay out the strips in the sequence shown, and stitch them together. Repress the seams in opposing directions as you work.

4 Section C uses four strips along the horizontal. Follow section C in the diagram to position the key fabric as you lay out the strips in the sequence shown. Stitch and press as before.

5 Section D is the smallest, needing only four lines of four squares. Repeat the process as before, using section D of the diagram as a guide.

3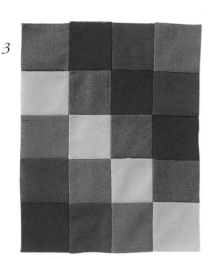

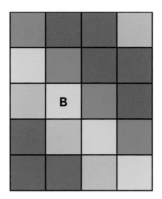

4

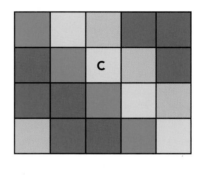

5

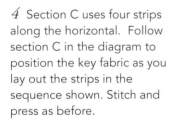

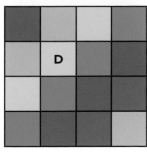

6 When the four sections are ready, stitch them together with three final seams—two horizontal and one vertical to complete the panel.

6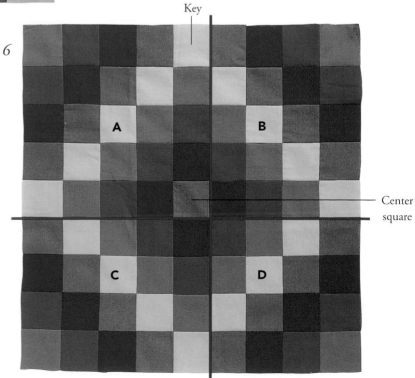

Key

Center square

English patchwork

English patchwork, which is sometimes referred to as paper or mosaic patchwork, is one of the methods of hand-stitching patches together. Each one is shaped by being basted to a paper template. The pieces are then placed right sides together and sewn using a tiny whip stitch through the edges, which are folded over the paper. Although this technique is time-consuming, it has the advantage of accuracy when awkward shapes are involved such as diamonds or hexagons. Its main advantage is that, with a little advanced preparation, it is a conveniently portable project.

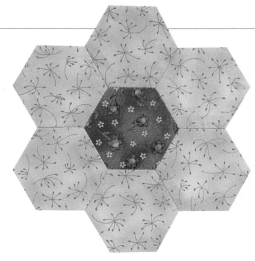

To design an English patchwork, use isometric or squared graph paper. Shapes can be combined as long as they all fit together without leaving any gaps. Make templates from graph paper glued onto card, or buy commercially available ones. Window templates enable you to frame a specific part of the fabric to position a motif.

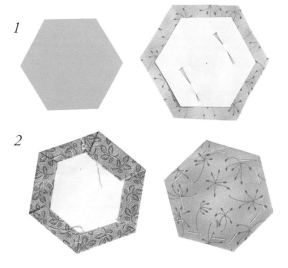

1

2

1 To make the papers, draw around a template onto good-quality sketching paper —if the paper is too thin, it will bend. It is important to cut the papers accurately, and cut out sufficient papers to start the project.

Pin the paper to the wrong side of the fabric and cut the fabric, adding a generous ¼" (0.75 cm) turning all around.

2 Baste the backing paper to the fabric, folding over the seam allowance. At the corners, fold the fabric over and secure with a stitch. Finish with a backstitch.

If the shape you are working with has an acute angle, reduce the bulk of the fold by trimming a corner off the fabric. Press

each patch to form a sharp crease around the edge of the paper.

3 When you have enough patches prepared, place two of them right sides together and oversew along the edges, beginning and ending with back stitches.

Work out the most economical way of stitching the patches together. If making a large item, it may be more convenient to work out a system of constructing units to be joined at a later stage. This will prevent the piece becoming large and unwieldy.

When the patches are all stitched together, the papers can be removed and re-used.

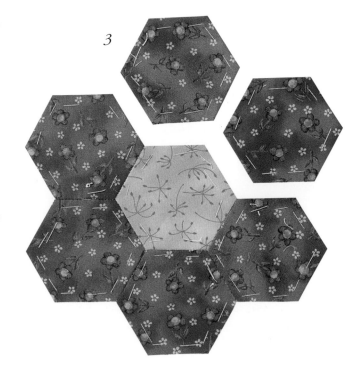

Alternative setting options

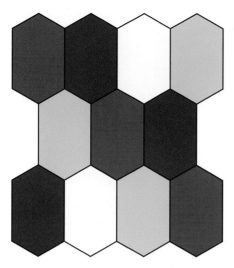

The long hexagon is sometimes referred to as the Church Window design.

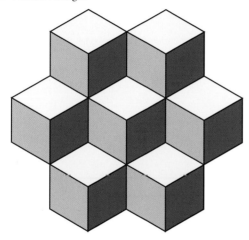

Baby Blocks or Tumbling Blocks create the illusion of a 3-D effect with diamonds in dark, medium, and light values.

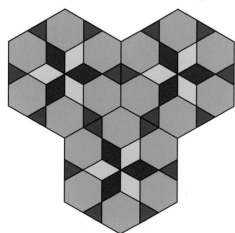

Stars, hexagons, and triangles are combined in this intricate design.

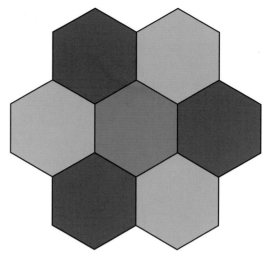

The most popular pattern is the repeated hexagon, often called Grandmother's Flower Garden.

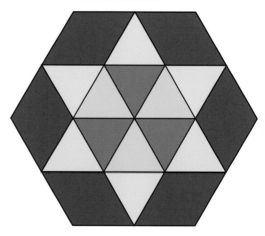

Triangles and diamonds are joined together to form hexagons.

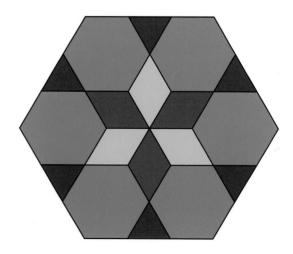

Diamonds, hexagons, and triangles form into hexagons.

Foundation piecing

Foundation piecing is a method of stitching patches to a translucent foundation material, onto which a pattern has been marked. It is good for ensuring accuracy with small shapes and sharp points. Patches are placed on the unmarked side of the foundation. The foundation can be made from a material that remains in the block, such as a sew-in interfacing, or it can be removable, such as tracing paper. There are advantages to both. Leaving the foundation in will stabilize the block and allow it to be stitched by hand. However, removable foundation needs to be sewn by machine, as tearing the foundation away will distress hand stitches. This block is a Roman Stripe, 2$\frac{1}{2}$" (6.5 cm) square.

1 Place the piece of foundation fabric over the block pattern. Secure lightly with masking tape and trace the pattern onto the foundation fabric. Mark a dotted line around the outside of the block. There is no need to mark the numbers as you can refer to the diagram for these.

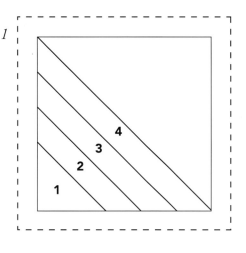

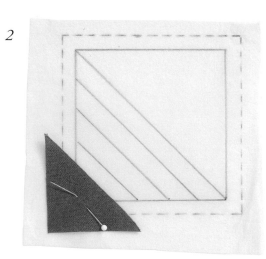

Note

The tracing has been drawn on both sides of the foundation simply to make the explanation of the technique clearer; you do not need to mark both sides.

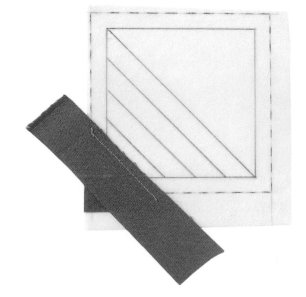

2 Begin with a patch for the small triangle of area 1. Cut a triangle of fabric that will adequately cover it and extend beyond the outer dotted line. Seam allowances are trimmed as you work, so there is no need to cut exactly. Position this piece right side up onto the foundation. Pin or use a light dab of glue to secure it.

3 Cut a strip of the second fabric wide enough and long enough to cover area 2. Place this right side down over patch 1. Pin to secure, turn the foundation over and stitch along the line that separates 1 and 2. Turn back and trim away the excess fabric beyond the seam to $\frac{1}{8}$" (0.5 cm); be careful not to cut the foundation.

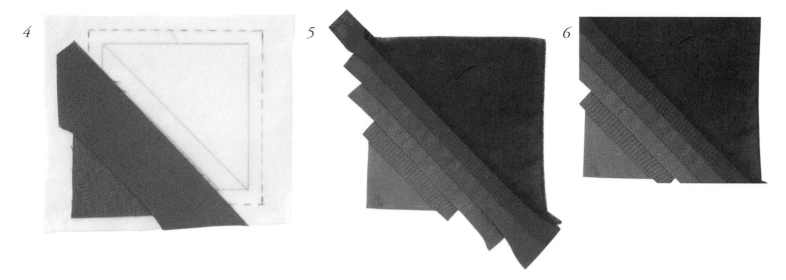

4 Flip patch 2 over so that you see the right side and press it flat against the foundation.

5 Add the next strip. Pin to secure, then turn the block over and stitch on the line between 2 and 3, as before. Turn back and trim the seam. Press the strip flat to the foundation.

Continue adding the strips, and then the large triangle, following the diagram.

6 When all the foundation fabric is covered, turn the block so that the diagram is visible and trim away the excess fabric along the outer dotted lines. This gives ¼" (0.75 cm) for joining the blocks. If using a removable foundation, leave it in until all the blocks are joined to avoid the edges stretching out of shape.

More foundation piecing

Flying Geese A Flying Geese strippy crib quilt showcases a collection of tiny fabric scraps.

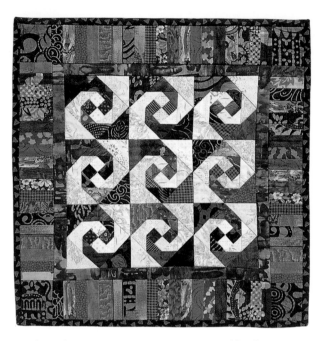

Snail Trail The interlocking shapes are created by the clever positioning of the dark and light fabrics within the blocks.

Turning Star Medallion The sharp points of the center star are easier to work using the foundation piecing method than would otherwise be possible.

Christmas Trees The Pine Trees block makes an appealing decoration in red and green fabrics.

Contemporary piecing project: Wallhanging

Although traditional pieced blocks form the basis of a contemporary approach to piecing, rather than setting them together in a regular grid, different elements are combined in an improvised manner. It is an opportunity to experiment with bold colors and experimental techniques and to produce works of art in their own right, or "sketches" for larger pieces.

Contemporary piecing can increase your confidence in the use of color and in your ability to make creative decisions about composition. A gallery of contemporary piecing follows on page 137. While a specific pattern is presented for the wallhanging in this project, take the chance to grasp the principles behind the construction, and enjoy creating original compositions.

Finished size
19" × 20½" (48.5 × 52 cm)
Fabric

Five fat quarters in contrasting fabrics.
22" × 24" (55 × 60 cm) batting
22" × 24" (55 × 60 cm) backing

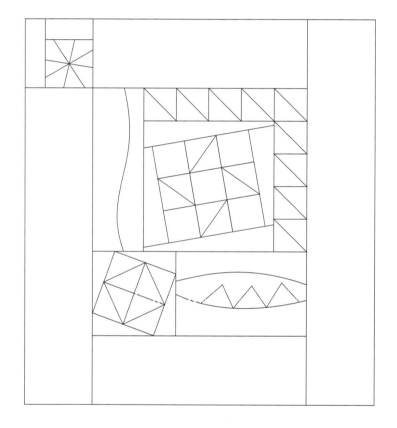

Four-patch blocks

1 Select two contrasting fabrics and cut a strip of each 2½" × 16" (6.5 × 41 cm). Place these, right sides together, and mark off squares along the length. Mark a zigzag diagonal line from corner to corner on each square, dividing each one into two triangles. Stitch a line ¼" (0.75 cm) away from the zigzag lines on each side of them. Cut the strip along the marked lines to divide into squares.

Cut along the diagonal line. Each square will yield two bi-colored squares. Press the seam allowances toward the darker side, then trim the small triangles of seam allowance, even to the edges.

1

continued on the next page...

2 Make a pinwheel block and another four-patch block, using eight of the bi-colored squares. Set them aside to be used in later steps.

2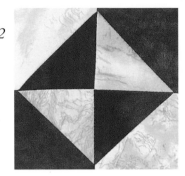

3 To make the central Friendship Star block, take one of the bi-colored squares as a guide for size, cut five more squares, four for the corners (yellow) and one for the center (pink). Stitch the block, as shown.

3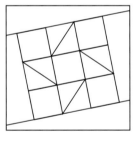

Adding the border

4 With a third fabric, add a 2¹/₂" (6.5 cm) wide border to the block on all four sides. Position the star block on a tilt to give the impression of movement.

Cut an 8" (20 cm) square of tracing paper and pin this to the bordered block, tilting the paper so that the corners touch the edges. Trim the border fabric to the paper outline.

4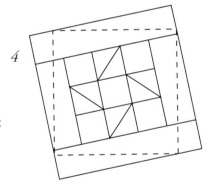

5 Make nine bi-colored squares in a different color combination following Step 1. Stitch together a four-square strip, and stitch it to the top of the block. Adjust the width of the block slightly, if necessary. Stitch together a five-square strip and stitch it to the right side, as shown.

5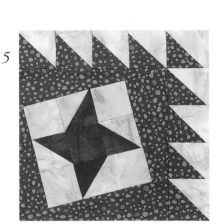

Curved seams

Strips joined with a curved seam add interest to the quilt.

6 Cut two strips of fabric 2¹/₂" (6.5 cm) wide and slightly longer than the plain edge of the central block. Place these on the cutting board right sides up and overlapping each other by 1¹/₂" (4 cm). Pin and cut through both layers, introducing gentle curves as you cut.

7 Discard the narrow edges of each strip. You will now have two pieces of fabric that fit snugly together with curved edges.

6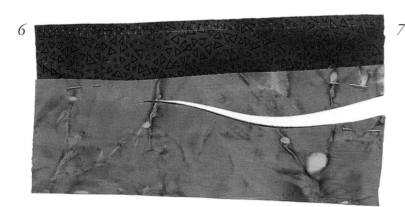

7

8

9

8 Place the two pieces right sides together (at this point it will seem as if they don't fit) and ease the raw edges together, pinning down the length of the strips.

9 Stitch, taking a scant ¹/₈" (0.5 cm) seam allowance. Press the seam over to one side, then press on the right side.

10 Add the curved strips to one of the plain edges of the block. Trim the length to fit the block.

11 Add a border to the undesignated small block made in Step 2, following the directions in Step 3; use a 6" (15 cm) square of paper, and tilt the block in the opposite direction from the Friendship star.

12 Prepare a panel of three curved strips (Steps 6 to 10) to fit the right edge of the block. Stitch the top two strips together.

10

continued on the next page…

Prairie points

These decorative triangles are inserted into a second curved seam unit, to give a 3-D feature. They introduce a flash of color and balance the composition.

13 Cut three 2¹/₂" (6.5 cm) squares of fabric. Fold diagonally across and press. Fold diagonally again. All the raw edges of the resulting triangles are now on one side. Pin in position on the lower raw edge of the curved strips. (See also Prairie points, page 142 to 144).

13

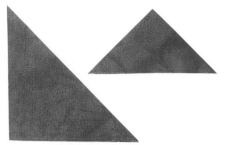

14 Add the third strip, catching the raw edges of the Prairie points in the seam.

Add the panel of three curved strips onto the block, and stitch the whole unit to the fourth side of the small main block.

14

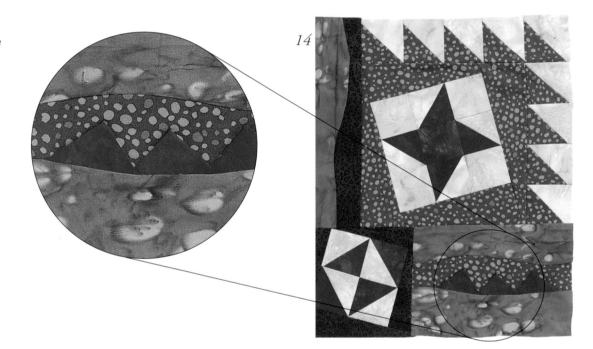

Pinwheel border

15 Trim the Pinwheel block made in Step 2 to 3" (7.5 cm) using a paper template placed on a tilt. Add a narrow strip of one of the outer border fabrics on two sides, then stitch the Pinwheel to one short end of the final border.

15

Outer borders

16 The outer borders can be made from more than one fabric, if desired. Cut these 4" (10 cm) wide. This will allow for the final curved shaping of the outer edges. Add the borders in sequence around the center panel.

Adding the batting and backing

20

17 Make up a piece of backing, slightly larger than the quilt top, from two pieces of fabric with a seam across the middle. Leave an opening in the seam; this is where you will turn the quilt right side out. Cut a piece of batting the same size as the backing.

18 Place the quilt top and backing right sides together, press, pin, then trim and shape the outer edges with gentle curves, with the wrong side of the quilt facing up so you can see how much of the border to cut when trimming and shaping.

19 Place the batting on a flat surface, then place the quilt on top of the batting, backing side up (the wrong side of the quilt top is now against the batting).
Reposition the pins from the quilt top so that they go into the backing and batting. Stitch all around the outer edges with the backing on top and the batting underneath. Use a walking foot on the machine, taking a generous ¹/₄" (0.75) seam.

20 Trim the batting close to the stitching and clip the corners diagonally to reduce bulk.

21 Turn the quilt to the right side through the opening in the backing. Finger-press the seam so it lies along the outer edge, then slipstitch the opening closed.

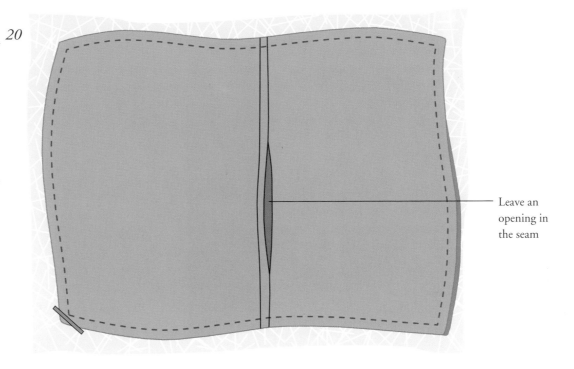

Leave an opening in the seam

Quilting

As with the piecing, the quilting can be free and improvisational, without the necessity to mark lines.
This wallhanging was quilted with a multicolored machine-quilting thread.

22 Quilt by hand or machine. Use the patchwork shapes as a guide to quilt, sewing in short straight lines. Quilt from the center outward. Where there are larger areas to be quilted, fill in the shapes with zigzag lines or curved lines on the curved seams.

continued on the next page...

More contemporary piecing

The main focus of this small quilt is an off-center Log Cabin block. Sawtooth edges, curved seams, and prairie points, with the addition of a Pinwheel in one corner of the border, complete the composition.

This example uses a more subdued color scheme. Monochromatic grays are teamed with various purple hues for a harmonious effect.

Another example that uses three small blocks combined with curved seams. This one has been embellished with hand-carved buttons.

This quilt was made up of five sections, which were then joined with curved seams to create the overall composition. The outer edges were bound with turquoise to enclose the dark border.

Special Effects

A variety of complex patchwork techniques can create a special effect in patchwork projects and be used to enhance quilts with beautiful textural interest. These special effects can be stitched by hand and machine, where appropriate.

With the exception of crazy quilts, the easiest fabric to use when trying out these techniques for the first time is cotton. However, as you gain more experience, try using silks or velvets, synthetics or sheers, because although these are challenging at times, they can give very pleasing and exciting results.

The wave panel and the folded star are both decorative panels suitable for pillows, journal covers, box tops, and greeting cards. Prairie points can be inserted into any seam or edge to add a decorative and textural dimension (see Contemporary piecing, page 131). Yo-yos (which are also known as Suffolk puffs), when applied to a background as decoration or stitched in groups, also provide interest. Cathedral window is an enduring and beautiful technique that can be used to show off a favorite piece of fabric. The same applies to crazy patchwork where precious pieces of luxurious fabric are showcased by embellishment with delicate embroidery stitches.

There are various strip patchwork techniques too, including Seminole and colorwash quilting.

Folded star

The folded star is made from rectangles of fabric folded into triangular shapes, arranged in concentric patterns. Use strong contrasts in fabric choices to make the star shapes stand out.

1 Cut a 6" (15 cm) square of foundation fabric. Mark the horizontal, vertical, and diagonal lines on the square by ironing the creases in.

2 Cut rectangles from two contrasting fabrics for the points of the star, each 1¼" × 2" (3.75 × 5 cm). For the sample shown, cut 20 rectangles in blue and 16 in green. Turn under and press a ¼" (0.75 cm) seam allowance along one long side of each rectangle. Press a crease down the center of each. Fold the corners down and press to make finished points.

2

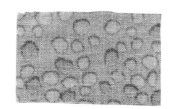

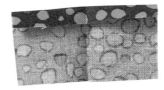

3 Place four blue points at the center of the foundation fabric, folded corners right side up. Take a tiny stitch in matching thread to secure each point. Baste the outer edge using small stitches to secure. The basting will be hidden by the next round of points.

3

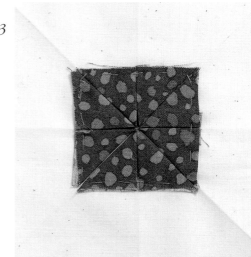

4 Place eight green points onto the foundation fabric, folded corners right side up. They should be ½" (1.5 cm) from the center point and secured with stitches.

4

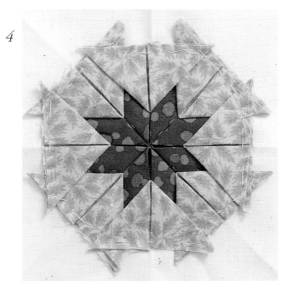

5 Continue adding points, alternating colors with each round. As the piece gets larger, add extra points to fill in the gaps.

6 Trim and bind the piece using a bias strip (see Bindings, page 248).

6

Wave panel

The wave panel uses folded strips inserted into a background fabric as tucks. Solid colors for the inserted strips provide the delicate contrast that adds to the effect as they are stitched down in alternate directions, before being lifted away from the background fabric to provide dimension. The panels can be inserted as blocks into cushions and patchwork quilts.

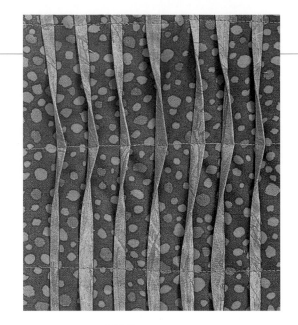

1

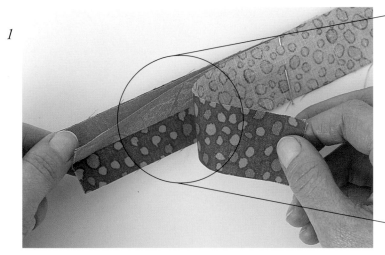

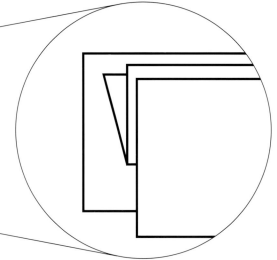

1 Cut 10 strips 1¹⁄₈" × 8" (3.5 × 20 cm) from the dark fabric, and nine strips 1" × 8" (3 × 20 cm) from the light fabric. Press the light strips in half lengthwise, wrong sides together. Place one of the folded light strips between two of the dark strips, right sides together and raw edges together.

2 Stitch a ¹⁄₄" (0.75 cm) seam along the long edges taking in four raw edges.

2

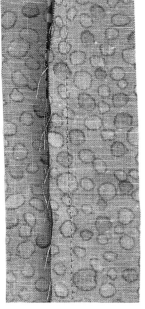

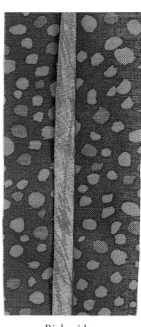

Wrong side   Right side

3 Continue adding the folded light strips between dark strips, until all are joined together. Press the panel so that all the tucks lie in the same direction. Trim the strip to 7¹/₂" (19.5 cm).

4 Stitch a line across the center of the panel at a 90° angle to the strips, anchoring the folded strips to the background.

5 Make two more lines of stitching halfway between the center and the sides, making sure that the tucks are stitched in the opposite direction to the center line. Finally, stitch along the side edges of the panel, forcing the tucks to lie back in the other direction again.

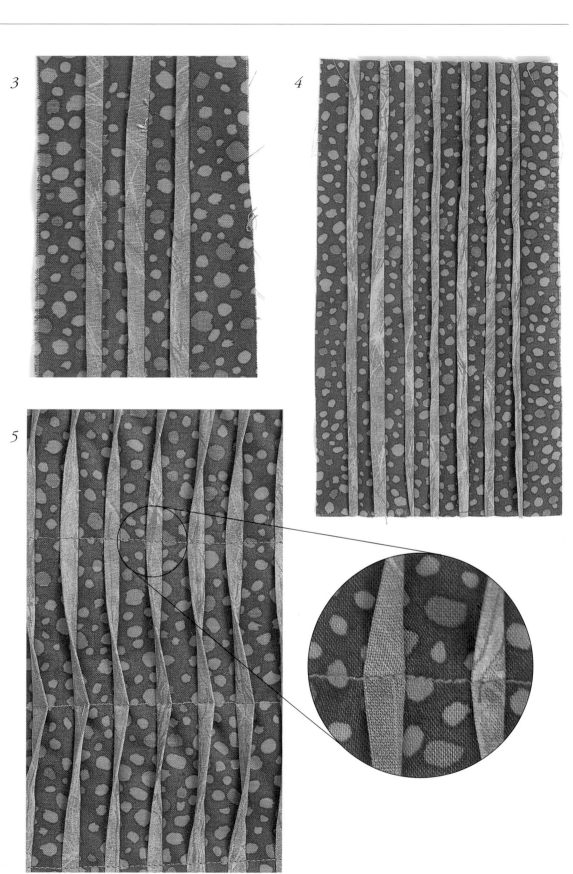

Prairie points

Prairie points can be prepared individually or in groups for insertion into any seam, for a 3-D effect, or stitched into an edge of a quilt for a decorative effect. There are three ways to prepare them, including quick-piecing, and each presents a different result in its effect. The advantage of making the points individually is that they can be made in different sizes and fabrics.

1 Cut a 3" (7.5 cm) square of fabric. Fold on a diagonal and again on the other diagonal.

2 Alternatively, fold the square of fabric in half, and fold down the two corners forming a double triangle.

3 To insert the prairie points, position them between the seam with the triangles touching point to point or overlapping.

Stitch the triangles onto one edge of the seam to stabilize them before stitching the seam.

1

2

3

Note

The ¼" (0.75 cm) seam allowance needed to attach the points will take up ½" (1.5 cm) of the original square.

Quick-pieced

This is a quick method of making a continuous band of prairie points that are evenly sized and spaced in one strip.

1 Cut a strip of fabric 4" (10 cm) wide and 18" (45 cm) long. Fold the strip in half lengthwise and press. Open the fabric and mark off 4" (10 cm) segments along the right hand side from the bottom to the top of the strip. On the left hand side, starting 2" (5 cm) up from the bottom, mark 4" (10 cm) segments again from bottom to top.

2 Cut on the marked lines from the outer edges to the center folded line.

3 Working on the bottom left square, with the fabric right side down, fold the bottom left corner in on the diagonal.

4 Turn the bottom point up to complete prairie point 1.

5 Repeat the first fold with the top left square. Fold up lower prairie point 1 to cover the start of prairie point 2.

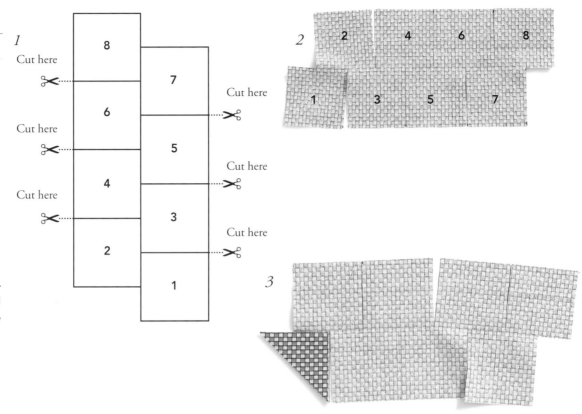

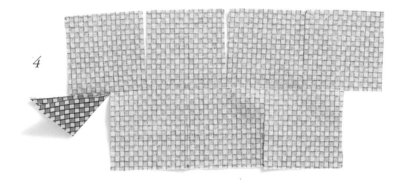

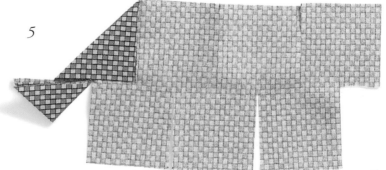

continued on the next page...

Prairie points (continued)

6 Make the second fold as before to complete prairie point 2, enclosing prairie point 1.

7 Make the first fold for prairie point 3. Fold prairie points 1 and 2 over prairie point 3.

8 Make the second fold for prairie point 3, so enclosing prairie point 2. Continue folding the segments, alternating from top to bottom until the band is complete.

9 Machine stitch along the raw edges, taking the smallest seam allowance you can in order to stabilize the band. When using this band in a quilt project, stitch to one side of the intended seam, raw edges together, before completing the piece.

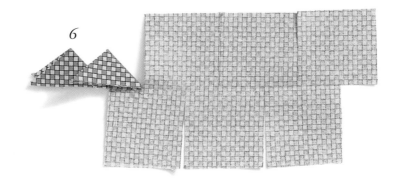

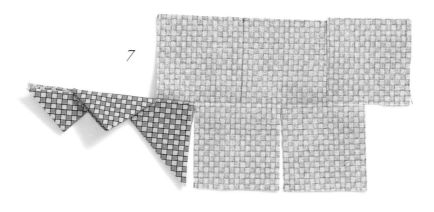

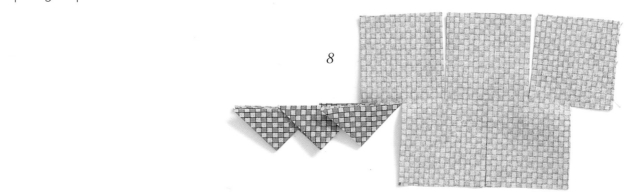

Yo-yos

Yo-yos are always worked by hand, and focus on a circular template, traditionally taken from a common household item such as a cup, saucer, or lid, to form a gathered circle of fabric. They may be drawn up loosely and another fabric may be inserted inside, or they can be stuffed, or embellished with beads or embroidery. Different sizes can be applied to a background as well as to each other. Yo-yos used in this way are particularly good for portraying flowers.

1 Use a template to cut a 3" (9 cm) diameter fabric circle (although you can make them any size desired). Turn a tiny hem around the outside, make tiny running stitches around the edge using strong thread.

2 Gather up the stitches tightly and secure the gathered fabric with strong stitches.

3 The yo-yos may be joined by over-sewing at point of contact with their neighbors.

Cathedral windows

Cathedral windows is a special piecing technique that reveals small "windows" of fabric within a folded and sewn background. The decorative windows can be precious pieces of fabric or embroidery, they can differ or present a unified match. This technique is popular for pincushions, which can be made by stitching two squares together to form a tube, inserting a cathedral window, and stitching top and bottom, stuffing before you close. The initial stages can be pieced by hand or machine, both of which are detailed here, but the inserting of the windows must be done by hand.

By hand

1 Cut a 6" (18 cm) square of fabric, turn a ¼" (0.75 cm) hem all around the edge, pin, and press. Mark the center of the square by pressing the fabric in half each way and open it out flat.

2 Fold the four corners into the center point, pin, and press.

3 Again, fold the four corners into the center, pin, and press.

4 Stitch the four center points together through all the layers to hold in place.

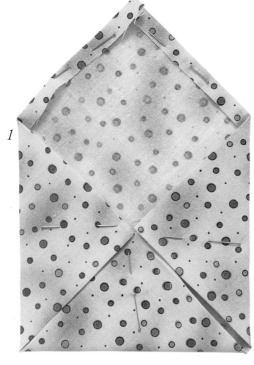

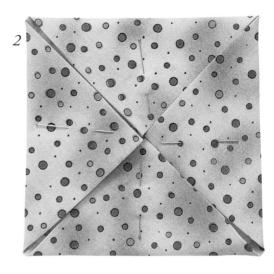

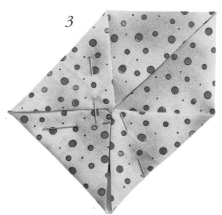

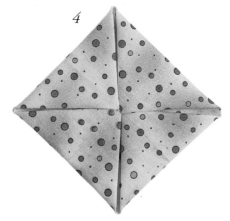

By machine

1 Cut a 6" (18 cm) square of fabric and fold in half, right sides together. Stitch the short sides together with a ¼" (0.75 cm) seam.

2 Clip the corners at the folded end to reduce bulk later and press the seams open. At the open side, bring the two seamed edges together so that the two pressed seams line up against each other. Stitch a ¼" (0.75 cm) seam leaving a gap to one side of the center large enough to turn the square right side out.

3 Press the seams open and turn the square through to the right side. Press again to ensure it is square and flat.

4 Fold the corners to the center, in the same way as in Step 3. Stitch the center points together through all the layers to hold in place.

1

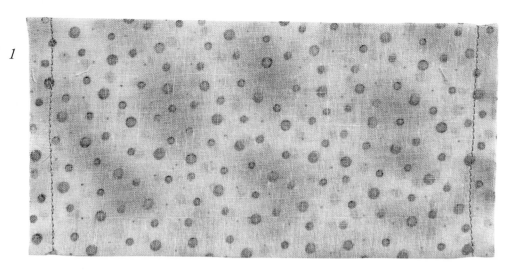

2

3

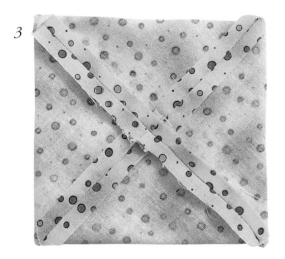

4

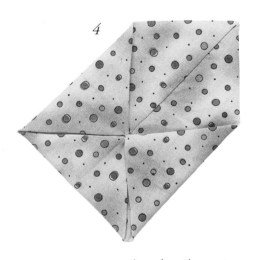

continued on the next page…

Inserting the windows

1 Make a number of squares by either method described, and stitch them together by placing them right sides together using a tiny oversewing stitch. The example here shows four squares stitched together.

2 Cut four "windows" of decorative fabric. To do this, measure between one corner and the stitched center of one square, and cut decorative fabric to that size. For example, if the distance from the corner to the center is $1\frac{1}{2}$" (4.5 cm), cut each window piece $1\frac{1}{2}$" (4.5 cm) square. Position the window fabric on top of interior diamond, as shown. If required, insert a square of batting cut slightly smaller than the "window" underneath it—this will create height and padding. Turn the folded edges of the background over the edges of that window and hem down neatly. If you want the decorative windows to appear up to the edge of the work, stitch the folded edges of the background round two edges of the window and take the other half of the window around to the back of the work. Neaten and hem down to finish. Otherwise, leave the half squares at the edges without windows.

1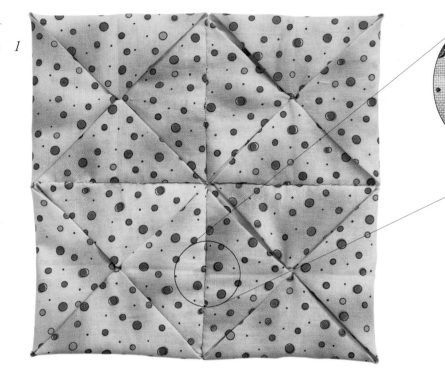

2

Crazy patchwork

Crazy patchwork is not hardwearing, but it can be really beautiful. It enables scraps of silks, satins, velvets, and other luxurious fabrics to be pieced and enhanced with embroidery stitches such as herringbone, feather, chain, buttonhole, or a combination of stitches, that cover the seams. The patches too can be embellished with beads, charms, and motifs, as well as ties, ribbons, appliqué, and tassels—even photographs and words can be introduced. There are two methods of piecing crazy patchwork described here.

Raw edges

1 Cut a square of foundation fabric approximately 8" (20.5 cm) square. Lay chosen fabric pieces onto the foundation fabric with each edge overlapping its neighbor by ¼" (0.75 cm). Trim as necessary. Pin and baste each piece, stitching through all the layers.

2 Continue until the foundation fabric is covered. These pieces may be fused if preferred, in which case the overlap between the pieces can be reduced. All the edges will be covered by decorative stitches.

Stitch-and-flip

1 Alternatively, pin the first piece right side up, starting in the center or in one corner of the foundation fabric. Take the next piece and place it right side down so that one edge lies along one edge of the first piece. Stitch through all the layers, ¼" (0.75 cm) from the raw edges. Flip the piece back to show its right side. Finger press or pin in place.

Take a third fabric and stitch it to another edge of the first two pieces and flip. Continue stitching and flipping until the foundation is covered.

2 Whichever piecing technique has been used, you can now embellish the patchwork, covering the seams with embroidery stitches.

Seminole patchwork

This pattern of patchwork was originated by the Seminole Indians of Florida, who used colorful bands to decorate clothing. Strips of different, brightly colored fabrics are first machine stitched together and then cut and reassembled into a variety of intricate patterns.

1 Cut strips of fabric in three contrasting colors, each 1½" × 30" (4.5 × 76 cm). Sew them together along the long edges using a ¼" (0.75 cm) seam allowance. Press.

2 Cut the strips into sections, each measuring 1" (3 cm) wide.

3 Sew the sections together, dropping the seams by one square each time, as shown, to make a Seminole band.

4 Take two more strips of fabric to contrast with the band, each 2" (6 cm) inches wide and stitch them on either side of the sectioned band, pinning to make sure that the seam just touches the corners of the band's central squares. The surplus fabric can be trimmed from the back to ¼" (0.75 cm).

1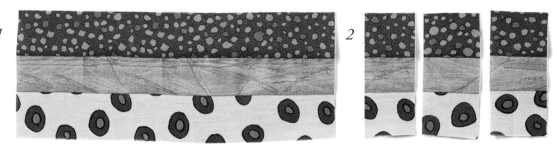

2

3

4

Alternative setting options

Stitching together the cut sections from strips in 1, 2 or 3 in each setting creates Seminole patchwork in different combinations.

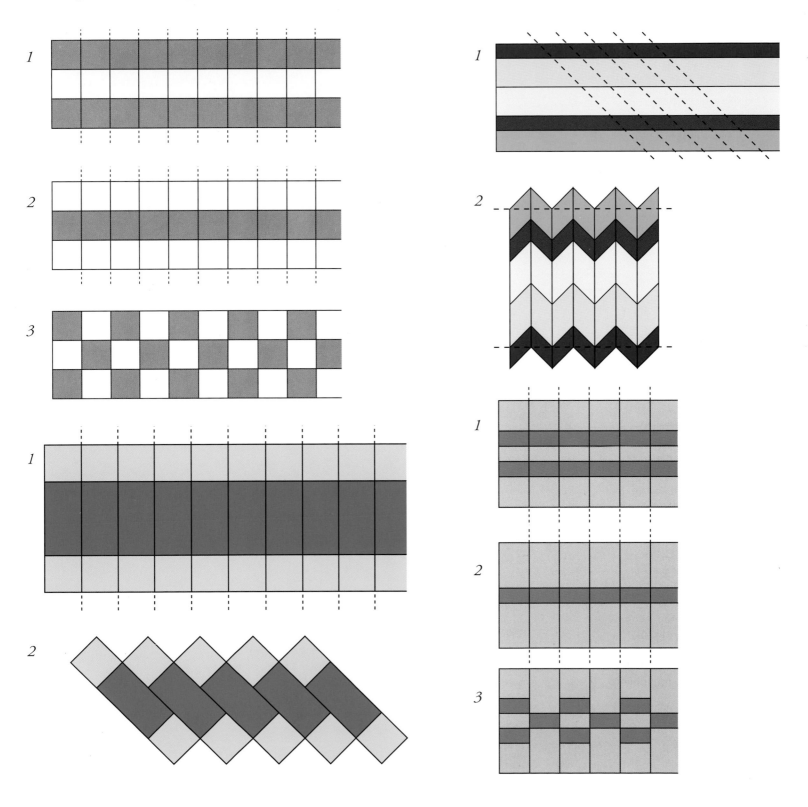

Strip patchwork

This technique involves cutting strips of fabric in differing widths, colors, and tones, then machining the sections together to create a new "fabric," which is then cut into shapes and stitched together to create further new designs and blocks. This techniques must be machine-, not hand-pieced, because the strips are cut into shapes after sewing. Hand stitches would fall apart, while machine stitching continues to hold the shapes.

1 Cut six strips 1¹/₂" (4.5 cm) wide and 6" (18 cm) long. Take two strips and pin them, right sides together, along one long edge. Stitch, using a ¹/₄" (0.75 cm) seam allowance. Press the seam to one side.

2 Attach further strips in the same way. Stitch from alternate ends of the strips to prevent the work becoming distorted. Press all the seams in the same direction.

    Alternatively, the strips can be machine stitched directly onto a foundation fabric. This can be paper—which is torn away after the stitching is complete—or muslin, or a very fine woven interfacing, all of which remain in the work.

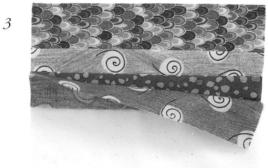

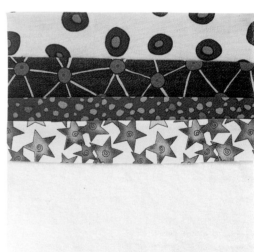

3 Cut a 6" (18 cm) square of foundation fabric. Place the first strip, right side up, along one edge of the square. Lay the second strip, right side down so that its long edge lines up with the long edge of the first strip and pin. Stitch, using a ¹/₄" (0.75 cm) seam allowance, and press the strip open.

    Attach further strips in the same way until the foundation fabric is covered.

4 It is possible to quilt the piece as it is stitched by laying a piece of batting on top of the foundation and stitching the strips through it. Care should be taken to ensure that the strips are pulled completely back over the batting before pinning the next strip as the batting is likely to make the fabrics bounce. An iron should not be used with many battings, so finger press and use pins instead.

Alternative setting options

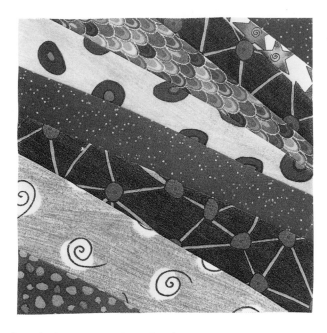

Introducing uneven strips and wedges gives movement to block designs.

Stripped fabric can be cut into bands and used as inserts in blocks.

Stripped squares can be stitched together to form a block.

Stripped fabric can be cut and pieced with solid pieces.

Watercolor quilts

Sometimes known as colorwash quilts, watercolor quilts blend squares of patterned fabric together and grades the squares from one tonal value or color to another across a quilt. The patchwork seams become blurred as secondary patterns are created. Floral prints are often used for this, as they blend together especially well.

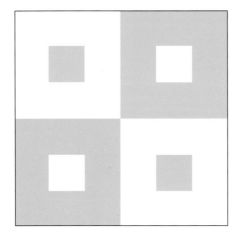

Start by making some tonal drawings in pencil. Shade to indicate value placements: light, medium, or dark. When you have a drawing you like, transfer the design to graph paper, to provide a grid where each square represents a square of fabric. Tracing paper may be laid over the design at this stage to work out a quilting pattern. The scale of the fabric squares that are used will reflect the size of the finished project, but usually squares of

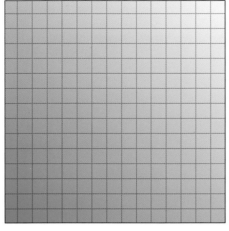
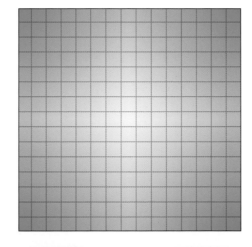
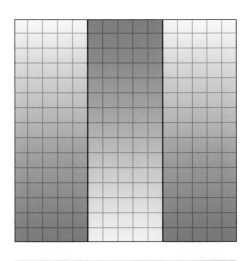

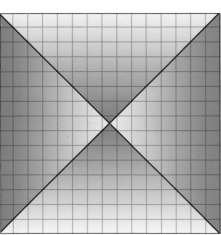
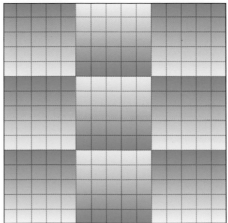
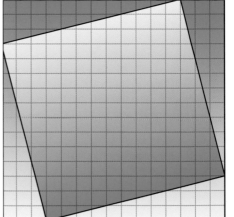

$1^{1}/_{2}"$ to $2^{1}/_{2}"$ (4 to 6.5 cm) finished to 1" to 2" (2.5 to 5 cm) are favored. Bear in mind that the larger the fabric squares, the more difficult it is to blend them from one square to another. The finished design uses 1" (2.5 cm) squares.

Gather and sort your fabrics into graded values from light to dark. The more fabrics you have, the easier it is to blend them. Use the wrong sides of the fabrics too to double your choices. Some fabrics may appear in two values; for instance medium dark or dark, according to which fabrics surround them.

1 Cut $1^{1}/_{2}"$ (4.5 cm) squares from all the fabrics and lay them out according to their values.

2 On a flat surface, arrange the squares into the design, referring to grid diagrams (see opposite.) Keep moving the squares around until you have achieved a design that pleases you.
   Start by stitching the squares together in pairs, taking them off the design surface carefully and then replacing them in their original position after the stitching is done. Then stitch the pairs into fours and the fours into eights and so on. This way there are fewer seams to match. Use a $^{1}/_{4}"$

(0.75 cm) seam throughout and a neutral thread. Press the seams toward the darker fabric where possible; otherwise, trim the darker seam allowance back to avoid shadowing on the light fabrics.

1

2

Note

To judge if the tones are working correctly, either half close your eyes or look through the viewfinder of a camera at the arrangement of squares.

Optical illusion

It is possible to capture optical illusions in pieced quilts where the contrast between patches can change the overall character of the quilt. Illusions occur through the clever use of tones in block designs, where the eye can be made to see some parts of the patchwork prominently, while other parts recede to the background. Log cabin is a prime example, where with careful selection of strips, making half the block from dark fabric and the other half from light, secondary patterns occur as the blocks are turned and set in different directions (see page 107).

Tumbling blocks is another classic example of optical illusion. Each hexagon block is made up of three identical diamond shapes, but by making one from dark fabric, one from medium tone and the other from light fabric, all placed in the same position in each hexagon, a 3-D effect is created which presents an optical illusion. Watercolor quilts too depend on the power of optical illusion to merge and contrast tones in the design. Some beautiful quilts below are examples of the possibilities for creating optical illusions when quilting.

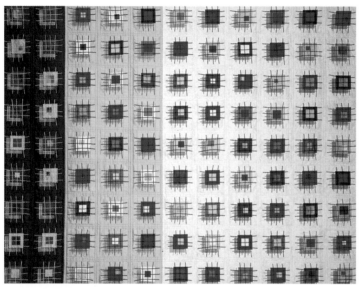

Kitchen Curtains by Sarah Impey.

Diagonal Illusion by Irene MacWilliam.

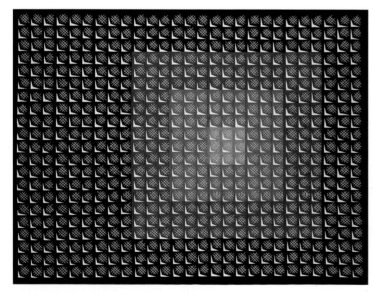

Cold and Frosty Morning by Sara Impey.

Settlement: Displacement by Valerie Hearder.

Fabric manipulation

Changing the surface of fabric is a way to create texture in your quilts. Once you have worked with the traditional piecing techniques, you may enjoy experimenting with the manipulation of fabric, changing its surface and creating exciting textures.

Basic ideas are explored in a series of samples for you to try. Use the resultant textured squares as blocks to be pieced in with your patchwork, to give unusual focal points or definition to your quilts. Combining different techniques together results in even more exciting possibilities.

All the techniques can be achieved with stitching by hand or by machine. With the addition of batting and quilting there is even more emphasis on the texture.

Embellishment may be added using beads, buttons, tassels, and found pieces such as seashells and feathers, as well as creative embroidery stitches.

In general it is simplest to start with cotton fabrics but try them all—with other fabrics such as silks, sheers, or even velvets—and you will get different results. The best part of all is that here you break the rules. Where normally you would cut to the straight of grain, instead try working on the bias. Instead of taking regular strips or tucks in equal size, experiment and try them thick, then narrow or irregularly cut. This is just a starting point for you to experiment. There are no mistakes in fabric manipulation, you are on a creative journey, and you can just keep inventing new textural effects.

Slashing

Slashing and its variation, chenilling, start with a stack of fabrics of various colors and textures. The stack is stitched and then the fun begins; cut into the layers to reveal hidden fabrics.

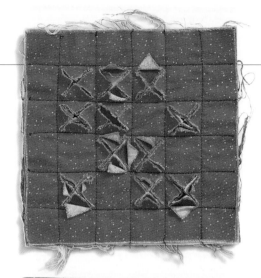

1 Cut a 6" (18 cm) square from five different fabrics, on the straight grain. Stack them one on top of each other, with right sides up, and pin them together.

2 Stitch grid lines 1" (3 cm) apart through all the layers, on the straight of grain. The grid may be marked on the top fabric for guidance, or you could sew through a paper pattern and tear the paper away afterward.

1

2

3 Use a pair of sharp scissors to snip through some or all of the layers on the diagonal, or bias. Take care not to snip the bottom layer or the sample may disintegrate completely. Cutting on the bias ensures that the fabric doesn't fray away completely. The different fabrics in the stack will be revealed as the fabrics are slashed.

4 Distress the fabric. This can be done by brushing with an old toothbrush or a suede brush, or running through the washer.

3

4

Chenilling

An alternative method of slashing is sometimes known as chenilling.

1 Cut a 6" (18 cm) square from five different fabrics, on the straight grain, and stack them on top of each other.

2 Pin them together. Sew parallel lines across the diagonal or bias, ½" (1.5 cm) apart.

3 Use a pair of sharp scissors to snip between the stitched lines, through all the layers except the bottom layer. The stitches should always be on the bias so that the fabric does not fray away completely.

4 Distress the fabric by rubbing, brushing, or by running through the washer.

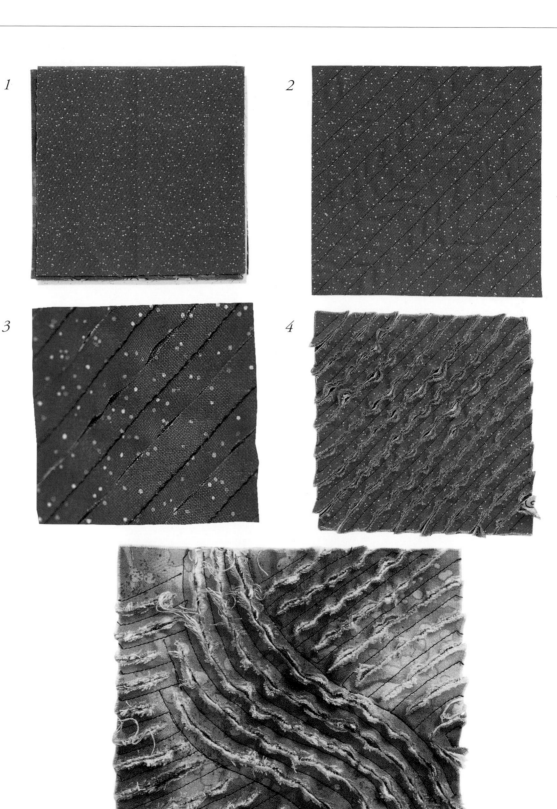

Fraying

These two techniques involve the pulling of threads to create a fringed edge. The pieces can be appliquéd onto, or used as inserts. In both cases they add interesting texture. The frayed sections always need some stitching to prevent the fabric from fraying away completely.

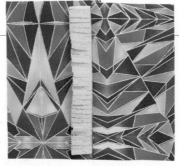

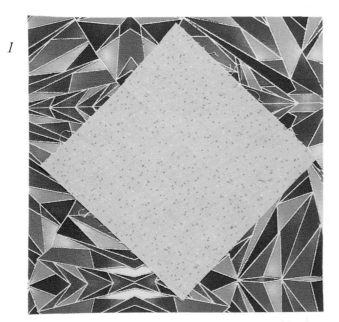

1

2

3

1 Cut a 4" (12 cm) square of fabric, on the straight grain, and pin it to a background fabric.

2 Stitch around the square about ¹/₂" (1.5 cm) from the edge to stabilize it, and to attach it to the background. Use a decorative stitch on your machine. Alternatively, stitch two rows of straight stitching.

3 Carefully fray the threads around the edges of the squares, using a pin. Stop the fraying two or three threads from the stitched line.

1 Cut a 1" (3 cm) strip of fabric on the straight grain and insert it into a seam so that ½" (1.5 cm) of the strip is left showing. The stitching of the seam will stabilize the fraying.

2 Carefully fray the threads of the strip.

3 If a chunkier effect is required, cut a 2" (6 cm) strip, fold in half lengthwise, wrong sides together, and press. Insert the strip into the seam so that the folded edge protrudes. Using a pair of sharp scissors, cut into the folded edge to create loops and then cut the loops to achieve the effect of a fringe. The fringe can be distressed further as desired.

1
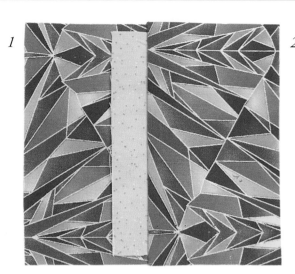

2
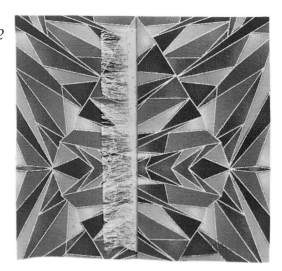

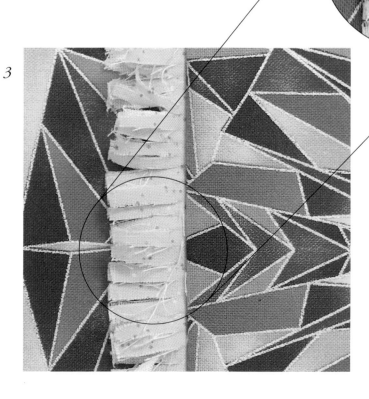

3

Weaving

Any of these woven panels may be stitched to a background to make a stronger finish and also to contribute to the finished design. Try experimenting with a mixture of strip widths, or weaves where the strips are not laid parallel to each other, or even use wedges instead of strips.

1 Cut or tear eight strips of fabric 1" (3 cm) wide and 10" (25 cm) long. Lay half the strips beside each other so that they touch. The process is easier if one end of each strip is pinned to a firm base such as a cork or polystyrene tile.

2 Weave the strips using a basket weave pattern.

3 For a dense result, butt the strips against each other. For, a lacier result leave spaces between the strips in one or both directions. The strips can be embellished before or after weaving, and stitching through the crossover point of the strips will make a much sturdier fabric.

4 Here, strips have been knotted before weaving and have been woven to reveal the background fabric.
  To create a soft, frayed edge to the strips, run them through the washer.

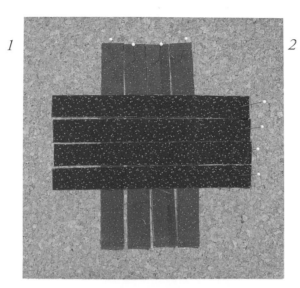

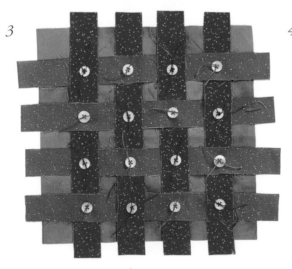

1 If a frayed effect is not required, the strips can be neatened first. Cut 10 strips of fabric 2"(5 cm) wide and 10" (25 cm) long, on the straight grain. Press the long sides to the middle, overlapping them by ¹/₄" (0.75 cm).

Cut a strip of batting to the width and length of the pressed strip and lay inside.

2 Pin the layers together and stitch down the center of the strip covering the overlapping area. Several rows of decorative stitching would be attractive.

3 The strips are now woven together as before, again pinning the edges to stabilize the weaving.

Pleating

Pleating is adding repeated folds to fabric. The folds can be regular or intentionally irregular and they are stitched into place in regulation order, or manipulated to create unusual, raised effects across pieced blocks.

1 Cut a piece of fabric 10" (30 cm) long by 5" (15 cm) wide on the straight grain of the fabric. Mark 1" (3 cm) divisions along both long edges. Leave enough space for a seam allowance at the edge. Pleat the fabric on the first set of marks. Using a matching thread, stitch along the fold using the edge of the presser foot to help with accuracy. The pleat should be ¼" (0.75 cm) wide.

2 Open the fabric out and fold on the second set of marks. Stitch the second pleat as before. Continue stitching all the pleats. Try to stitch up one pleat and down the next. If all the pleats are stitched in the same direction, the sample will distort. (This might of course be what you want!)

Press all the pleats in the same direction. Stitch a ¼" (0.75 cm) from the edge to anchor all the pleats.

3/4 Mark divisions across the top of your work. In the samples shown the divisions have been varied. (If the divisions are even, the result looks more like the Wave panel, see Special Effects, page 140). Sew along these markings, holding the pleats down, in alternate directions, or in pairs.

Box pleating

1 Cut a 6" (15 cm) square of fabric. Mark 2" (5 cm) divisions along the sides (do not draw lines across the fabric because they will show).

Fold along the first set of marks and stitch using a matching thread and a ¹/₂" (1.5 cm) seam allowance.

2 Open up the fabric and repeat the process to make the second pleat.

3 Press the pleats flat so that they look like box pleats.

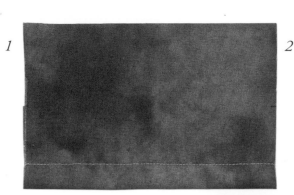

4 Mark 2" (5 cm) divisions along the other two sides of the square. Stitch the pleats as before, crossing over the previously pressed pleats.

5 Embellish the central crossings with cross stitch, buttons, beads, tassels, or quilting ties.

Gathering

Gathering fabric is achieved by running a straight stitch along an edge and drawing the thread up carefully, to shorten the dimension of the fabric and create a textured surface of irregular, loose, and informal folds.

Gathered strips

1 Cut a strip of fabric, 2½" (6 cm) wide and twice as long as the block width required. Sew along the long edges, within the ¼" (0.75 cm) seam allowance, using strong thread, and a running stitch or a long machine straight stitch.

2 Pull up the gathers, making sure that the thread ends do not pull out, until the strip is the length required. Distribute the gathers evenly.

3 The strip can now be inserted between two flat pieces of matching or contrasting fabric. Place the gathered strip and flat strips right sides, long edges aligned, and stitch a ¼" (0.75 cm) seam. Gently press the seam allowances toward the flat strip.

4 To create a curved strip, pull the two long edges in such a way that one edge is gathered tighter than the other. Cut out the shape in the foundation fabric and arrange the gathered strip to fit it exactly. Stitch the strip to the foundation to stabilize the curves.

1

2

3

4

Gathered squares

1 Cut a rectangle of fabric 7" x 3½" (17.5 x 9 cm). Sew along both long edges by hand with a running stitch, or long machine straight stitch. Carefully pull up the gathers, making sure the threads do not snap or pull right out. Gather up until you have a 3½" (9 cm) square, and distribute the gathers evenly.

2 The squares may then be stitched together in blocks, for insertion into a pieced work.

1
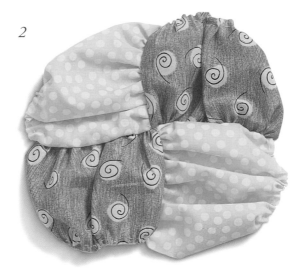

2

Ruched fabric

1 Cut a 10" (25 cm) square of fabric. Sew a running stitch across the fabric, stop, turn, and come back without breaking the thread until the return. Repeat the rows of stitching until the fabric is covered. Repeat at right angles to the previous rows.
   Carefully gather up the stitches on one side. Then gather up on the other side until the fabric is completely ruched.

2 Stabilize the work by stitching the ruched piece to foundation fabric cut to the same size as the finished ruched piece.

3 Stitch solid strips all around the ruched fabric to show off the effect.

1
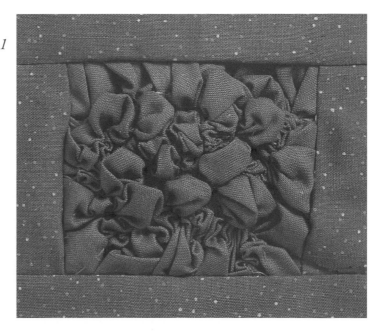

Pintucking

Pintucks are tiny folds in fabric, stitched to create delicate raised lines. The stitching can be regularly patterned, or applied freestyle, crisscrossing across the fabric.

The zipper foot is ideal for machine stitching pintucks as it allows for sewing close to the folded edge. Pintucking shapes and curves is more easily done by hand.

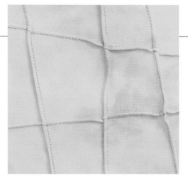 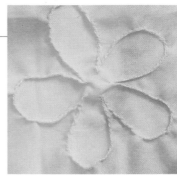

Machine stitched

1 Fold the fabric, wrong sides together to create the first pintuck. Position the foot on the folded edge, and stitch along the fold.

2 Open out the fabric and refold a second pintuck. Stitch and unfold. Continue folding and stitching one tuck after another, in a regular format or randomly.

1

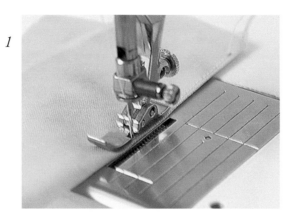

2

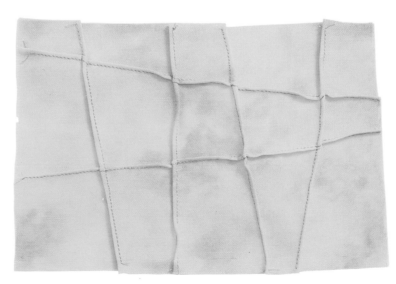

Hand stitched

1 To provide a stitching guide, mark a design onto tracing paper and baste the outline onto the fabric by stitching through the paper. Once the outline is clear, gently tear away and discard the paper.

2 To pintuck in straight lines, fold the fabric on the basted line, wrong sides together, and take tiny running stitches through both layers, no more than $^1/_8$" (2 mm) from the fold. Open out the fabric to reveal the pintuck.

3 To pintuck curves, insert a threaded needle $^1/_8$" (2 mm) inside the basted line and bring it up $^1/_8$" (2 mm) outside the basted line. Take a tiny stitch and bring the needle back to the inside. Work five or six stitches and then pull the thread taut, gathering up the stitches and raising a pintuck.

For tight curves, the stitches on the inside of the curve should be even smaller than those on the outside.

4 Pintucking with overcast stitching gives a rope-like edge. Bring the needle up $^1/_8$" (2 mm) to the left of the basted line. Take the thread across the line and make a small stitch from right to left under the line, bringing the needle up a small distance in front of the previous place. Keep making stitches in the same direction staying $^1/_8$" (2 mm) away from the basted pattern line on both sides. After five or six stitches pull

1

2

3
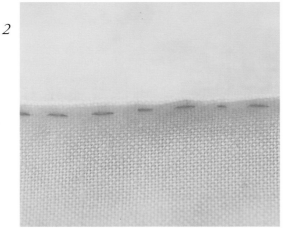

the thread taut to raise the pintuck and continue.

To finish, stretch the tucked fabric, pin to a padded board, and fix the tucks by holding a steam iron just above the surface. Allow to cool and dry before removing from the board.

4
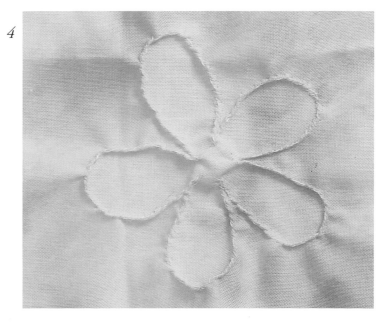

Origami

The ancient Japanese art of paper folding is brought to quilting using cotton or muslin which, while not folding as crisply as paper, does have the advantage that any fold on the bias can be rolled back and stitched to add variation.

1 Cut a 6" (15 cm) square of fabric. Fold in half, wrong sides together, and press. Open the fabric out and fold the fabric in half the other way and press again.

2 Open the fabric right side up. Using the pressed fold to guide you, take a ½" (1.5 cm) pleat and pin. Continue by turning the fabric in the same direction each time and take ½" (1.5 cm) pleats on all four sides of the square. The four pleats must all face in the same direction.

1

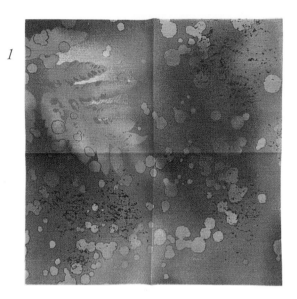

3 Once all the pleats are in place, manipulate the fabric flat and into a twisted square. This takes a little manual dexterity and some perseverance, but once achieved becomes easier.

2

3

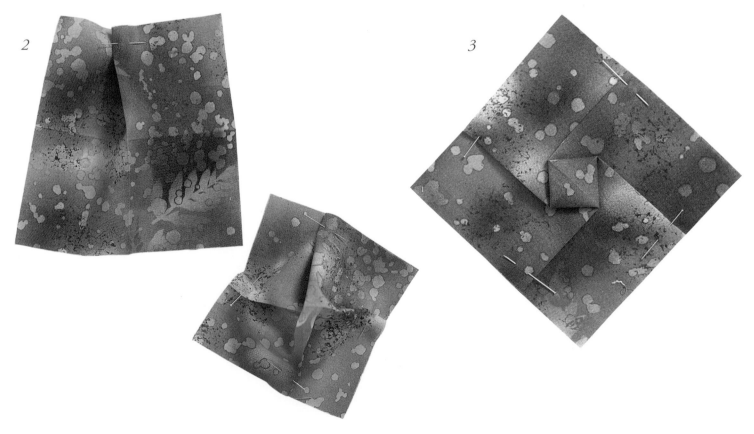

Couching

To manipulate fabric for a textured effect or to embellish your quilts with original additions, such as beads, ribbons or perhaps seashells, use the technique of couching. It simply means holding objects or threads onto a background fabric with the use of a decorative stitch.

1 Couching can be made decorative with the use of embroidery stitches. The most commonly used stitches for this are cross stitch and herringbone stitch, but try experimenting with other sewing machine stitches too.

1

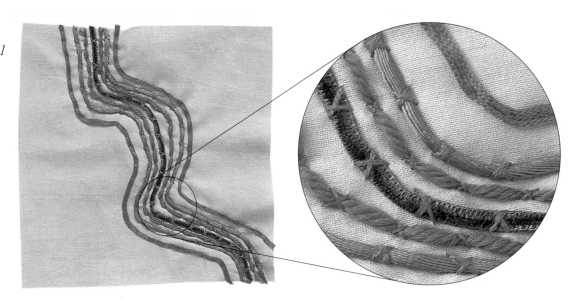

Knitting

By knitting with strips of fabric you can create novelty patches for insertion into patchwork quilts or contemporary pieces. Any fabric is suitable and it is a good way to use up favorite fabric scraps that are too precious to discard. As long as you staystitch the edge to prevent it from ravelling, it can be cut and pieced into your projects just like any other patch of fabric.

1

1 Tear, or cut fabric strips ¹/₂"(1.5 cm) wide and as long as possible to provide a running length. Roll the strips into a ball. Use thick needles and a plain knit stitch. If possible begin using a new strip of fabric at the beginning of a new row, but if not, run the new strip in as you continue knitting.

Appliqué styles

Appliqué can be one of the most rewarding techniques within the realm of patchwork and quilting. It is possible to use the simplest of shapes to create a naïve or primitive design. In one of the easiest methods, freeform shapes are applied to a background fabric with a blanket stitch, a method that folk art lovers and children enjoy. Country-style quilts and related items often use this form of appliqué.

Ideas for appliqué designs and patterns can be found in many places. Children's coloring books are a great source of inspiration. Motifs on wallpaper, drapes, and carpets can often be adapted for appliqué and used on an item that is being made for a specific room.

Nature is another great source of inspiration both for shapes and color. You can use appliqué to represent a favorite flower, or go into greater detail by applying several different fabrics for one flower and further embellishing with embroidery to create more realism. Those who enjoy gardens can stitch appliqué designs and also have the pleasure of seeing the appliquéd version long after the real thing has ceased to bloom.

The fine paper-cut designs of Eastern Europe make wonderful appliqué designs. Their intricacies, while perhaps a challenge for the novice, can easily and successfully be replicated—by all abilities—using the technique of shadow appliqué.

Patchwork and quilted items that are made with a seasonal feel and for periodic use can be enhanced with appliqué shapes and designs. These items frequently take their lead from nature's seasons or our holiday festivals, or special family occasions.

Appliqué is an art form found throughout the world, taking on the cultural influences of individual countries. It is often found in countries where patchwork and quilting are not established local needlecrafts.

No matter what type of design interests you, be it the simplest or the most intricate imaginable, appliqué—both by hand and machine—can be a very enjoyable method of interpretation. Several different appliqué techniques are described and demonstrated on the following pages and many are then applied in the appliquéd project on page 190.

Hawaiian

Hawaiian appliqué is said to have originated from visiting missionaries to Hawaii, who took with them their skills in patchwork and quilting, and taught these to the islanders. Hawaiian women adapted the technique to create designs inspired by the fauna and flora of their islands. Fabrics were in short supply, and it became the practice to use only two fabrics—one solid color for the background and another for the "paper-cut" design. The undulating lines created by echo quilting represent the waves surrounding the islands. Traditionally, this design would have been large enough to fill a bed-sized quilt.

1 Mark the design onto a card template. Add a ¼" (0.75 cm) allowance around the outside of the drawing and cut out the template.

1

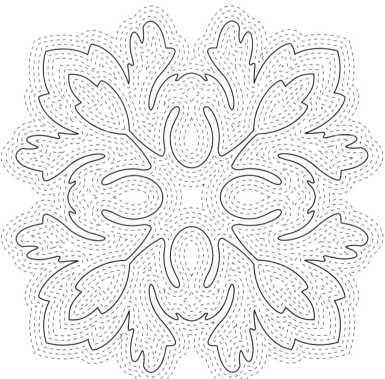

continued on the next page…

2 Alternatively, to create an original design, fold a piece of paper in half, then in half again. Fold this on the diagonal. Mark the design onto the folded paper and cut around the shape.

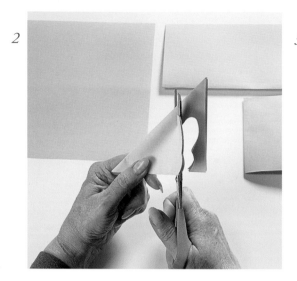

3 Open it out to see if it appeals—if not try again! Once satisfied, refold the paper and make a template by placing the folded paper on a piece of card and drawing around it, marking a ¼" (0.75 cm) seam allowance.

4 Fold a square of fabric in the same way as the paper, with the wrong side out. Place the template on the fabric and trace around it.

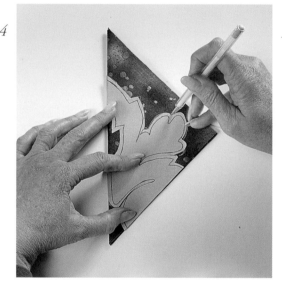

5 Using a good pair of scissors, carefully cut out the design through all the layers of fabric. Do not open it out at this stage.

6 Fold the background fabric in the same way that you folded the paper, to find the center. Unfold and place right side up on the table. Place the folded, cut-out design onto the background, aligning the folds with the creases on the background fabric.

7 Carefully unfold the cut design onto the background.

8 Securely baste the design onto the background fabric.

9 Hand-stitch the design to the background fabric using the needle-turn method (see page 63), clipping into the curves and into the V shapes to release any tension in the fabric.

10 Remove the basting. Layer the backing, batting, and quilt top; baste.

11 Quilt, using echo quilting (see page 217), both inside and outside the pattern.

8

9

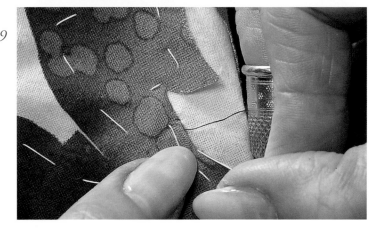

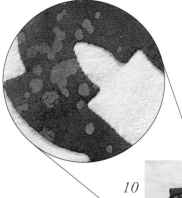

10

11

Shadow appliqué

Shadow appliqué is one of the easiest techniques to achieve successfully and the end result is very effective. Shapes are fused onto the background fabric using either a permanent or a temporary fusible adhesive, and then sheer fabric is laid over the whole item. These layers are further layered with batting and backing and all the layers are basted together. A running stitch is worked around each shape, holding it in position and quilting it at the same time.

Sheer fabrics like chiffon, organdy, organza, and voile—often in white or a pale color—are used for the covering layer to create a soft and muted effect. The fabrics used for the appliquéd shapes should therefore be strong and bright. Solid colors create a better result than prints.

1 Cut out the shapes for the appliqué and bond them onto the background fabric in the desired location.

1

Note

If the shadow appliqué is to be used on an item for which you do not want batting (like clothing), simply proceed without it or the backing fabric.

2 Once the design is complete, place a piece of the sheer fabric—slightly larger than the background fabric—on top. Place these two layers on top of a piece of batting and backing fabric, both cut larger than the top two layers.

3 Carefully baste all layers together to prepare for quilting.

2

4 Thread a needle with a strong quilting thread or a cotton perlé. Stitch a row of quilting stitches around the edge of every shape in the design, adding any further stitching required to create detail such as veins in leaves, etc. This stitching holds the layers together, trapping the appliqué shapes and quilting at the same time. More quilting may be added to the background areas if desired.

3

4

Stained glass

This exciting appliqué style takes its name from its source of design—stained glass. The fabrics used should have a vividness of color found in stained glass works. Silks, satins, synthetics, and hand-dyed fabrics have this element of pure saturated color, and because these fabrics can be placed onto a foundation fabric, there is no need to ensure they are of the same type. Black is used in the appliqué to represent the lead found in stained-glass windows. This need not be the rule, however, it does make the bright colors glow.

Use cotton fabric to create the bias for the lead (as it is easier to handle than other fabrics—see Celtic appliqué, page 180), or buy ready-made. Some purchased varieties can be temporarily bonded in position by being ironed in place ready to be stitched.

The foundation fabric should be lightweight and a light color, to form an invisible foundation on which to place the shapes in your design.

1 Trace your selected design onto a foundation fabric. Create templates for the areas that you wish to fill with bright colored fabric. There is no need to add seam allowances, as the shapes will just touch each other and the bias strip will later cover the raw edges where they meet.

1

2 Mark out the shapes onto the paper backing of fusible adhesive and iron it onto the wrong side of the fabrics. Cut out the shapes and peel off the paper backing.

3 Place the shapes, right side up, onto the foundation fabric in the correct location, allowing the edges to just touch each other. Iron the shapes to fuse them onto the foundation fabric.

4 Once all the shapes are in place, the bias strip can be added. Analyze the design and start where the end of the bias strip being added will tuck under another piece of bias strip later. If using a bias that can be temporarily bonded in position, iron it once you are sure it is in the correct place.

5 Pin or baste the strip ready for stitching. You can either hand or machine appliqué the strips to the foundation fabric. If using the machine, top stitch along both edges of the bias strip, or use a narrow open zigzag stitch with a matching thread or invisible monofilament. Alternatively, a twin needle can be used, stitching along both edges of the bias at the same time.

2

3
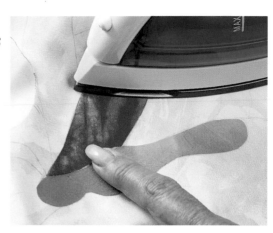

4

5

6
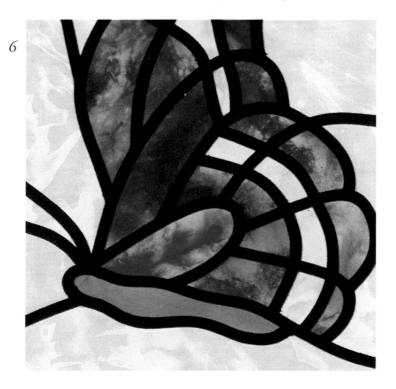

6 To complete, machine stitch alongside each edge of the bias strip. There is no need to add extra quilting to other areas.

Celtic

This form of appliqué is based on ancient Celtic designs of interwoven lines often found on religious buildings and artefacts. Today, these patterns are as popular as ever, and provide a rich source for embellishment. Because the designs are mainly curving in nature, bias tubes are used to allow the fabric to turn corners easily. The tube is made without any joins, to avoid bulk. Ready-made tubes come in packets of several widths, or there are plastic pressing bars for making your own bias tubes (see page 33).

1 To create the bias tubes, begin by finding the true bias of the chosen fabric: fold the selvage edge of the fabric diagonally, making a 45° angle.

2 From the triangle of fabric created, cut strips of fabric along the diagonal, twice the desired finished width, plus twice the seam allowance. The seam allowance for bias is normally at least 1/8" (3 mm), but if you find this too difficult to work with, allow for a wider seam allowance and trim off the excess after stitching.

3 Fold the strips in half lengthwise, wrong sides together. Stitch approximately 2" (5 cm), using your determined seam allowance. Insert the pressing bar into the tube just stitched to ensure that it is of the correct width. If the bar will not fit, decrease the seam allowance. If the fabric tube is too big for the bar, increase the seam allowance. Stitch all the tubes.

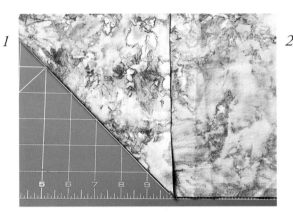

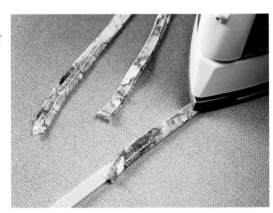

4 Insert the pressing bar into a tube and twist it until the seam and seam allowances are on one side of the bar and cannot be seen on the other side. Press the seam in one direction, moving the pressing bar through the tube until the bar is released at the other end. Repeat for each tube.

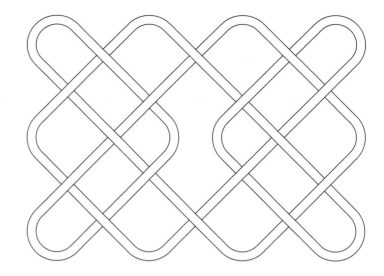

5 Trace the Celtic design onto the background fabric by drawing a line through the center of the double lines of the design. When the design weaves under a section, stop drawing and start again on the other side of the section. This will help you see when the tube being appliquéd should weave under another tube.

6 Place one of the bias tubes so that the end starts in an "under" position and ensure it is long enough to reach the next "under" location.

You may decide to appliqué as you go or place all the tubes in position for the complete design and baste them in place before blind stitching.

Begin hand stitching the bias tubes to the background fabric. Stitch the inside of a curve first so as not to overstretch the bias.

When you encounter a junction where the tube being stitched will go over another that is not yet positioned, leave a gap in the stitching for a tube to weave under later. Stitch any gaps closed as you stitch the "under" weaving tube in position. Each time you come to an "under" location, check to be sure that the bias tube you are using will reach the next "under" junction. If it will not reach, cut the bias tube off so that the end will be in the center of the tube that will pass over the top of it. Insert a new tube so that the ends just touch or slightly overlap, and continue stitching.

6

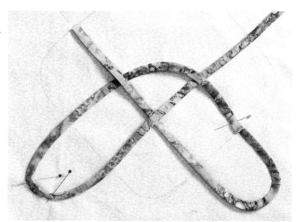

3-D

Both hand and machine appliqué can be embellished with the addition of 3-D elements. This is sometimes achieved by the manipulation of fabric, creating ruches, tucks, folds, and texture. On other occasions an element of the appliqué—such as a leaf or a petal of a flower—is made separately and then attached, either by tucking it under another part of the appliqué, or by stitching it to the background fabric and the main design. The possibilities are endless and it is great fun exploring.

Here are the basic steps on how to create 3-D, free-standing daffodil flower heads and buds, attached to hand-appliquéd leaves. On page 184, rose petals with leaves that are attached under a portion of appliqué are demonstrated.

3-D daffodil flower heads

1 Mark and cut white fabric into simple petal shapes. Place two petals right sides together, and machine stitch the edges leaving the lower edge open. Repeat five times to create six petals. Clip any curves as necessary. Turn the petals right side out and press. Fold or gather the open end to create a pleat.

2 Place the six petals in the appropriate location on the background fabric to create the flower head. Secure temporarily with pins or by hand stitching.

1

2

3 To create the flower center, cut out two circles of yellow fabric—one large and one small— and a small piece of batting, if desired. Fold under the edge of the large circle and work a running stitch around the edge. Place the large circle, face-down, in the center of the petals, the batting in the center of this circle, and the small circle, face-up, on top of it. (See Yo-yos, page 145.)

4 Stitch the inner circle to the background fabric, securing the outer circle, the batting, and the petals of the flower at the same time.

5 Pull the thread running around the edge of the larger circle so that it gathers up over the smaller circle in the center.

6 Tie off the ends of this thread or use it to stitch the gathers to secure.

3

4

5

6

3-D daffodil flower buds

1 Cut a circle of fabric for each flower bud. Fold each circle in half, wrong sides together.

2 With the folded edge at the top, roll the top right and top left edges to the middle. Stitch all the raw edges together. Blindstitch the bud to the background fabric in its appropriate location.

1

2

continued on the next page…

3-D rose head and leaves

1 Sandwich batting between two layers of fabric, chosen for leaves, right sides out. Using a short, straight machine stitch, outline the shape of each leaf. Cut out the leaves, then satin stitch around the edges. There is no need to satin stitch the portion of the leaves that will tuck under other shapes.

2 Invert the design and trace it out onto the wrong side of the background fabric. Place and stitch the leaves in position on the right (unmarked) side of the background fabric.

3 Place the fabric chosen for the flower head, right sides up over a layer of batting. Place both layers over the right side of the background fabric, and secure with pins. This gives extra dimension to what would otherwise be a flat portion of the appliqué.

4 Stitch the shape from the wrong (marked) side of the background fabric.

5 Trim the excess flower fabric and batting away close to the stitched line.

6 Satin stitch over the lines of stitching holding the fabric and batting in place.

1
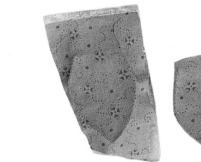

2

3

4

6

5

Embellishing with embroidery

Early forms of crazy patchwork (see page 149) were the perfect way to show off embroidery stitches. Using fabrics such as velvets, satin, and brocades left over from the making of ballgowns to create what today are called throws, was the pastime of ladies. Hours were spent in embellishing the luxury fabrics with rich embroidery stitches.

Today, embroidery is an exciting embellishment to appliqué. There are wonderful threads available for this stitching and fine details that would be difficult, if not impossible, to appliqué, such as the tendrils of plants, or a bird's eye or beak, or facial features, are embroidered to add depth, or create illusion and atmosphere to appliqué designs.

Embellish appliqué with embroidery stitches such as a stem stitch or French knots, or more freeform, random stitching either by hand or machine. You may prefer to use hand embroidery to keep a consistent, soft feel to the appliqué, as in the apple blossom at right.

Some of the decorative embroidery stitches available on sewing machines can be used to embellish the center of a flower or the edge of a petal. Alternatively, you could use free motion machine embroidery.

In the seascape below right, an appliqué design has been completed first and free motion machine embroidery has then been used to "color" areas on or around the shapes.

The embroidery not only adds the embellishment desired but quilts at the same time, giving further texture to the finished item.

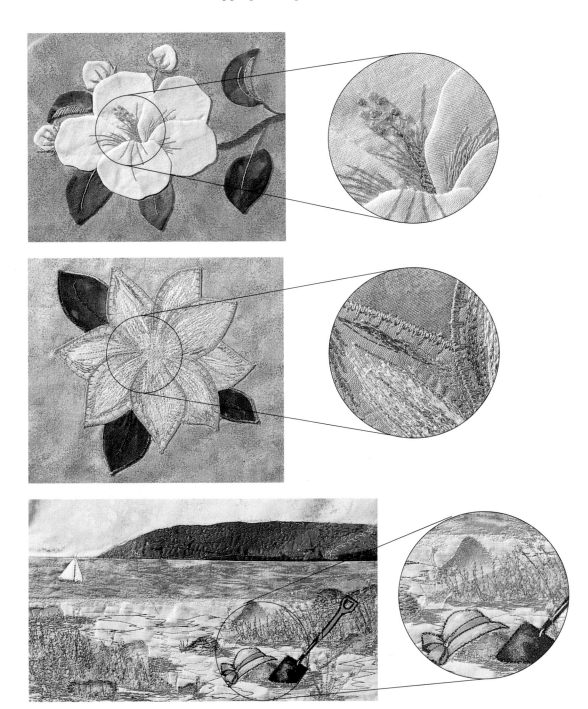

Reverse

In reverse appliqué, the fabric that is the prominent part of the design is placed underneath the background fabric. This background fabric is then cut away to reveal the color and pattern beneath, and the edges of the background fabric are stitched to the fabric below, using the needle-turn method (see page 63).

Two very distinctive forms of reverse appliqué are used by the Kuna Indians living on islands off the coast of Panama, and the Hmong people of Laos, Vietnam, and Thailand. Natural form and folklore inspire the mainly asymmetrical designs used by the Kuna Indians. The designs by the Hmong people are inspired by nature, but their reverse appliqué designs are usually symmetrical, much more intricate, and can also include embroidery. To create a simplified form of reverse appliqué, have a copy of the design available for reference as you progress.

1 Mark an outer line of the design onto the right side of the background fabric. Cover a square of contrasting fabric, right side up, with the background fabric, also right side up. Baste these two layers together following the outline.

1

2 Cut the background fabric, ¼" (0.75 cm) inside the marked line, clipping the seam allowance on any curves. Take care to cut the top layer of fabric only.

Using the needle-turn method, appliqué the foundation fabric to the contrasting fabric now exposed. Cut away the excess contrasting fabric from the back.

3 Mark the next portion of the outline onto the first contrasting fabric. Cut a square of the second contrasting fabric, and place it right side up, into position behind the work previously stitched. Baste, following the marked outline.

4 Cut through the top layer (the first contrasting fabric) ¼" (0.75 cm) inside the drawn design to reveal the new layer of fabric. Appliqué the first layer onto this fabric as before, using a needle-turn stitch.

5 Repeat the process using a third contrasting fabric, and marking the final trace outline. Baste, then cut and needle-turn stitch to complete the design.

2

3

4

5

Broderie perse

Broderie perse developed during the eighteenth century out of a desire to use the brilliantly colored fabrics that were manufactured in India and imported into the West. The motifs printed on these fabrics were cut out and appliquéd onto a base fabric. The technique got its name because it was thought to resemble Persian embroidery. It is used with great effect today when worked on a small scale to enhance appliqué designs, rather than for the design of a whole quilt, as would have been the case in earlier centuries.

1 Select elements from your chosen fabric that can be used individually within an appliqué design.

2 To machine stitch, first cut out the motif exactly to size, and fuse the shapes onto a background fabric. To hand stitch, cut the motif with an allowance to turn under the edges. Stitches can either be unobtrusive, using a monofilament thread, or decorative, using contrasting threads. These examples show the effects using five different types of stitch:
(a) machine blanket stitch,
(b) hand blanket stitch,
(c) machine zigzag stitch,
(d) machine zigzag stitch using monofilament thread, and (e) hand blind stitch.

3 To prepare the flower and the stems, cut out and fuse each shape. Position on the background fabric. Press to fuse in place. Machine satin stitch the stems.

4 Use monofilament thread to hand appliqué the bunch of flowers and the cat to the background fabric, turning under the edges as you stitch (see page 69).

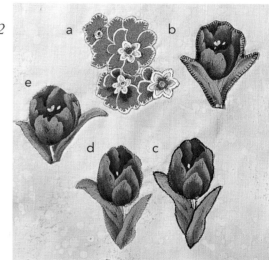

Landscape

Piecing, appliqué, or a combination of both disciplines, can be used to create charming landscape designs. Whatever method is used, an impression rather than a literal representation should be the aim.

A starting point might be a landscape photograph, a postcard from a tropical location, or a scene from your imagination. Observe that in scenery, those areas further away are grayer in tone to areas that are closer, which are brighter and contain truer colors. Bear this in mind when selecting fabrics for the different areas. Fabrics that have a textured appearance rather than prints may be better for achieving the desired look.

3

1 Start with the fabric for the sky, and fuse this onto the lower portion, the mountains. Then fuse the foreground in place.

1

2 Cut out and fuse further elements into place, building up the landscape. To avoid a build up of the fusible adhesive, which may cause the appliqué to become stiff, fuse each shape to its neighbor only along the outer edge.

3 Add embroidery and quilting stitches—either by hand or machine—to create illusion and detail.

2

Appliquéd project: Wallhanging

This elaborate wallhanging incorporates many elements of hand and machine appliqué, drawing on several of the techniques described on pages 173 to 189. Step-by-step, you build up the picture, beginning with Celtic appliqué, using fused shapes, adding 3-D leaf and flower elements, and broderie perse motifs, concluding with some delightful embroidery embellishments.

Finished size

23" × 18" (80.5 × 46 cm)

Fabric

1 fat quarter background fabric
1 fat quarter basket fabric
½ yd. (45 cm) fabric for border and binding
1 long quarter for frame between border and background
Various fabrics for flowers and leaves
1 yd. (1 m) backing fabric and sleeve

Other materials

Fusible adhesive
2¾ yd. (2.5 m) piping cord
25" × 30" (62.5 × 75 cm) batting
Scraps of batting for 3-D flowers and leaves
Threads to match or complement fabrics for piecing and appliqué
Machine embroidery threads to match or complement flower and leaf fabrics
Monofilament thread for machine quilting around basket and flowers
Quilting thread for background hand quilting
Pencil for tracing design onto fabric
Stabilizer

1 Cut a piece of background fabric 15½" × 20½" (38.75 cm × 51.25 cm). Trace the drawing onto the wrong side of the background fabric.

Trace the basket portion of the design onto the right side of the background fabric for the Celtic appliqué (page 180) that will create the basket weaves.

2 Cut and fuse 10 round leaves from your chosen fabric with fusible adhesive. Position one round leaf behind the basket on the right side. Fuse it in place, right side up. Stitch around the shape to secure.

Use the chosen basket fabric to make bias tubes ½" (1.25 cm) wide and long enough for the basket handle, and bias tubes ³/₈" (1 cm) wide and long enough for the top and bottom edges of the basket. Make ¼" (0.75 cm) tubes for the body weaves of the basket. Pin and baste the bias tubes in place to create the basket, and hand stitch.

1

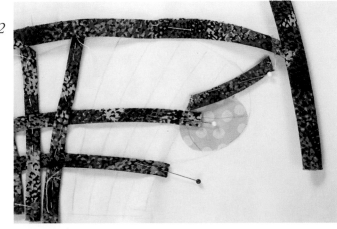

2

continued on the next page...

3 Follow the diagram to determine in which order the 2-D leaves should be stitched to the background fabric. Those that are positioned under another leaf should be stitched first. The large leaves will have a layer of batting behind them to add dimension. On the right side of the background fabric, place a piece of batting in the appropriate position. On top of this, place the chosen leaf fabric, right side up. Secure with pins.

4 Using a short stitch, machine stitch on the reverse side around the leaf shape being applied. Stitch on any drawn vein lines as you go, so that you will see where to place the decorative stitching. Turn the unit over again and trim the excess fabric and batting back to the line of stitching. Repeat the process with or without batting until all the 2-D leaves have been stitched in place.

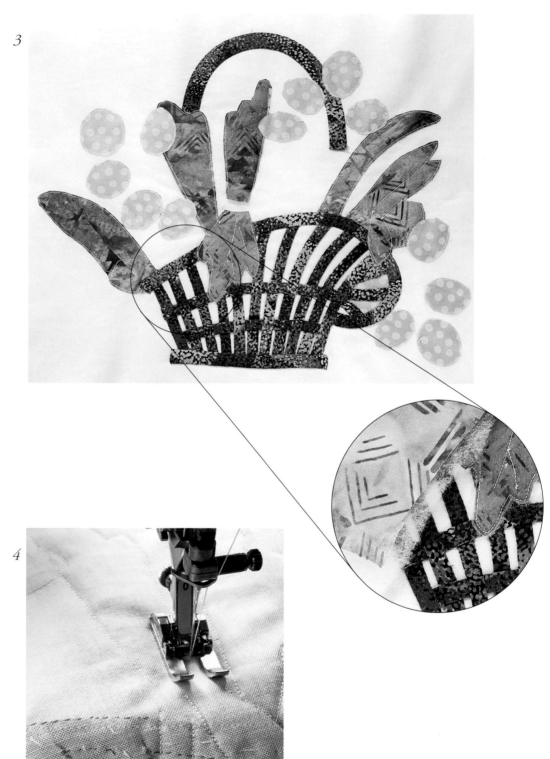

5 For the 3-D leaves, make a sandwich of two layers of leaf fabric with batting in the middle. The fabric should be right side out on both the top and bottom of the sandwich. Make a tracing of the leaves onto a piece of tracing paper. Place the paper tracing on top of the fabric sandwich and secure with pins. Machine stitch on the lines for each leaf. Tear off the paper. Cut out each leaf, cutting close to the stitched line. Place the leaves on a stabilizing material. Using a matching thread, satin stitch around the edge of each leaf. Remove the stabilizer according to the manufacturer's instructions. Set aside until Step 10.

5

6 Analyze the drawing to work out which of the flowers are to be stitched first. As with the leaves, place a piece of fabric slightly larger than the flower shape in position, right side up on the right side of the background fabric. Turn the unit over and stitch along the drawn lines on the back, as well as on the lines for the outside edge of the shape. Turn the unit over and trim away the excess fabric and batting. If a flower has one or two leaves tucked under its petals, pin the leaves into position before stitching on the lines of the flower, catching in the edges of the leaves under the flower.

6

7

7 For the broderie perse flowers, cut an appropriate motif from your chosen floral print fabric. Do the same for the butterfly. Fuse the flower shapes in position.

continued on the next page…

8 Once all the 2-D shapes are secured in position, place a piece of stabilizer large enough to cover the entire area of the appliqué behind the background fabric. Machine satin stitch around each shape. One or more of the decorative stitches on your machine can be used very effectively—especially on the flower petals. Apply the decorative stitching to the shapes in the same sequence as the application of shapes to the background.

8

9 Work the yo-yo flower in position (see 3-D appliqué, page 182).

9

10 Position the 3-D leaves in the correct location. Using a narrow satin stitch, stitch the center vein of each leaf, carrying the stitching up to join the stem line. Create the stem line with a row of narrow satin stitches. Once stitched, twist the leaf to give a slight curl, for realism and dimension.

11 Create the three freestanding 3-D flowers. Make a sandwich with the chosen fabrics and batting, as for the 3-D leaves. Place a lightweight paper tracing of the flower shape on the sandwich and stitch on the line around the outside edge of the flower. Remove the paper, cut out the flowers, and place on a stabilizer. Satin stitch around the edge of each flower and add embroidery embellishments. When satisfied, remove the stabilizer.

10

11

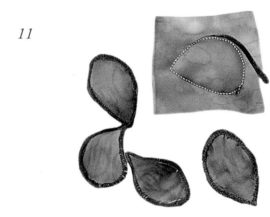

Follow the same method to create the 3-D butterfly. The flowers and butterfly will not be added until the quilting of the wallhanging has been completed.

Frame and border

1 Cut the frame fabric ³/₄" (2 cm) wide, fold in half lengthwise, wrong sides together, and press. Pin the strip onto the background fabric, along the top and bottom edges, and the two sides, aligning all raw edges. Baste.

Cut the border fabric into 2¹/₄" (5.75 cm) wide strips. Pin these strips to the background fabric, aligning the frame fabric along all raw edges. Machine stitch all layers together, allowing a ¹/₄" (0.75 cm) seam allowance. The corners can either be mitered or butted.

1

To complete the wallhanging

1 Cut the backing and batting 2" (5 cm) larger on all sides than the background fabric and borders. Baste the three layers together. Machine quilt, using monofilament thread, around each shape. Hand quilt the lines that radiate from the center of the design.

1

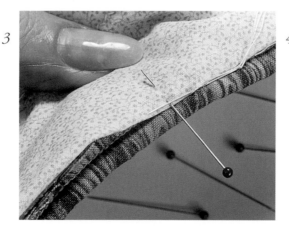

2

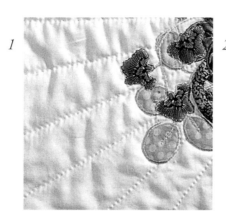

2 To pipe the edge of the hanging, cut a straight strip of border fabric wide enough to wrap around the piping cord plus two ¹/₄" (0.75 cm) seam allowances. Place the piping cord lengthwise down the wrong side of the fabric strip, bring the edges together, and using a zipper foot and matching thread, stitch as close to the cord as possible.

Fold the backing fabric back, away from the edge. Align the raw edges of the covered cord and the border fabric. Stitch the cord, the border, and the batting together, close to the cord. Trim the batting back to the stitched line.

3

4

3 Trim the backing fabric to size, allowing ¹/₂" (1.5 cm) seam allowance on all four sides. Turn this seam allowance under, and blind stitch the backing to the sandwich along the row of stitches made when the cord was added to the border.

4 Stitch the 3-D flowers in place. Secure the butterfly by stitching it to the background either side of the body. Embroider the antennae, taking care that the stitches go only into the background fabric and batting and not through to the backing fabric.

continued on the next page…

Appliquéd project: Wallhanging (continued)

5 Make a sleeve (see page 252) and stitch it to the back, ensuring that the stitches are not visible on the front. Hang it and enjoy!

5

Wholecloth quilts

Before the advent of printing onto textiles, decorative designs had to be applied, pieced, or sewn onto fabrics to produce a pattern. Sewing large pieces of cloth together with a quilting stitch combined the decorative effect of those stitches with the warmth provided by stitching several layers together. These plain quilts have become known as wholecloth quilts. Various styles evolved: in colder northern climes, an inner layer of padding, or batting, was added, whereas various styles of corded and stuffed work were developed in Southern Europe and the Near East.

Originally, quilting motifs tended to be regional, but as people migrated, so these styles spread and have, to some extent, intermingled. In the USA, several distinct wholecloth quilt styles relate back to those brought in by immigrant settlers. Many whitework quilts, for example, are akin to the elaborate corded and stuffed work found in southern France. In Britain, two definitive styles from south Wales and the northeast of England have been retained. Amish quilts, on the other hand, combine the large patchwork pieces of Welsh quilts with the free-flowing feathers of the English Durham quilts in a new and distinctive style.

Nowadays, the making of wholecloth quilts is not restricted to hand stitching. The old designs have been adapted and updated to suit machine quilting, and exciting new designs are continually evolving.

The simplest form of wholecloth quilt is the strippy quilt, in which wide strips of alternating colored fabrics are joined together. The quilting designs usually (but not always) follow the length of the strip. The strips used to be made of fabrics left over from making plain quilts, but could also include patterned or even pieced fabrics. The type and width of strips, and the variety of quilting patterns used on them, make this the most diverse style of wholecloth quilt.

Other wholecloth quilts are made from a single piece of fabric. As it may not be possible to find fabric of sufficient width, panels of fabric are often joined together to make a larger piece. It is usual to have a center panel of fabric with adjacent strips, rather than a seam down the middle of the quilt top.

Backing fabric may also be joined to make a larger piece, but to avoid bulky areas, the seams must not lie in the same position as those on the quilt top. Once quilted, they will be barely visible under the pattern.

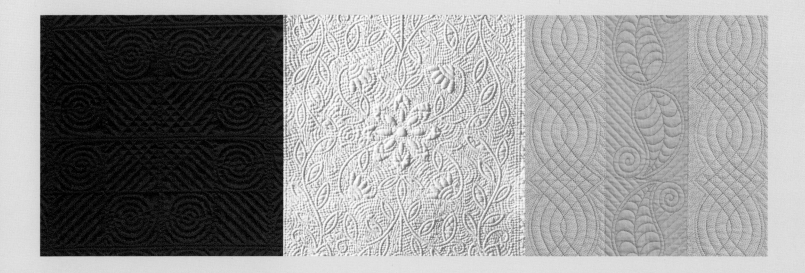

Designing wholecloth patterns

The first step in making a wholecloth quilt is to design and draw out the quilting pattern. Design is not something that all quilters are comfortable with, but this need not deter you, should you wish to make one. The easiest option is to buy a ready-marked quilt top on bleached or unbleached muslin. These designs provide excellent starting points for making wholecloth quilts, and can obviously be adapted. For quilters with more confidence, templates, both commercial and homemade, can be arranged into pleasing original designs.

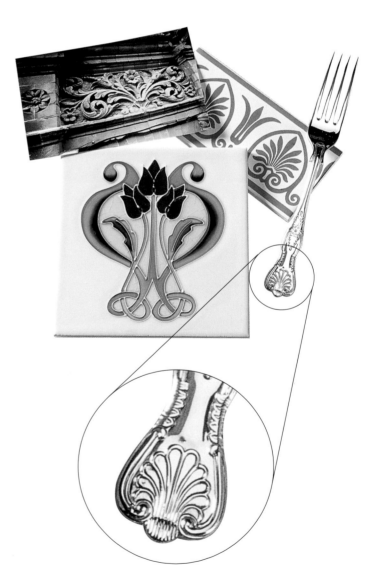

Should you wish to use fine fabrics, or to choose a colored fabric, commercial patterns are available. Some quilting books contain layout drawings with templates that can be drawn up or enlarged on a photocopier.

Inspiration for original patterns may come from many sources. Old quilts are the most obvious design source. Combining the best of several old quilts into an entirely new quilt will provide valuable insight into how designs were laid out in the past as well as setting an interesting challenge. Inspiration can come from other crafts: look for designs in plasterwork, wrought iron work, and carvings in decorative stonework and old wooden furniture. Even silverware can provide motifs that can be arranged into a wholecloth quilt design. Here, the motif has been inspired by a silver fork.

1 Quilting motifs usually display symmetry. When drawing out a motif, draw only the bare minimum. Tracing mirror images and repeat components will be more accurate than further drawings.

2 The motif may be arranged to form the central pattern of a quilt.

3 The addition of several smaller motifs will give added interest, and can also be arranged in a different way to form the basis of a border design. At the corners, added interest can be given by positioning further motifs relating to the central design, or by ensuring that a border design continues around the corner in an unbroken line.

Once the design is finalized on paper, you are ready to start the quilt. Turn to page 226 for the next steps to hand quilt your design.

4 The area between the center motif and the borders is filled in with a background quilting design. This is usually one of several variations of pattern based on simple straight lines.

1

2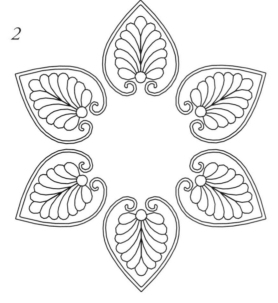

3

4

Sashing and borders

Once you have completed all the blocks for a quilt, and decided on the setting of the blocks, you need to assemble them and add sashing and/or borders. There are many setting possibilities open to you (see page 72), some of which contain sashing between the blocks to create individual designs. This can be either simple sashing or sashing strips with cornerstones.

Sashing is made up of strips of fabric that separate the blocks. They can change the tone and color of a quilt. You can create a bold look or a soft look by choosing different colors for the sashing. If you choose the same color as the background of the blocks, it will make the blocks appear to "float." Sashing strips create unification between what might otherwise be uncoordinated blocks. It is always wise, therefore, to choose the sashing fabric after you have completed all the blocks. Take the blocks to a quilt store and lay them on a variety of fabrics. Do not try to select fabric for sashing by simply taking swatches of fabric or by trying to choose in advance. Sashing fabric can make or mar a quilt, so make your choices with care.

It is tempting to cut sashing strips wider than is advised here to make a quilt bigger; however, this is not advisable, as the blocks can look disjointed if too far apart. To increase the size of a quilt, increase the number of blocks or increase the number and size of the borders.

Once the body of a quilt is complete, consider the borders. Borders need to complement a quilt in both color and style. They should never look as though they were an afterthought as the entire effect may be spoiled; so should be awarded the same amount of consideration as the main body of the quilt.

Medallion-style quilts are a series of borders round a central block. When adding borders to a quilt, accurate measurements need to be taken. If this is not done, the quilt will have wavy edges and will not lie flat.

Simple sashing

As a guideline, sashing strips should be no wider than one quarter of the finished block size: the sashing for a 12" (30 cm) block should be no more than 3" (7.5 cm), and no more than 2¼" (5.5 cm) for a 9" (23 cm) block.

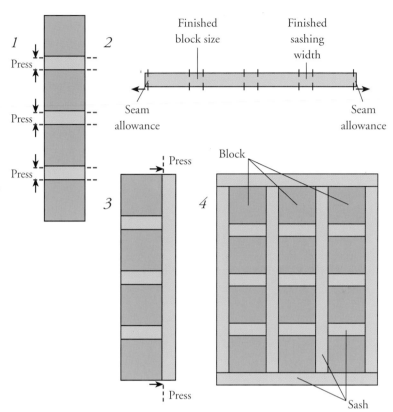

1 Cut the sashing fabric into short strips the same length as the blocks and one quarter as wide plus ½" (1.5 cm) for the two seam allowances. Join a column of blocks by stitching sashing strips between each pair. Press all seam allowances toward the sashing.

2 Measure the length of the columns of blocks and cut long sashing strips to this length. These strips will need to be cut parallel to the lengthwise grain. Mark the seam line positions from the blocks onto the strips. This

will help to line up the blocks and keep the quilt top square.

3 Pin and stitch the strips to the pieced rows matching the marks. Press all the seams toward the sashing strips.

4 To prepare the sashing for the top and bottom of the quilt top, measure the width of the quilt and cut sashing strips to this size. Mark the seam positions onto the sashing strip as in Step 2. Pin and stitch the strips to the quilt, and press all the seams toward the sashing.

Sashing with cornerstones

The addition of cornerstones to sashing can add a further dimension and introduce another fabric. The corners can be small pieced blocks or plain fabric. They are always square and the same size as the width of the sashing.

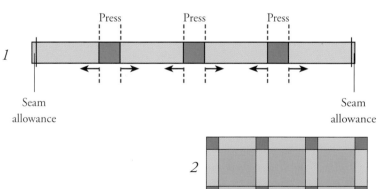

1 Cut the sashing fabric into short strips the same length as the blocks and one quarter of the width and stitch to the blocks, as in Step 1 of Simple Sashing. Join each column of blocks by stitching sashing strips between each pair; in addition, stitch sashing strips to the top and bottom of these columns. Press all the seam allowances toward the sashing.

2 The long strips of sashing are made up of sashing pieces sewn together with cornerstone squares in between. Cut the sashing fabric into short strips the same length as the blocks and one quarter of the width. Either cut basic squares of fabric or prepare small pieced blocks for the cornerstones; these should be the same size as the width of the sashing pieces. Stitch

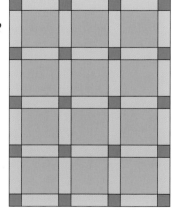

together the strips of sashing and cornerstones into long strips the length of the columns of blocks. Press all the seams toward the sashing.

3 Stitch the long strips to the columns of pieced blocks, matching the seams as you go (see above).

Measuring for borders

Measure the quilt in three places on the horizontal and three on the vertical: the two parallel edges (A and B in the diagram) and in the middle of the quilt (C in the diagram).

Add the measurements for A, B and C for the vertical together and find an average: A + B + C, divided by 3 to find the length of the two vertical borders. Repeat the measurement on the horizontal to find the length of the two horizontal borders. For simple sashing, reduce the length of the horizontal borders by twice the width of the border. For mitered corners, keep the full length of both the horizontal and the vertical borders. Measurements need to be taken for each border as it is added. Never simply cut a strip and sew it into place, trimming away any surplus. This can present difficulties, especially if you go on to add multiple borders.

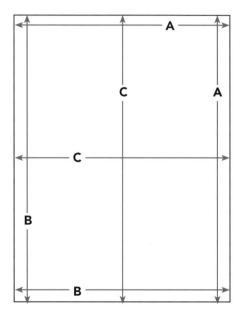

Strip borders with corner blocks

Corner blocks make interesting additions to simple, straight borders.

1 Measure the quilt top in both directions. Cut border strips the length needed, and cut corner blocks the size of the width of the border strips. These corner blocks can be pieced blocks, if preferred. Sew the blocks onto either end of one of the sets of border strips, either onto both sides or the top and bottom. Press away from the corner blocks. Stitch the plain borders to the quilt top first, and press toward the added border. Stitch the borders with the corner blocks to the quilt, matching the seams as for butted seams (see page 51), and press toward the added borders.

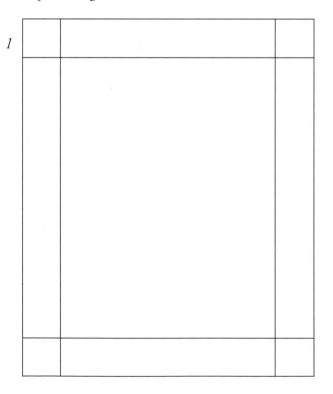

Simple borders

The simplest style of border is made up of straight strips. You may choose to add one, two, or three strips. Lay a variety of fabrics alongside the quilt top in order to determine which of them gives the effect you desire. If just one fabric is used, the border needs to be wide enough to frame the quilt body, but not so wide as to overpower the rest of the design. If using two fabrics, the inner border will be the narrower of the two, and usually the lighter or brighter. Outer borders are usually darker in value and intensity in order to frame the overall quilt. The most common number of simple borders used to frame a quilt is three. All three need to differ in width and tone.

1 Measurements for simple borders need to be taken at each stage. First, measure the side borders and cut strips lengthwise from the border fabric. Alternatively, you can cut borders from the width of the fabric and stitch the pieces together, either with straight seams or angled seams, depending on personal preference. Note that angled seams do not show so much once quilted.

2 To piece the strips at an angle, lay them right sides together at right angles. Draw a line across the corner, as shown, and sew on this line. Trim away the excess and press the seam open.

3 When you have made and cut strips for the sides, pin at the center first, then at the ends, and ease along the quilt edge as necessary. Stitch to the quilt and press toward the borders.

Measure the quilt along the top, middle, and bottom to find the length of these two borders. Cut, pin, and stitch as before. Press toward the added borders.

Any subsequent borders are added in exactly the same manner. There are no definite rules about adding sides before top and bottom. It is fine to add top and bottom before sides instead; just remember to measure the lengths accordingly.

1
2
3

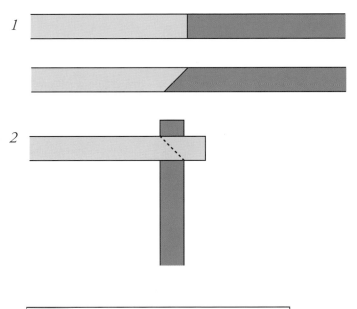

Borders with mitered corners

On most occasions, borders to quilts will only require straight corners. However, if a border is in a striped fabric, it creates a more pleasing frame if the corners are mitered, allowing the stripes to flow around the corner.

1 To calculate dimensions for mitered borders, measure the length of the quilt top, plus twice the chosen width of the borders, plus 5" (12.5 cm) for overlap. For example, if the border is to be 4" (10 cm) wide and the quilt 70" (178 cm) long, you will need to measure:
70" + 4" + 4" + 5" = 83"
(178 cm + 10 cm + 10 cm + 12.5 cm = 210.5 cm). Cut border strips to this size.

2 To attach the border, mark the mid-point of the quilt edge by measuring half the length of the quilt less the outer seam allowances.
  Pin the border strips onto the quilt, working from the center to the seam allowance edges. Stitch between the seam allowance points. Stitch the border around all four sides in the same manner.

3 To create the miter at each corner, work on a flat surface onto which you can iron. Press one border flat in the direction of the other border. Press the adjacent border flat and then fold it to create a 45°-angle so that it lies exactly on top of the first strip. Press this crease in place. Open out the quilt top and fold it right sides together with the borders lying exactly on top of each other. Stitch along the creased line. Repeat for the other corners. Trim away the excess fabric and press the seams open.

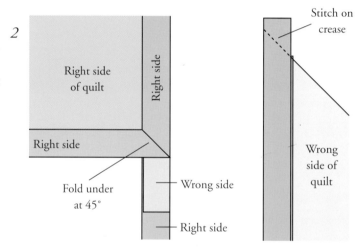

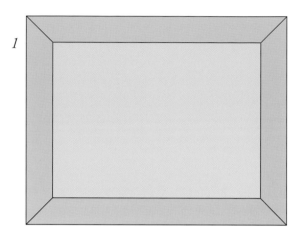

Pieced block borders

Borders can be created from a collection of blocks sewn together to create borders of the correct length. The choice is infinite: checkerboards, four-patch blocks, nine-patch blocks, sawtooth borders from half-square triangle units, and flying geese borders, to name but a few. Measure accurately and always ensure the borders are the correct length before sewing to the quilt.

QUILTING TECHNIQUES

Machine quilting

Machine quilting is a partnership between you and your sewing machine. This section takes you through the basic procedures for getting started with machine quilting and also for being at ease with your sewing machine. Once you have mastered some of the techniques, you will find it liberating to complete your quilts with patterns that are totally unique and, as machine quilting is quicker than hand quilting, you can make many more quilts!

The first thing to remember is that nobody ever went straight onto the freeway on the day they started to learn to drive. And so it is with machine quilting. Practice is the order of the day, and if you follow these instructions and make some samples before quilting your precious quilt top, then you will feel confident about tackling larger and more intricate projects. You will gain confidence with practice.

Machine quilting also gives you an opportunity to use some wonderful threads and exciting fabrics that are on the market today. Be bold and never be afraid to try something new.

Machine quilting was at one time frowned upon by purists as a "lazy" way to complete a quilt. Due to some amazing, award-winning, machine-quilted quilts entered into international quilt shows, machine quilting has been accepted by the quilting world as more than just a quick and easy way to complete a quilt. It has become an art form in its own right.

There is never simply one way to achieve anything, so try out a variety of techniques and see which ones suit you and the sewing machine accessories you have. There are no quilt police, so do not be put off by rules. If you find a method of quilting that gives good results, then stay with it.

Preparing the equipment

Get to know your sewing machine! Machine quilting will become easier the more you do it, but first you need to know about certain special features on your machine and how to use them.

There is such an array of sewing machines available today that you will need guidance from your sewing machine dealer to find the one that is right for you at the price that suits your pocket. For machine quilting, you will need a good straight stitch, a satin stitch, and the ability to lower the feed dogs for free motion work. You will also need a walking foot and a darning foot.

To get the best results, make sure that your machine is clean and in good working order before you start.

A large table with plenty of room around the machine is important and, ideally, the machine should be set into the table to give you a flat surface. If this is not possible, there are plastic extension tables available for most sewing machine brands.

A swivel chair that can be raised and lowered is ideal for sewing at the machine. A table or ironing board placed just to the left of the machine and butting up to its table helps to take the weight of the quilt and prevents dragging. Quilters sometimes ask how it is possible to get the bulk of the quilt through the small gap of the machine arm. Rolling the quilt makes it simple, and you will find it easier the more you quilt.

1 Clean your sewing machine: look in the instruction book to find out how to remove the bobbin and brush away the build up of fluff, which can affect tension and stitching. If your sewing machine uses oil, find out from the manual where to put it for smooth running.

Decide on the color thread you wish to use on the back of the quilt and fill several bobbins, to avoid running out at a crucial moment.

Always use a new needle for each project to achieve good results. The quilting needle is especially good for invisible or monofilament threads used for quilting in-the-ditch and on multi-colored fabrics. When using heavier weight embroidery threads for embellishment, use embroidery or top stitch needles.

1

continued on the next page...

Preparing the equipment (continued)

2 You will need a walking foot, which has metal feet underneath that "walk" the three layers through the machine. This prevents pulling and puckers occurring underneath the quilt as you sew. You will also want a darning foot, preferably one that has a see-through area so that you can see where you are going. Ask your dealer for the correct feet for your machine.

2

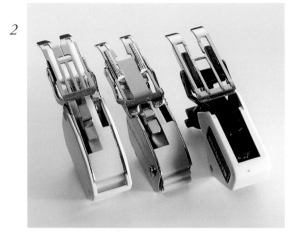

3 Sit comfortably at your sewing machine, directly in front of the needle, at a height where your arms can rest on the table.

Ideally, have your sewing machine set into a special table to give you a flat space around the machine and to prevent drag on the quilt. Clear the space behind the machine so that the quilt will move forward and not bunch up behind the arm. As you feed the quilt through the machine, roll the bulk under the machine arm for easy maneuverability and position your hands as shown to keep the area under the machine as taut as possible.

Special quilting gloves are available to grip the quilt as it goes through the machine.

3

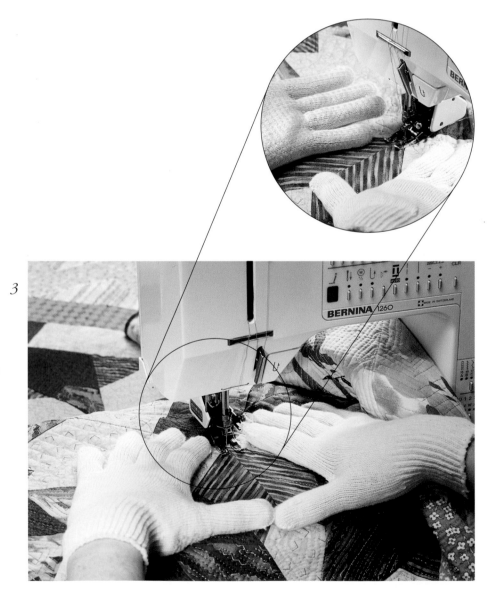

Preparing the quilt sandwich

To prepare to quilt, a layer of backing, batting, and the top fabric have to be attached together to form the quilt sandwich. This is particularly important as it is vital to eliminate any pleats and puckers that can form if this step is not carried out properly.

The layers can be basted together with thread, however, it may be difficult to remove the basting thread without tearing the machine stitches. There are three alternative methods. Whichever method is used for keeping the layers together, and it is a matter of preference which you choose, it is important to make sure that all layers are smoothed out and that they are secured at regular intervals.

If you have to join pieces of fabric to make the backing, cut off the selvage before sewing so that the fabric will lie straight. Make sure that any seams are to one side of the center and that they are pressed open to reduce bulk. Iron the backing and the top very carefully before layering the quilt sandwich to eliminate any creases. This is the last chance to do so before quilting.

Use a large table or the floor to ensure that you have a space larger than the quilt. Fold the quilt top in half and place a large colorful pin at the half way mark. Repeat with the batting and the backing. Place the backing flat on your chosen surface, smoothing out any creases as you go. Secure the edges with pins or masking tape to make the backing fairly taut. Matching the marking pins, place the batting over the backing and smooth into place. Repeat with the quilt top.

Pin basting

This is probably the most popular method for basting the layers together. Safety pins of 1" (2.5 cm) size are the best as they leave very small holes that will disappear as you quilt.

Starting in the center, place the pins at regular intervals, as shown. Avoid pinning across pieced lines, as the pins will get in the way when you are quilting. Smooth out the quilt top as you go, to ensure there are no creases or pleats. Remember that the more safety pins you put in, the better the chance of holding the quilt together securely while quilting.

Remove the safety pins as you quilt. Store them open in a box, ready for the next time you quilt.

continued on the next page…

Quiltaks™

For a faster method of basting the quilt layers together, use a product called Quiltak™. It consists of a plastic gun with a needle; the taks are made of plastic and are shot out of the needle through the fabric.

You need a plastic grid underneath the quilt top so that when the gun is fired, the taks go straight into the layers.

You need to place many more taks than safety pins to make the layers secure. Beware of using taks with delicate fabrics as the holes left by the taks are large and do not disappear.

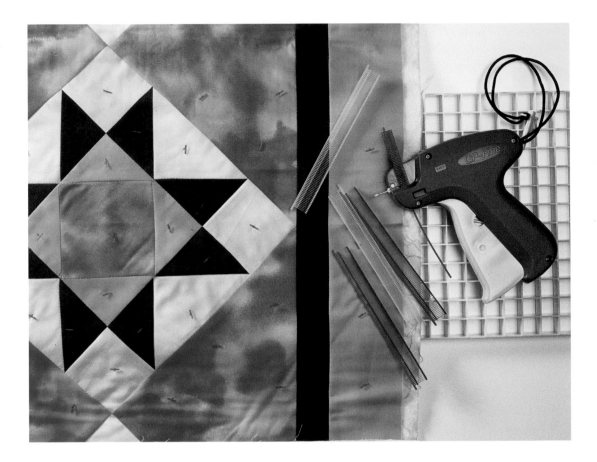

Fabric adhesive spray

This is by far the most costly way to baste your quilt, but it is very quick and easy. There are several makes of fabric adhesive spray available, some stickier than others and some clog the machine needle. Great care must be taken to ensure you have good ventilation when using these sprays.

Pin and lay out the layers of your quilt, as before. Shake the can and spray in lines across the quilt backing from top to bottom. Carefully match the half-way pins and smooth out the batting over the backing, eliminating creases as you go. It is possible to peel off the batting as you go and re-position if necessary. Spray the batting as above. Carefully match the half-way pins and smooth out the quilt top over the batting and backing, eliminating creases as you go.

The spray will eventually disappear, but if you wish, you can wash the quilt to remove it and to give your quilt a softly rumpled look.

Marking and using stencils

One of the joys of machine quilting is that, once you are comfortable with it, there is very little need to mark designs on the fabric. You can use the width of the walking foot and the darning foot as guidelines for several quilting patterns. When you have become proficient at free-motion quilting, the sky is the limit and no marking is required.

Sometimes, however, it is necessary to follow a certain pattern that has to be exactly marked, such as designs that need to fit onto borders or form part of a block. You can either design these yourself by taking a motif for your quilt design and developing it, or you can take advantage of the many stencils that are available. Remember that those stencils that allow for a continuous line of stitching are by far the easiest to use when machine quilting. There are many stencils made especially for machine quilters, and several books with continuous line designs.

Marking with pens, colored pencils or chalk

There are many different types of pen on the market, some that are water soluble and others that fade over time. Always test the pen on a spare piece of fabric so that you can be sure that the trail it leaves will disappear.

Similarly, there are several different crayons, some of which are water based and others oil based, but still test them out first.

Chalk pencils are also very useful and can be found in quilting and art supplies shops. The marks they make can usually be removed with a toothbrush. When marking straight lines as you might for a grid design, use powdered chalk in a special container with a wheel for dispensing. These are also available in quilt shops and the chalk can be brushed off the finished piece.

1 Cut a 10½" (27 cm) square of cotton, batting, and backing fabric. Place the stencil centrally on the cotton square. Carefully mark with the marking pen through the stencil holes onto the fabric. Remove the stencil and join the lines. Make the quilt sandwich (fabric basting spray has been used in this sample).

2 With the contrasting thread, machine quilt along the marked lines.

3 Remove the marking using water in a misting spray bottle. Leave the sample to dry.

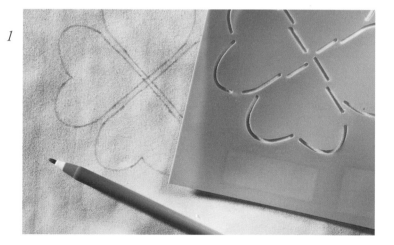

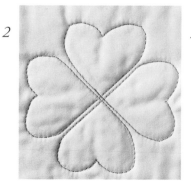

continued on the next page…

Marking borders

There are many stencils that fit borders, or you might like to make up your own design, perhaps taking an element from your quilt blocks that lends itself to enlarging or reducing to fit a border. You can either use them before you have prepared the quilt sandwich, when they lie flat, or after you have quilted other areas.

1 Start by laying the stencil or your design on the corner and check that it is exactly in the middle of the corner. Ensure the stencil is equidistant from the edges of the block or interior of the quilt and that there is enough space on the outer edge to add the binding after quilting. Mark through the stencil, moving it along to continue the design.

Move the stencil to the remaining three corners and proceed as above. You will now be able to work out whether the stencil fits the border exactly. If not, you can adjust by enlarging or reducing it. Complete the remaining three borders to match the previous one.

2 You may not want to mark the border. Instead, you can mark the stencil or your own design onto tracing paper and pin this to the quilt sandwich.

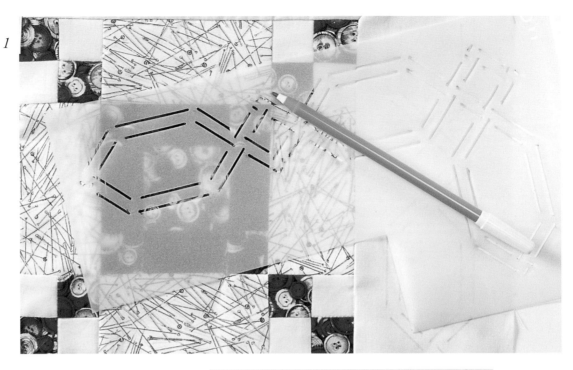

1

Trace four corner sections. Measure the length of each of the sections of the border and cut several lengths of paper to fit, allowing for enough space to overlap when pinning to the quilt. Adjust the design at the center point of the border if you need to, and ensure that you have made all four borders exactly the same.

Pin all the corner sections and then carefully pin the rest of the paper, one border at a time.

3 Machine quilt either with the walking foot, if the design does not have too many curves, or free motion with the darning foot. Carefully remove the paper to reveal the quilted border.

2

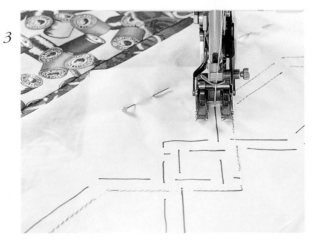

3

Straight-line quilting

There are several ways of quilting straight lines. Try the methods outlined below several times and see which one suits both you and your machine. The most important element is to secure the stitches at the beginning and end of your quilting and to avoid a knot of stitches either on the top or bottom of your quilt. Some quilters start by bringing the bottom thread up to the top of their work.

Stopping and starting

1 Little stitch: Adjust the straight stitch to the smallest length. Sew five of these tiny stitches and then turn the stitch length to one measure higher than the normal stitch length. Continue sewing and when you get close to the end of your stitching line, turn the stitch length to the previous small stitch and sew five stitches.

2 Fix stitch: If your sewing machine has a "Fix" button, use it at the beginning and end of the quilting.

3 Forward, reverse, forward: Start the line of stitching with three stitches normal length. Reverse to the beginning. Stitch forward as usual. At the end of the quilting line, reverse three stitches and then go forward three stitches.

Grid quilting

1 Quilting a grid, or cross-hatching, has been popular for hand quilters over centuries, and on the sewing machine it is a very simple technique. It is useful for enhancing blocks and larger spaces between blocks. Study the diagram to follow the direction of stitching to achieve a continuous line.

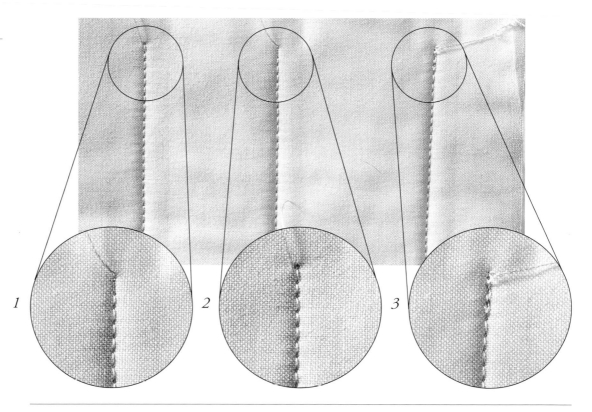

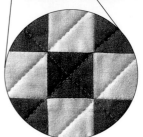

continued on the next page...

Quilting in-the-ditch

1 Stabilizing the blocks and borders of your quilt is the first step to achieving good results. Study the blocks on your quilt to see how you can achieve a continuous line while quilting in-the-ditch.

2 Stitch in the seam lines around the blocks, using an invisible or monofilament thread so that the stitches are hidden. Use a quilting needle size 75 or 90. It is easier to stitch on the side against the seam allowances.

3 Continue around the borders. Once this has been done, you can go ahead with quilting designs without fear that the back of the quilt will crease and pucker. It also allows for greater flexibility in embellishing your quilt.

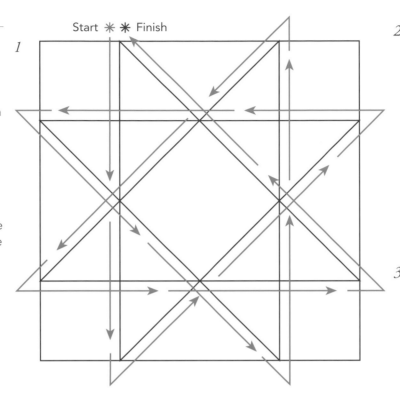

1 Start ✳ ✳ Finish

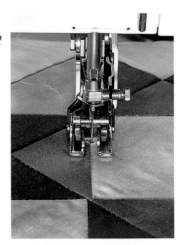

2

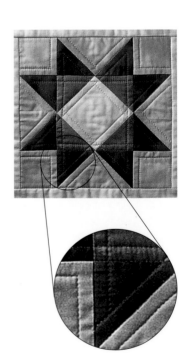

3

Outline quilting

1 Having stabilized the block, you can outline the design by using the width of the walking foot as your guide. Use the diagram to follow the direction of stitching the block in a continuous line. Sew on the inside of the star lines to create a secondary design. Using the width of the walking foot as your guide, sew outside the star to outline it.

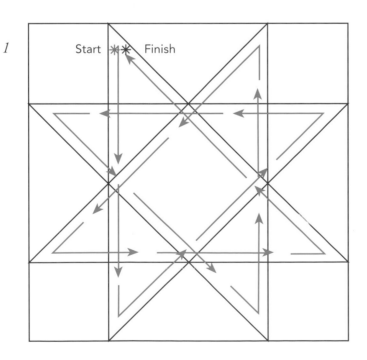

1 Start ✳✳ Finish

Free-motion quilting

Once you have mastered this technique, you will be able to develop your quilting skills to create masterpieces. At first you may feel out of control, but just remember to breathe and that practice makes perfect. The design possibilities are endless and this technique also gives you a chance to try out colorful threads available to quilters today. Just think of it as drawing with a needle.

You will need a sewing machine that is able to cover or drop the feed dogs—usually a switch under or at the back or front of the machine arm. As they are not gripping the fabric, this allows you to move the quilt under the foot without being restricted to straight lines. It also means that you will need some control over how slowly or quickly you do this, as your speed will determine the stitch length.

You will need a darning foot, a quilting needle if using regular thread or monofilament and an embroidery needle if using rayon. Machines with a needle-down facility are ideal for free-motion quilting.

Starting and stopping

1 Machines differ and many have a "Stop" or a "Fix" button, which secures the thread. Test your machine to find the method that suits you. Practice the most important element: to secure the stitches at the beginning and end of your

quilting and to avoid a knot of stitches either on the top or bottom of your quilt.

Use the needle-down facility. Take a few stitches almost on the spot, then gradually guide the quilt under the foot and move the fabric back and forth and up and down until you find a comfortable rhythm and an even stitch. As you come to the end of the stitching, take a few stitches almost on the spot to secure the threads.

1

2 Start again, and guide the quilt around, going from side to side and up and down. Try writing your name.

2

Stippling and other effects

Once you are comfortable with the basics of free-motion quilting, try some more stitching effects. Make a quilt sandwich about 12" (30 cm) square and divide it up into smaller squares so that you

can experiment. The sections here show stippling, large and small (also called meandering), straight-line stippling, curls, leaf patterns, flowers, and a few others. You can have fun making up your own designs by making up several practice quilt sandwiches.

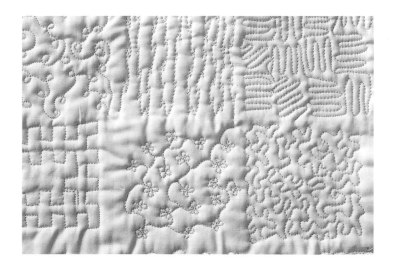

Contour quilting

Once you have mastered free-motion quilting, and you become used to creating special effects in plain spaces, try free-motion quilting on a block. The design shown here contours the block design with a figure eight and ends up looking like circles and semicircles. Once practiced, it is easy to achieve and enhances many designs. Lower the feed dogs and put on the darning foot.

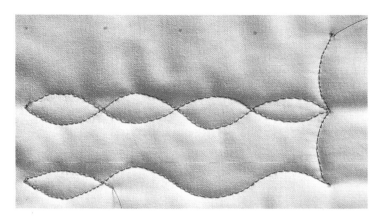

Prepare a sample quilt sandwich and mark off a square using a blue marker pen with five dots across and five down, 1" (2.5 cm) apart. Sew a few stitches almost on the spot and, starting in the left-hand corner, stitch a semicircle to the next dot. Turn 90° and stitch down from dot to dot in a curved vertical line, making semicircles in a figure eight formation until you get to the last dot. Stitch up vertically, sewing from dot to dot in semicircles in a figure eight formation until you reach the top line. Continue in this way until you have covered the vertical lines. Turn the sample 90° and continue along the horizontal lines. Finish where you started.

You can apply this technique to many blocks. It lends itself well to Flying Geese.

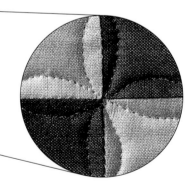

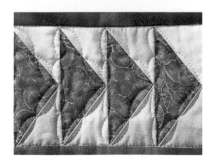

Echo quilting

When using a motif in a quilt, it can be greatly enhanced by quilting around the outline of the design. Depending on the shape of the motif, it is possible to create interesting lines that echo its design and shape.

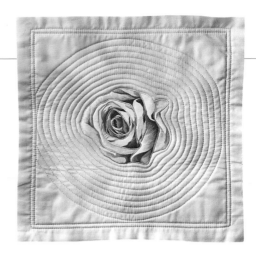

1

1 Fuse or appliqué a motif onto the center of a 12" (30 cm) square sample quilt sandwich. Use the satin stitch foot, an embroidery needle, and the feed dogs up. With a variegated rayon thread, and a small satin stitch, sew around the motif to give extra depth to it and also to secure it firmly to the foundation fabric.

2 Change to the darning foot and lower the feed dogs. Change the thread to one matching the foundation fabric. Start stitching from a part of the motif that extends onto the background and secure the thread with a few stitches almost on the spot. Now stitch around the motif with an even stitch using the width of the darning foot as a guide.

2

Trapunto

To give your quilt designs a raised look, thus adding dimension to the quilting, use trapunto. This is the term given to the method of layering batting behind the chosen pattern to make the designs stand out. The preferred type of batting for trapunto is 100 percent cotton of the softer variety. Two extra layers are added behind each quilting design, and once the design has been quilted and the waste batting cut away, a further layer of batting is added to the quilt sandwich in the normal way. Heavier types of batting are unsuitable, as they add too much weight to the quilt.

Trapunto adds extra dimension to a quilting pattern.

1 Fold a 12" (31 cm) square of tracing paper in half and then half again to find the center. Trace the chosen design onto the paper, making sure that you have centered it. Find the center of a 12$\frac{1}{2}$" (32 cm) square of cotton by lightly folding it in half and then half again. Pin the paper, matching up the centers onto the cotton square, placing pins around the edge.

2 Place two 9" (23 cm) squares of batting together. Pin them accurately under the design, from the front. Drop the feed dogs on the sewing machine and put on the darning foot.

1

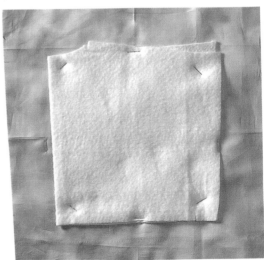

3 With Wash-a-Way™ thread in the needle and a light colored thread in the bobbin, free-motion quilt around the design (see page 215). Remove the paper carefully, in order to avoid pulling the stitches.

4 With small, sharp scissors, cut away the surplus batting at the back of the work.

5 Make the quilt sandwich with 13" (33 cm) squares of backing and batting, pinning them into place with safety pins. Thread the needle with thread that matches the quilt top, and put matching thread in the bobbin. Free-motion quilt around the design, following the line of stitches that you made with the Wash-a-Way™ thread.

6 Stitch a line 1" (2.5 cm) in from the edge of the sample to form a square, and stitch a second line $1/8$" (3 mm) from the first to form a frame. Stipple quilt with a small stipple between the square and the trapunto design.

7 When all the stitching is complete, pin the sample onto your design board or a flat area covered with some muslin, and spray it all with a fine mist sprayer to dissolve the Wash-a-Way™ thread.

3

4

5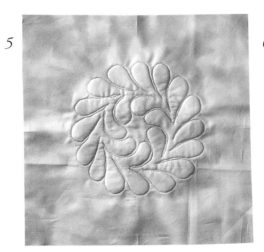

6

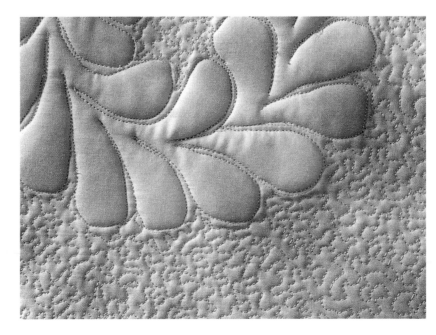

Machine-quilted project: Wallhanging

Almost all of the machine-quilting methods described in the preceding pages are included in this blue and yellow medallion quilt. In-the-ditch, outlining, echo quilting, free motion around shapes, contour quilting, and stippling are all presented here. A large Variable Star block forms the central focus of the quilt and is surrounded by three borders of Square-in-a-square blocks, Flying Geese, and several dark narrow frames. Now that you have practiced machine quilting on your samples, you can go ahead and enjoy making this pretty quilt.

Finished size

43" × 43" (110 × 110 cm)

Fabric

A variety of 100 percent cotton fabrics, width 44" (112 cm):
¼ yd. (25 cm) bright floral
1 yd. (1 m) gold
1 yd. (1 m) royal blue pattern
¼ yd. (25 cm) pale gray pattern
1 yd. (1 m) dark blue
1 yd. (1 m) focus fabric with motifs
½ yd. (50 cm) pale lemon
¼ yd. (25 cm) mid-blue
½ yd. (50 cm) gray, blue, yellow
  pattern

1½ yd. (150 cm) backing
48" × 48" (122 × 122 cm) batting

Other materials

Threads: gray and yellow, for piecing
  invisible monofilament and yellow,
  for quilting
¼" yd. (25 cm) fusible adhesive
Needles: 80/11 for piecing;
  130/705 H-Q (75) for quilting
Machine feet: ¼" (0.75 cm) foot;
  walking foot; darning foot
Rotary cutting equipment

Central star block

Cut: one 7½" (19 cm) square of bright floral; four 4" (10 cm) squares of gold; eight 4" (10 cm) squares of royal blue pattern; four 4" (10 cm) squares, four 4" × 7½" (10 cm × 19 cm) rectangles of pale gray pattern.

Draw a diagonal line on the wrong side of all the squares, except the pale gray ones.

1 Place a gold square on each of two opposite corners of the bright floral large square, right sides together. Pin in place and sew along the lines. Cut away the outside waste fabric. Press the gold corners back.

1

2 Repeat with the remaining two corners. Press the corners back to reveal the square.

3 Place a royal blue square on the right-hand corner of a pale grey rectangle, right sides together. Sew along the line, allowing a ¼" (0.75 cm) seam allowance, and cut away the outside waste fabric. Press back the corner.

4 Repeat Step 3 on the left-hand corner. Press back the corner. Make four.

2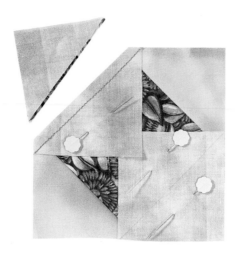

3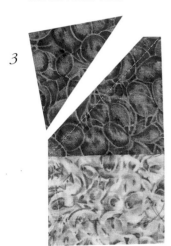

4

5 To assemble the block, lay out the pieces, add the pale gray squares to the corners. Sew the units together in three rows. Sew the rows together to form the square.

5

Frame 1

Cut strips of dark blue fabric: two 1½" × 14½" (3.75 × 37 cm); two 1½" × 16½" (3.75 × 42 cm).

Sew the shorter strips to the top and bottom of the block and press outward. Sew the remaining two strips to the sides of the block and press outward.

continued on the next page...

Border 1 (Square-in-a-square blocks)

Cut: 20 4$\frac{1}{2}$" (11.5 cm) squares of focus fabric with motifs; 80 2$\frac{1}{2}$" (6.5 cm) squares of pale lemon.

Draw a diagonal line on the wrong side of all the squares.

1 Place a pale lemon square exactly on two opposite corners of a focus fabric square, right sides together. Pin in place and sew along the lines. Cut away the outside waste fabric and press the lemon corners back. Repeat these steps with the remaining two corners. Make 20 blocks.

1

Arrange the 20 blocks around the central medallion. Sew together two strips of four blocks and sew these to the top and bottom of the

center block. Sew two strips of six blocks and sew these to the remaining two sides. The block should now measure 24$\frac{1}{2}$" (62.25 cm) square.

Note

When using fabrics with specific motifs, cut them so that the motifs appear in the center of the square. A square ruler is very helpful for centralizing the design.

Frame 2

Cut strips of dark blue fabric: two 1$\frac{1}{2}$" × 24$\frac{1}{2}$" (3.75 × 62.25 cm); two 1$\frac{1}{2}$" × 26$\frac{1}{2}$" (3.75 × 67.5 cm).

Sew the shorter strips to the top and bottom of the block and press outward. Sew the remaining two strips to the sides of the block and press outward.

Border 2 (Triangles)

Cut: eight 4$\frac{1}{2}$" (11.5 cm) squares of mid-blue; four strips 4$\frac{1}{2}$" × 13$\frac{1}{2}$" (11.5 × 34.5 cm) of gray, blue, yellow pattern; four strips 4$\frac{1}{2}$" × 17$\frac{1}{2}$" (11.5 × 44.5 cm) of gray, blue, yellow pattern.

1 Draw a diagonal line on the wrong side of all the mid-blue squares. Place a square on the corner of one end of the shorter strips and sew along the line. Place another square on the next short strip, sew along the line and trim the waste on the outside corner.

2 Press back both corners. Sew the two strips together. Repeat with the two remaining shorter strips and the four longer strips. Sew the

two shorter strips to the top and bottom of the center medallion, matching the center seams of the mid-blue triangle to the center seams

of the first border. Sew the remaining two longer borders to the two remaining sides.

1

2

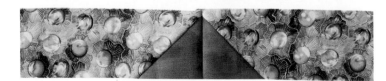

Frame 3

Cut strips of dark blue fabric: two 1$\frac{1}{2}$" × 34$\frac{1}{2}$" (3.75 × 87.75 cm); two 1$\frac{1}{2}$" × 36$\frac{1}{2}$" (3.75 × 92.75 cm).

Sew the shorter strips to the top and bottom of the block. Sew the remaining two strips to the sides of the block and press outward.

Border 3 (Flying Geese)

For Flying Geese, cut: 96 2" × 3¹/₂" (5 × 9 cm) rectangles of royal blue; 192 2" (5 cm) squares of gold.

Draw a diagonal line on the wrong side of all the gold squares.

1 Place a gold square on the right hand corner of a royal blue rectangle, right sides together, and sew along the line. Cut away the outside waste fabric. Press back the corner.

2 Repeat on the left corner. Press back the corner.

3 Make 96 Flying Geese units. Sew the Flying Geese together in strips of 12. Join two strips together so that the Flying Geese are "flying" toward each other. Sew a strip to the top and bottom of the quilt.

For corner squares cut: four 3¹/₂" (9 cm) squares of bright floral; 16 2" (5 cm) squares of gold.

Draw a diagonal line on the wrong side of the gold squares.

4 Place a gold square on the right-hand corner of a bright floral square, right sides together, and sew along the line. Trim away the waste fabric and press back. Repeat on the other three corners.

1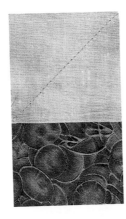

2

3

4

Frame 4

Cut: six 1¹/₂" (3.75 cm) strips in dark blue, across the width of the fabric.

Join the strips into a continuous line. Measure across the width of the quilt and cut two strips to this measurement. Sew these strips to the top and bottom of the quilt and press outward. Measure the length of the quilt and cut two strips to this measurement. Sew the remaining two strips to the sides of the quilt and press outward.

continued on the next page...

Appliqué

Cut four motifs from the focus fabric, leaving a ¼" (2.5 cm) seam allowance.

Iron the fusible web to the wrong side of the motifs.

Cut around the motifs carefully. Peel off the backing paper and place a

motif centrally on each of the four mid-blue triangles and press.

Prepare the quilt sandwich

Measure the size of the quilt and cut the backing and the batting 4" (10 cm) larger. You may have to join pieces of fabric to make the width for the backing. Using your preferred method, either safety pins, Quiltaks™, or spray (see page 209), baste the backing to the batting. Then baste the top to the batting.

1 Quilt in-the-ditch around the Central star block; around Frame 1 both sides; all Square-in-a-square blocks; Frame 2; around the triangles of Border 1; Frame 3; around the Flying Geese of Border 3; Frame 4. This will secure your quilt and keep it square. Grid-quilt the star of the Central block and outline quilt the pale gray.

2 Free-motion quilt around the motifs of Square-in-a-square blocks and stipple quilt the pale lemon.

3 Use a stencil to quilt Border 2. Start at the corners and arrange your design so that any change in the

1

2

3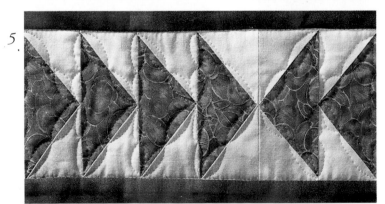

4

5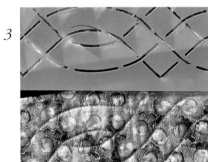

pattern takes place away from the corner. Depending on the complexity of the stencil, you can either free-motion quilt or use the walking foot.

4 With a small satin or zigzag stitch, quilt around the four motifs on the mid-blue triangles. Echo quilt around the motifs.

5 Contour quilt around the Flying Geese, going down one side and up the other to keep the quilting continuous.

Binding

Measure the perimeter of the quilt and cut dark blue strips 2½" (6.5 cm) wide. Join them in a continuous strip to match the length of the perimeter. Fold in half along the length and iron flat. Attach the binding (see page 248).

Attaching the sleeve

Make a sleeve (see page 252) and stitch it to the back, ensuring that the stitches are not visible on the front. A hanging sleeve will help your quilt to lie flat and straight against the wall. The pole slips out of the sleeve when you need to wash or store the quilt.

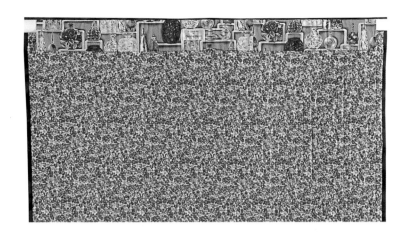

Hand quilting

Hand quilting gives a soft line to quilting patterns and especially provides finished quilts with an appealing drape. The process is much slower than machine quilting but far more personal. It can also be very sociable, from sitting sewing with the family while watching TV, to joining in a quilting bee with the local quilt guild or small group of friends.

The purpose of quilting is simply to hold the three layers (top, batting, and backing) of a quilt together. That this can be decorative and add texture to the finished quilt is a huge bonus! Enough quilting stitches (about 70 percent) need to go through all three layers of the quilt to hold it together. With practice, nearly all stitches will eventually go through, but do not worry if stitches are smaller on the back than they are on the top —this is quite normal.

It is very important to try to get the stitches evenly sized and spaced. Smaller stitches come with practice, but even stitches come through hard work! A little quilting every day will help keep the hands and eyes coordinated: if this is impossible, have a practice piece to work on for the first 10 minutes to regain rhythm before resuming work on a project.

Choice of quilting design is very personal, but here are a few general guidelines. When quilting patchwork, try to find designs that cover the work but avoid bulky seam intersections. Curved designs will give added dimension to the geometry of a patchwork quilt, whereas straight lines will accentuate the curved motifs of appliqué. Designs with straight lines and gentle curves will be easier to quilt than tight spirals and feathers. The latter are not impossible for beginners; they just take longer!

This section describes several ways to hand quilt, but there are many more variations on those methods. Similarly, there are many different quilting products for you to choose from. Quilting stitches and the best sequence for hand-quilting are demonstrated, from getting started to undertaking a wholecloth, hand-quilted crib quilt. Experiment until you find products and a style that suit you.

Relax and enjoy your hand quilting.

Preparing fabrics and equipment

Although choice of fabrics has been covered elsewhere (see pages 14 to 20), it is worth reiterating that tightly woven fabrics will be difficult to quilt by hand.

Choice of batting is also important. Most hand quilters find that a good quality 2 oz (70 g) polyester batting is the easiest to use.

To achieve an even tension with hand-quilted work, it is best to use a quilting frame of some sort. A 14" (35 cm) hoop is probably the most affordable and portable, but there are many other options available from beautifully crafted floor-standing frames to small wooden hoops. If using a hoop, please remember to take the work out of it when not quilting to avoid hoop marks.

The best needles for quilting are called betweens. Start with a size 9 or 10 and graduate to the smaller size 12. These needles are very sharp, and it is best to protect both top and underneath fingers during the quilting process. There are many varieties of thimbles and finger protectors for you to choose from.

The most important piece of equipment used in hand quilting is you, so pay attention to posture and eyesight. Make sure that you sit in a comfortable, well-supported position with a good light source. Best stitches are not achieved in cramped and ill-lit conditions.

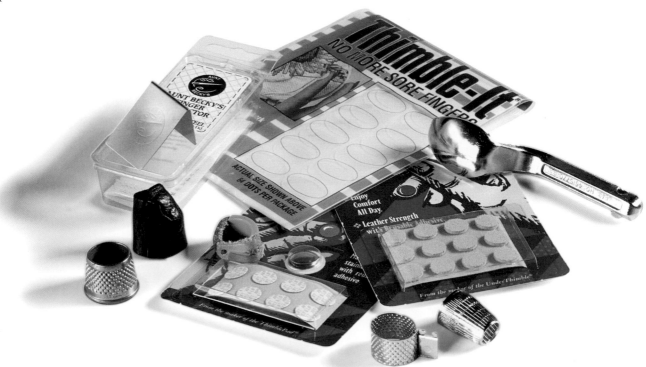

continued on the next page...

1 The first step is to mark the quilting pattern on the fabric. If you are using a freestanding frame or are quilting patchwork, you may find the best method is to make or buy stencils and mark them as you go.

2 If using solid fabrics, mark the pattern on paper using a fine black indelible pen. Pin the fabric over the pattern and trace the design onto the fabric. With dark fabrics a light box may be used.

3 To assemble the quilt sandwich, cut the top fabric, batting, and backing fabric to size. The batting should be 1" (2.5 cm) larger than the top fabric, and the backing 1" (2.5 cm) larger than the batting. This is to allow for take-up during the quilting process. Ensure the fabrics are smooth and wrinkle free. Lay the backing fabric down, wrong side up, position the batting centrally over it and, finally, lay the marked top fabric down, right side up.

4 Using a long thin needle and cotton basting thread, baste across the quilt in parallel lines 3" (7.5 cm) apart.

1

2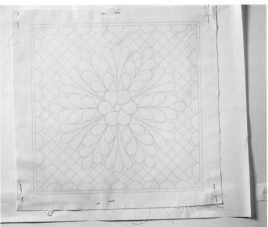

3  *4*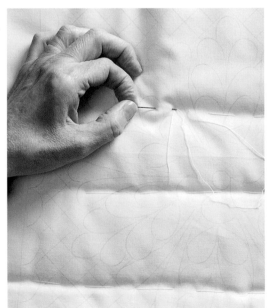

5 Now baste a second row of similar lines, rotated 90° to form a grid. Pin-basting is not recommended when using a hoop.

Positioning the hoop frame

1 Place the inner ring of the hoop under the quilt sandwich in the center of the piece. Gently pat down the work so that it is not taut across the hoop.

2 Open up the screw on the top hoop, and then place the hoop onto the inner ring. Check that the work is wrinkle free before tightening the screw to secure.

It is important to have enough "give" in the work contained in the hoop; too tight a tension will make quilting difficult.

The quilting stitch

Quilting needles are small, so cut your thread at an angle to facilitate threading. It will help to have a contrasting background, so thread dark colors against a light background, and vice versa.

Hand quilting will be far more pleasurable if the fingers are protected in some way. It is usual to wear a thimble on either the first or middle finger of the top hand and another thimble or finger protector on the corresponding finger of the underneath hand.

Start quilting from the middle, and progress toward the edges. This allows any little tucks in the backing fabric to be gradually pushed out to the edges of the quilt.

Making the knot

1 Hold the needle in your sewing hand. In your non-sewing hand, hold the tail end of the thread furthest from the needle. Bring the end of the thread in your non-sewing hand around in a loop to lie along the needle toward the eye, and hold this end with the thumb and first finger of your sewing hand.

2 With your non-sewing hand, take a portion of thread lying near the tip of the needle and, working away from yourself, wrap this around the needle three times (the number of times will vary according to the thickness of thread).

3 Without letting go, push the needle through the threads to complete a French knot. This will be secure and not unravel in the quilt.

4 Slide the needle into the batting and under the line that you are about to stitch, ¼" (0.75 cm) away from your starting point. Bring the needle up at the beginning of the stitching line. Pull the thread through so that the knot "pops" between the threads of your fabric and into the batting. If the knot does not appear to want to go through, do not force it, but start over: you may have split a thread of your fabric, and forcing the knot through will make a hole. Any small tail of thread can be dealt with by sliding the needle under it and rotating the needle until the thread disappears.

1

2
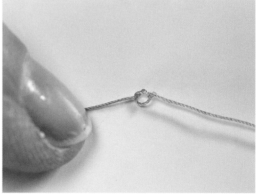

3

4

Starting

To demonstrate the positioning of thimbles, sheer fabrics have been used in these steps.

1 Put the needle into the fabric and onto the underneath thimble at a perpendicular angle. Bring the thimble on the top hand into position so that the needle is balanced between the upper and lower thimbles.

2 Bring the thumb of the sewing hand forward and rest it on the thimble finger of the underneath hand. This will help to bring the needle back up to the surface without creating tension in the wrist of the sewing hand.

3 Angle the needle back toward the fabric *and at the same time* slide the underneath thimble in the same direction. The needle should skip off the edge of this thimble and reappear at the surface.

4 Once the needle is back at the surface, move the underneath thimble just enough to allow the needle down through the work. Now angle the top thimble back up to insert the needle onto the underneath thimble to start another stitch.

1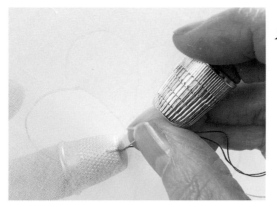

2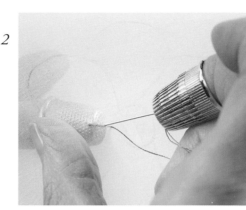

3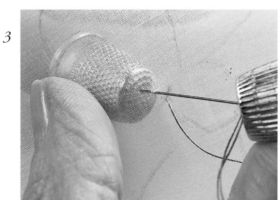

4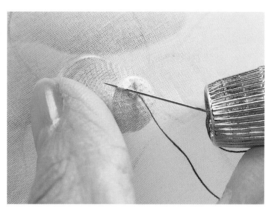

5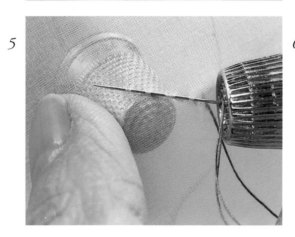

6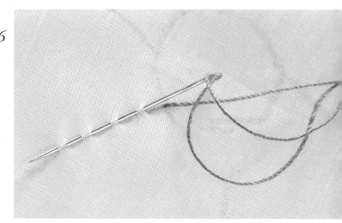

5 At first, you may only manage one stitch at a time. However, with practice, you will be able to get several stitches onto the needle at the same time. Then it is possible to check that stitches are even before pulling the needle through. It also speeds up the quilting process considerably.

6 When you have enough stitches on the needle, pull it through. Be careful not to pull the thread too tightly. The stitch tension should be similar to regular hand sewing.

continued on the next page...

Finishing

It is best to start and finish threads at "junctions" in your quilting design (marked as red arrows at right). If you start and finish in the middle of a smooth curve for example, the join may interrupt the smooth flow of the design.

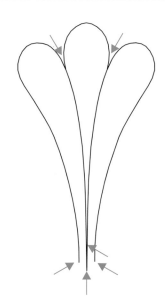

1 To finish, allow enough space for one last stitch. Hold the thread exiting the fabric with the non-sewing hand and bring the needle around, away from you, to form a loop.

2 Wrap the thread twice around the needle and pull the needle through. Gently tease the knot down toward the quilting until there is only enough thread between the fabric and the knot for one last stitch.

3 Put the needle into the batting to form the last stitch. Ideally the needle should also travel underneath a pattern line yet to be stitched as this will further anchor the thread.

4 Bring the needle and thread up to the surface and "pop" the knot into your work. Pull the thread taut and snip carefully. The end should vanish into your work when the tension on the thread is relaxed.

1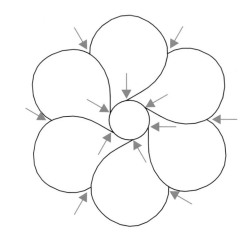

2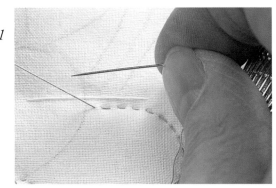

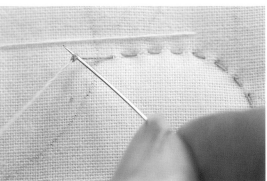

3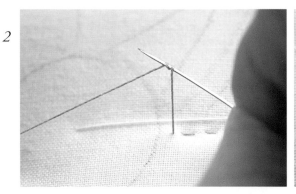

4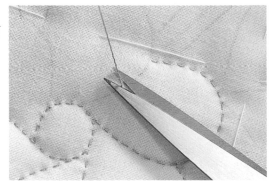

Traveling

It is useful to be able to "travel" from one line of stitching to the next without having to stop and restart every time.

1 Insert the needle into the batting but not through to the back of the work. Bring the point of the needle back up to the surface as far away as possible and pull the needle partway through.

2 Keep the eye of the needle buried in the batting, and rotate the needle 180°.

3 Now using the needle backward, bring the eye up to the surface at the point where a new line of stitches will commence. If you need to rotate the needle more than twice, then the distance from one quilted area to the next is too great and you should finish off the thread.

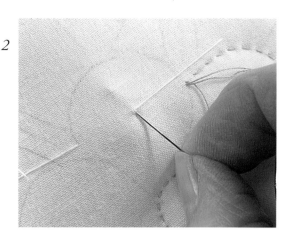
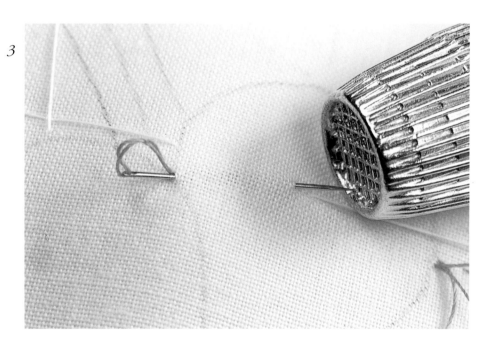

Stab stitch

Stab stitch is invaluable when trying to quilt through the bulky seams of a patchwork quilt. It is essential to work with a freestanding frame. The top hand pushes the needle down vertically through the quilt sandwich, and the bottom hand pushes it back up to the surface. Only one stitch at a time is made this way, and so the process can be quite slow. A drawback is that stitches on the reverse side of the work are frequently untidy.

Lap quilting

Some quilters find stitching easier without a frame. Instead of manipulating the needle through the fabric, here a longer needle is held still and the fabric fed onto it by the non-sewing hand. Because the work gets bunched up in the non-sewing hand, it is essential to baste the top in a 1¹/₂" (4 cm) grid before starting. Great care must be taken to ensure that work doesn't pucker from pulling the threads too tightly!

Quilting sequence

When quilting background patterns such as cross hatching, it is best to have the starting and finishing points stitched before you begin the background quilting.

1 Stitch the pattern elements on either side of the area to be filled.

2 Stitch the background quilting. Gradually work your way around the quilt. (Note that basting a towel to the edge of the work will extend the working area of the hoop to the edge of the quilt).

1

2

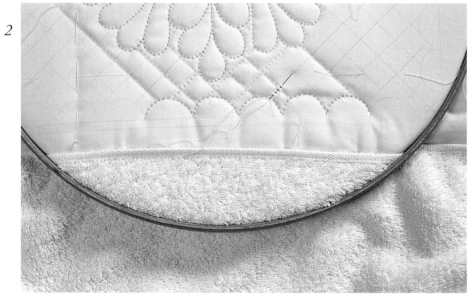

Quilt as you go

To quilt large items in a manageable and portable way, each patterned block is quilted separately and the finished blocks are then assembled into a complete quilt. For best results, leave the outer ½" (1.5 cm) of each block unquilted.

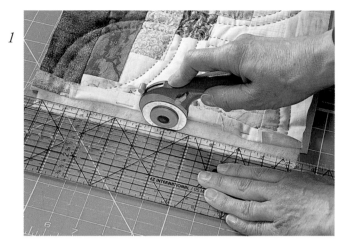

1 Fold back the quilted top and the backing fabric of a block, and trim the batting to the exact size of the finished block. Trim the top fabric to ¼" (0.75 cm) larger than the batting, and the backing to ½" (1.5 cm) larger than the batting.

2 Join the top fabrics, right sides together, and stitch a ¼" (0.75 cm) seam.

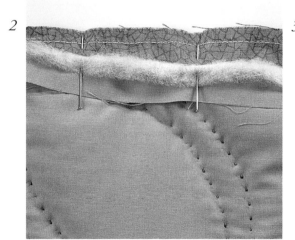

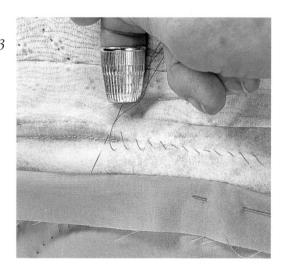

3 Fold the backing fabric away, and whip stitch the batting pieces together.

4 Fold in one backing fabric seam allowance to overlap the seam allowance of the second block. Slip stitch into place. Continue to assemble blocks into rows and then join the rows together in the same way.

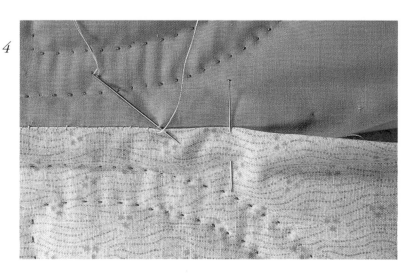

Hand-quilted project: Crib quilt

This beautiful wholecloth crib quilt will give you ample opportunity to practice design and hand stitching.

While it is necessary to use solid fabrics to show a wholecloth quilt to advantage, fabric choice is not limited to 100 percent cotton fabrics. Providing a fabric is not woven too tightly (which will make quilting difficult), there is a wonderful assortment of silks, satins, sateens, and lawns to be used, in addition to the usual quilting fabrics. The backing fabric should be of similar weight and weave to the top fabric but can be of different fiber content. Solid fabrics in a complementary color or small calico prints are ideal choices.

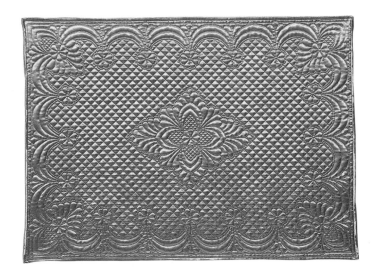

Finished size

31" × 42" (79 × 107 cm)

Fabric

1¹/₂ yd. (1.4 m) top fabric
1¹/₂ yd. (1.4 m) backing fabric
32" × 45" (82 × 115 cm) lightweight polyester batting

Other materials

Quilting thread, two shades darker than the top fabric
Quilting thread to match top fabric
Basting thread
Betweens quilting needles
Basting needle
Quilting hoop or frame
Removable fabric marker
Thimbles
Scissors
Tracing paper and fine line black marker pen.

1
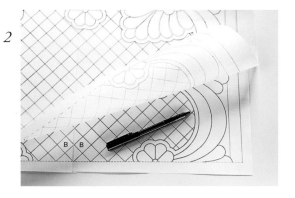

2
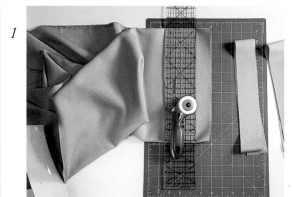

1 Wash and iron any cotton fabrics. Make sure other fabrics are wrinkle free. Cut four 2" × 45" (5 × 115 cm) strips from the top fabric for the binding and set aside for Step 6.

2 Enlarge the pattern by 150 percent using a photocopier. Trim along dotted lines and join together with clear tape, matching points A to A and B to B. Trace the design onto tracing paper with a fine line black marker pen. Flip the completed tracing and join to the photocopy along the dotted line to make a master pattern for half of the design.

continued on the next page…

3 Lightly fold (but do not crease) the top fabric in half, and line up and pin to the center edge of the master pattern with right side of the fabric up. Position and pin the rest of the fabric in place and trace the design onto the top fabric with a washable fabric marker. If using dark top fabric, a light box will be useful.

4 When one half of the design is marked, unpin the top fabric from the master pattern. Rotate the top fabric 180° and realign the centers of both pattern and quilt top. Repin and trace the second half of the design. The quilt top marking will now be complete. Alternatively, a whole master pattern may be drawn by tracing and joining a second half master pattern. The whole quilt top can then be marked without having to move the fabric.

5 Start quilting in the middle of the work. Use the darker quilting thread for the pattern elements and the matching thread for the background quilting (cross-hatching). Gradually work out to the edges of the quilt. Do not stitch the outer line enclosing the design.

3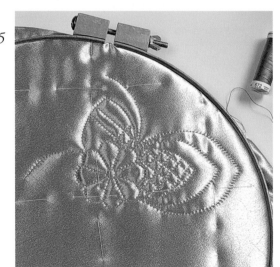

4

5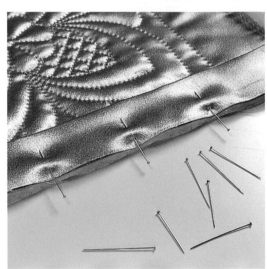

6

Completing the quilt

6 Pin the quilt top into the correct shape and steam—do not iron it. Leave it pinned out until it is completely dry. Measure length and width through the center of the quilt to calculate the amount of binding needed. Trim the quilt to the outer marked line of the design.

7 Fold the binding in half lengthwise, wrong sides together, and press. Attach binding with a ¹/₂" (1 cm) seam, and hem in place. It may be helpful to mark a line ¹/₂" (1 cm) in from the raw edges of the folded binding as a stitching guide.

Sign, date, and enjoy your wholecloth quilt.

Special hand-quilting techniques

As well as the huge choice of quilting patterns available, hand quilting offers a variety of decorative techniques. These range from the simple use of buttons or charms in tied quilting, to the more labor-intensive, 3-D effects of corded quilting. Exciting new threads may be used in different ways, which big stitch and sashiko quilting show off to great advantage. Give your quilt a new dimension by experimenting with these techniques.

Tied and button quilting

While the function of quilting stitches is to hold the three layers of the "sandwich" together, the following techniques are quick and easy alternatives to the quilting stitch. These are the best methods to use when quilting very thick and puffy battings in comforters, which would be impossible to hand or machine quilt.

Tied quilting

Knot the three layers together with decorative threads, yarns, or ribbons. It is usual for ties to be placed where seams meet rather than in the middle of a patch of fabric. It is up to personal preference whether the decorative tails are made to lie on the front or the back of a quilt.

1

1 Pin-baste the quilt sandwich together with either straight pins or safety pins. This will provide an opportunity to decide on, and mark, the placement of ties to be made.

2 Thread a needle with yarn, cotton or ribbon and make a stitch through all three layers of the quilt across a seam junction. Leave at least a 1"

(3 cm) tail of thread, make another stitch on top of the first, again through all three layers.

3 Snip the thread leaving at least a 1" (3 cm) tail. Tie the two tail threads together in a square (reef) knot. When all

ties are complete, trim the tails to the same length, usually about $1/2$" (1.5 cm).

Button quilting

A variation on tied quilting, this method uses buttons or charms sewn through the three layers to anchor the quilt together.

Note

These methods are not suitable for use on quilts for small children as the buttons and knots could constitute a choking hazard.

Corded quilting

Cording is an early technique that can be found in many examples of seventeenth- and eighteenth-century whitework in the United States and Britain. Sometimes known as Italian quilting, it can be used alone or in conjunction with other types of quilting.

Any design can be used for cording provided the quilting lines can be adapted to form channels. As can be seen from the illustration, filling these channels with yarn will give a raised effect to the work. To show this, it is better to use a flat or very low loft batting.

Method with natural fibers

Originally, wool and, occasionally, cotton were used for corded quilting. To avoid the effects of the cords shrinking when washed, the following method is used:

1 Mark the design onto the top fabric. Place this onto a piece of muslin and baste together. Hand quilt all the channels that are to be corded and remove the basting.

2 To begin cording: with the wrong side facing, insert a darning needle threaded with trapunto wool into the beginning of a quilted channel and weave through.

3 Each time the needle is brought up out of a channel, leave a loop of yarn when re-inserting the needle. These loops will allow for yarn shrinkage when the work is washed. Any intersecting cord should be cut when it overlaps another cord.

4 To assemble the finished piece, place the corded piece onto batting and backing fabric and baste together. Quilt any other uncorded parts of the design. In thread that matches the top fabric, quilt a second line of stitches 1/4" (0.5 cm) around the outside to hold the corded lines in place.

Method with synthetics

With the availability of modern acrylic yarns which do not shrink when washed, a simplified, and speedier, method is used.

1 Mark the design onto the top fabric. Place over layers of muslin, batting and backing fabric, and hand quilt the channels to be corded. A flat or very low loft batting will give the best results.

2 Using a blunt darning needle and acrylic yarn, insert the needle carefully under the top fabric and thread the yarn into the quilted channel. Leave a small amount of extra thread at the beginning of a corded channel.

3 When the needle will reach no further, bring it back up to the surface. Pull the needle through and then re-insert the needle into the hole just made in the fabric. Continue to cord until you reach a "junction" in the design.

4 At each "junction," carefully snip the yarn close to the top fabric. Start a new thread to continue in another direction.
  Depending on the size of the channels, several lengths of cord may be used to fill each one. If this is necessary, bring the needle up to the surface at a different place each time.

1

2

3

4

5 When all the cords are in place, carefully trim back all the spare yarn and, with a blunt needle or a fingernail, gently tease the fabric fibers back into place over the holes. Hold the work in both hands and tug gently several times in each direction. Any remaining ends will disappear.

5

Shadow quilting

This attractive variation on corded quilting will add subtle color to the overall effect. With this technique almost sheer fabrics are used, allowing the colors of the yarn used in the cording process to show to best effect. Batiste and fine white cotton lawn fabrics are ideal. The sample illustrated was made using the modern method with cotton lawn. Yarns need to be very bright as the shadowing effect really mutes their colors.

Either corded quilting method may be used (see page 242), but before you start, check that the top fabric does not allow the muslin or voile to show through.

If using synthetic yarn, take extra care when re-inserting the needle. It must go into *exactly* the same hole made when the needle was brought to the surface. If just one thread of top fabric becomes trapped, the yarn will not vanish back into the channels but will leave a visible mark on top.

When cording is complete, gently scratch any holes in the fabric closed with a fingernail.

Washing the finished work in warm water will remove any visible markings and will help close any small gaps left in the fabric by causing the fibers to swell.

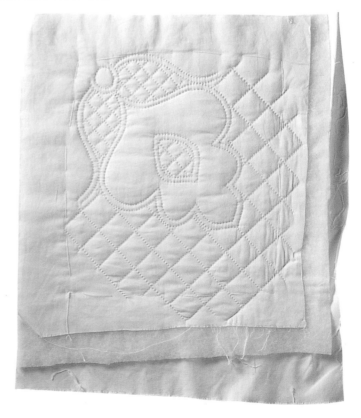

Sashiko

Sashiko is a traditional Japanese form of stitching that was used to sew two layers of fabric together to strengthen and give added warmth to clothing. Sashiko is a folk art with regional differences in design being handed down from generation to generation. Traditionally, the stitch is sewn onto indigo fabrics with coarse white thread, and each stitch represents a grain of rice. The gaps between stitches are smaller than the actual stitches with the ratio of stitch to gap being 3:2.

Modern Sashiko uses colors other than the traditional indigo and white, but color contrasts still need to be strong. Sashiko pieces are often used as bags, tablecloths, table mats, and wallhangings. Nowadays, thin flat batting is often added to make true quilts.

There are many Sashiko patterns to choose. Some are based on squares, circles, diagonal lines, and even hexagons. They symbolize simple aspects of nature and everyday life. The illustrations show examples of traditional patterns.

To make a Sashiko piece, mark the designs onto the top fabric and baste the top layer onto a backing fabric.

It is usual to use a large needle to accommodate the thick threads used in this technique and you may require stitches to be made one at a time. Do make the stitches as regular as possible and take care that where stitches meet, they do so neatly. Knots must be either buried between the two layers of fabric or left at the back of the work. If the latter method is used, add a backing cloth when stitching is complete.

Matsukawa Bishi

Nowake (Pampas)

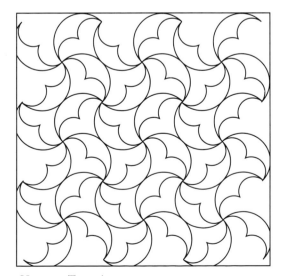

Hanmaru Tsunagi

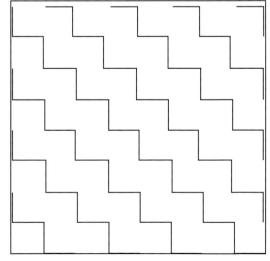

Dan Tsunagi

Big stitch quilting

Big stitch quilting is a blend of traditional hand quilting and Sashiko, popularized by American quilter, Jo Walters. It can be used on both pieced and solid quilts using quilting patterns from either tradition. As with traditional Japanese quilting, coarser threads are used to create a big stitch with a stitch to gap ratio of 3:2. There is an exciting variety of thicker threads from which to choose—variegated threads, for example, really show to advantage when used for large stitches. However, the technique demands accuracy because irregular stitches will be very visible. Care needs to be taken where stitching lines cross over or meet to ensure that "junctions" are as neat as possible.

Traditional Welsh design stitched in a variegated thread.

A combination of piecing, appliqué and traditional Sashiko patterns.

Finishings

Once you have pieced and quilted your quilt there are a number of ways to finish the edges. This chapter deals with binding of the edges using either straight or bias binding, or lapped binding finished by stitching in the ditch. The most common finish is either to bind in a matching or contrasting colorway.

If the center of your quilt is very busy in its design, or the colors are very strong, you may choose a binding to match the borders of your quilt, to give the effect of the edges of the quilt simply floating away. A contrasting fabric as your choice for the binding will make a stronger statement.

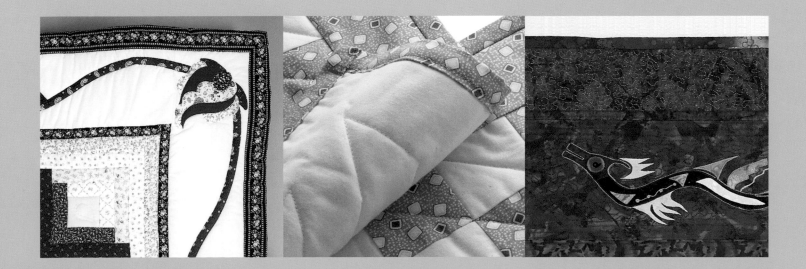

Binding

Squaring the quilt

Trim away any excess backing fabric and batting to the size of the top layer. Use a long ruler and square up the corners; make any adjustments at this stage. If some distortion has occurred during quilting which has resulted in wavy edges, the quilt will need to be blocked square before the binding is attached. To do this, lightly steam the quilt and pin out square onto a design wall or in a carpeted floor space. Leave to dry out, then remove the pins.

Preparing the bias binding

Binding can be made from straight strips or from bias strips. Straight binding can be cut from the width of the fabric and an ideal width is either 2¼" or 2½" (6.5 cm or 7.5 cm). To calculate the number of strips you need, measure the total distance around the quilt and divide by 40. For example, you will need eight strips for a quilt measuring 72" × 90" (183 cm × 228 cm) but 12 strips for a quilt measuring 120" × 120" (305 cm × 305 cm).

Bias binding is cut from the true bias of a square of fabric, and to make a large amount of bias binding very quickly, without the bother of having to join it before use, prepare continuous bias binding. The method is best reserved for large quilts.

The following table gives some example of the yield from different size squares

Continuous bias binding

1 With the wrong side upper most, mark A, B, C, and D at the edges of the square. Fold the square on the diagonal (bias) and cut on this fold.

2 Sew A to B right sides together with ¼" (0.75 cm) seam.

3 Press the seams open. Draw lines on the wrong side of the resulting parallelogram at intervals spaced apart the width of the bias you require.

4 With right sides facing, bring edges C and D together. Drop the seam down one bias width at the top and bottom. Match the marked lines and stitch with ¼" (0.75 cm) seam.

5 Press the seam open. Cut strips following the marked lines, starting at the dropped seam end, and ending at the other dropped seam end.

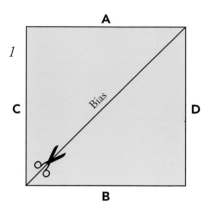

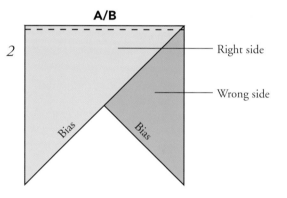

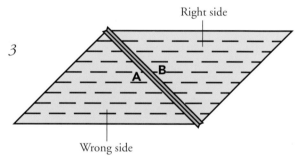

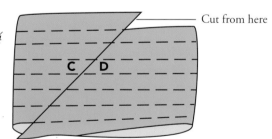

Standard measurements

Bias width	Fabric square 18" × 18"	Fabric square 27" × 27"	Fabric square 36" × 36"
2¼"	144"	324"	578"
2½"	129"	291"	518"

Metric measurements

Bias width	Fabric square 50 × 50 cm	Fabric square 70 × 70 cm	Fabric square 1 × 1 m
6.5 cm	385 cm	754 cm	1.55 m
7.5 cm	334 cm	654 cm	1.33 m

Joining binding strips

1 To join binding strips with a bias seam, lay two strips on top of each other, right sides together, crossing at right angles. Draw a line across the diagonal and stitch on this line. Trim the excess ¹/₄" (0.75 cm) from the seam.

2 Press the seam flat. Repeat until you have all the lengths joined together. Fold in half lengthwise, wrong sides together, and press.

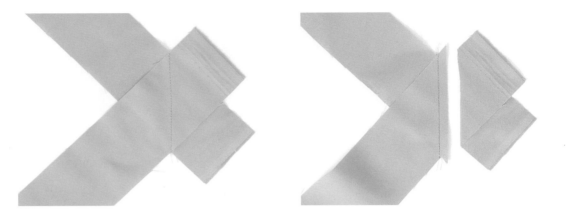

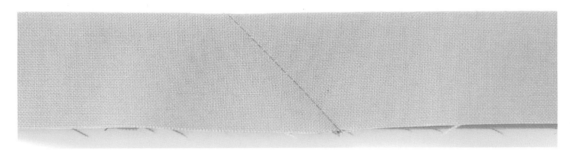

Attaching binding to the quilt

1 Lay the binding around the quilt, raw edges of the binding against the raw edges of the quilt top, starting halfway down one side. Check no joins fall at the corners. Adjust your starting point, if necessary. Leave a long tail and begin stitching with a backstitch to secure.

2 Machine stitch to the point exactly ¹/₄" (0.75 cm) from the corner of the quilt. Stop, reverse, and cut the thread. Fold the binding away from the quilt to create a 45° fold in the binding.

3 Fold the bias back down on itself with the fold flush with the edge of the quilt. Stitch, starting right from the edge, and sew toward the next corner.

1

2

3

4 Continue until you have stitched around all corners. Stop stitching when you are 12" to 15" (30 to 45 cm) away from the starting point.

With the quilt flat, cut the right-hand tail straight, about halfway along the gap. Lay the other tail on top. Measure an overlap equivalent to the width of the binding strips. For example, if your strips were cut 2¹/₄" (6.5 cm), then the overlap will be 2¹/₄" (6.5 cm). Cut the tail straight.

4

continued on the next page…

Binding (continued)

5 Pick up the ends of the binding, unfold it, and bring the right sides together. Lay them exactly on top of each other and pin. Mark the diagonal and sew across this diagonal line.

6 Check that the binding fits by pulling it out straight. If all is well, and no adjustments need to be made, trim the excess triangle and press the joining seam open.

7 Fold this piece of binding in half, wrong sides together, and lay it flat along the edge of the quilt. Pin in place and stitch around, finishing just after your initial starting point.

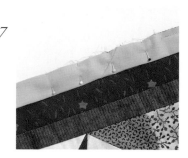

8 Fold the folded edge to the reverse side of the quilt and slip stitch it into place using a blind stitch. Work toward the corner, making a stitch at the seam line and folding the fabric into a miter. Stitch to secure, and carry on toward the next corner. Front side miters will automatically fall into place.

Lapped binding

1 Prepare four binding strips, as before, each 2" (5 cm) longer than the quilt sides. Machine stitch the binding to one side, allowing excess to extend off the ends. Wrap the folded edge to the back and pin in the ditch of the seam from the front. Stitch from the front in the ditch of the seam, catching the fold on the back. Bind the opposite side in the same manner.

2 Trim the excess binding to the corners. Apply binding to the remaining sides and trim the ends to ½" (1.5 cm).

3 Tuck the ends under before wrapping the folded edge to the back to form a neat corner.

4 Finish by stitching in the ditch to thoroughly secure the binding.

Display and care of quilts

Quilts were made to enjoy. Exhibit them, display them on your beds, hang them on the walls, use them, or give them away as gifts. However, if your quilt collection is burgeoning you will want to find the best way to store them away and take measures to protect them. This section discusses the cleaning and repair of quilts.

Many quilters find their bed quilts also make wonderful wallhangings. Included here is instruction for incorporating a hanging sleeve in order to display your quilt. If hanging quilts from walls permanently, take them down every so often to give them a rest from the strain of hanging.

Storage

The best way to store a quilt is flat on a bed, either in everyday use or layered up with other quilts and covered with a sheet to protect them from light. If you wish to store your quilts on display shelves, place acid-free tissue paper between the folds and between the quilts and the shelf for protection. Quilts can be wrapped around cardboard tubes with layers of acid-free tissue between the rolling. You can also buy acid-free cardboard boxes for storage. However, cotton pillowcases make adequate storage. Every month, refold the quilts to avoid permanent crease lines, and if possible, give your quilts a breather and lay them out on a bed for a few days.

Hanging

The simple addition of a pocket or sleeve to the top edge of the back of a quilt will enable it to be hung for display. The sleeve needs to be deep enough to carry a curtain rod or flat board.

To accommodate a flat board, cut the fabric four times the width of the board plus 1" (2.5 cm). For example, if the board is 2" (5 cm) wide, you need to cut fabric 9" (23 cm) wide. For a round rod, cut fabric five times the diameter of the rod plus 1" (2.5 cm). For example, if the curtain rod has a diameter of 2" (5 cm), cut fabric 11" (28 cm) wide.

1 Cut strips of fabric the width desired and piece together end-to-end to measure the exact width of the quilt from edge to edge. Turn down 1/2" (1.25 cm) at each end and stitch. Fold the strip in half lengthwise, wrong sides together.

2 Stitch 1/2" (1.25 cm) from the raw edges and press the seam flat. This side is the back of the sleeve. Pin this to the top of the quilt, aligning the edge with the seam line of the binding. Blind stitch in place by hand, and then stitch the bottom edge of the sleeve to the quilt.

Cleaning

Vacuuming

This method of cleaning puts the least stress on a quilt. Lay the quilt out flat on a sheet and use the soft brush attachment. Vacuum both sides of the quilt. If the quilt is fragile, cover it with fine nylon or muslin before vacuuming.

Dry Cleaning

Antique silk or wool quilts must be dry-cleaned but be sure to engage a reputable cleaner with experience of cleaning exceptional textiles. Relevant museums and quilt historians would be able to provide advice and contacts in your area.

Washing and drying

Most cotton quilts can be hand washed. Before washing any quilt, always test for colorfastness by wetting a tiny area of each fabric and blot with paper towels to see if any dye adheres to the paper.

To hand wash, half fill a bathtub with warm water and mild, pure soap powder.

Lay a sheet at the bottom of the bath and then lay the quilt in on top. Agitate gently; do not rub or abrade the surface of the fabrics. With the aid of the sheet, and perhaps a friend, lift the quilt clear and drain as much water as possible. Rinse with as many changes of water as necessary. Drain again, pressing out as much water as possible. Do not wring.

Roll the quilt in towelling to absorb as much moisture as possible, and then dry flat, ideally outside on a warm day. Lay a dry sheet on the ground and position the quilt face down out of strong direct sunlight. If you have to dry a quilt indoors, lay the quilt flat on layers of towels, also tested for colorfastness, which you will need to replace as the quilt dries.

Quilts made from synthetic fabrics can be machine washed on a gentle cycle. First test for colorfastness using bleach-free detergent. They can be dried in a dryer on a cool setting. Place a towel in the dryer with the quilt to reduce excessive creasing and to speed the drying process.

Remove the quilt from the dryer while it is still damp and complete the drying process flat as for hand-washed quilts.

Repairing

Quilts that are in regular use will eventually deteriorate or become damaged in some way. The most common damage is seams wearing out. This is easily rectified with invisible hand stitches. If however, the damage is more extensive, there are ways to make running repairs. Torn or worn fabric patches can be replaced by making a template of the damaged patch and matching, or near-matching, fabric to the size plus seam allowances. Press seam

allowances to the wrong side of the new patch. Pin and then baste the patch exactly over the worn patch. Stitch in place by using a blind appliqué stitch.

If the quilt needing repair is an antique or very delicate, it is worth talking to quilt conservationists first. They may not recommend repair but rather might suggest covering the damaged area with a single layer of net stitched with long straight stitches along the seam lines.

Resources

Mail order sources for quilting supplies:

Keepsake Quilting
Route 25B, PO Box 1618,
Center Harbor,
NH 03226-1618
(800) 865 9458
www.keepsakequilting.com

Omnigrid, Inc
1560 Port Drive
Burlington,
WA 98233
(800) 755 3530

Threadart
13121 Louetta Rd #125,
Cypress,
TX 77429
(281) 373 0230 or
toll free 1-866-224-4088.
www.Threadart.com

The Quilt Room
20 West Street.
Dorking.
Surrey RH4 1BL
44 (0)1306 877307
www.quiltroom.co.uk

Strawberry Fayre Fabrics
Chagford
Devon TQ13 8EN
44 (0) 1647 433250
www.strawberryfayre.co.uk

Contributors

Katharine Guerrier has been making quilts since 1980 and has been teaching patchwork and quilting workshops since 1985. Katharine's work draws on the traditional motifs of pieced patchwork, developing them to give a contemporary feel and use of color as an important part of the design process. Katharine contributed the Introduction, and the chapters on Design, Patchwork and Piecing, and Specialty Piecing. Her quilts are featured on page 65 (left): Pinwheel Zigzag; page 68: Snail Trail Variation; pages 98 and 100: Sampler quilt; page 108: Log Cabin quilt; page 136: Contemporary pieced wallhanging; page 130: foundation pieced quilts.

Anne Walker contributed the chapters on Fabrics, Equipment, Cutting and Stitching Techniques, Sashing and Borders, Finishings, and Display and Care of Quilts. Anne's love of geometry and pattern developed into an interest in patchwork, which in turn led to her teaching numerous workshops and to her publications, including *Patchwork Pocket Palette* and *The Weekend Quilter* series. Anne is involved with education programs and the development of the City and Guilds in Patchwork and Quilting.

Christine Porter is Director of Cabot Quilting Conferences, founded in 1994 to enable top quilters of many nationalities to meet and learn from some of the best teachers in the world. She is also involved in fabric design with Woodrow Studio, a leading quilting fabric manufacturer. Christine has won awards for her quilts and regularly teaches at the Quilters Affair, Sisters, Oregon, The Pacific International Quilt Festival, The World Quilt & Textile Show, Mid Atlantic Quilt Festival, and the Appalachian Quilting Festival. Her recent book is *Quilt Designs from Decorative Floor Tiles*, Christine contributed the chapter on Machine Quilting, and her *Jazzy Quilt* is featured on page 2; wallhanging on page 220 and 225; and Trapunto quilt on page 218.

Rebecca Collins was introduced to patchwork when living in West Africa and she began teaching her love of the craft to others; her success can be measured by the 14 students who have gone on to make prize-winning quilts. Rebecca has contributed to *The Quilter's Handbook*, and *Quick and Easy Projects for the Weekend Quilter*, *Quilting Masterclass*, and to *Patchwork and Quilting* and *Traditional Quiltworks* magazines. She exhibited her quilts at the IQA Quilt Show in Houston, in Europe and in the UK. Rebecca contributed the section on Appliqué Stitches and the chapter on Appliqué Styles, and her wallhanging is featured on page 190 and 196; Christmas Comforts sampler quilt page 200 (right) and 204, and on page 252.

Since making her first wholecloth quilt in 1994, **Sandie Lush** has been a regular prizewinner taking awards both for design and her fine hand quilting skills. Her quilts have twice won championships and have been exhibited in Europe, Australia and Japan. In the United States they have featured in The World Quilt and Textile Fair and have won prizes at both the Quilter's Heritage Celebration in Pennsylvania and the International Quilt Festival at Houston. Her quilt *Moonflower* was awarded first place in the Merit Quilting category in Houston in 1997. Sandie's quilts are featured on pages 9, page 197, 198 and 199, 242 and 243, 251 (right), and she wrote the chapter on Wholecloth Quilts and Hand Quilting.

Susan Chapman was introduced to patchwork and quilting while living in New York. She now teaches quilting throughout the UK, including the acclaimed City and Guilds' course. Her quilts have received several awards, and she has written for a series of revision primers in patchwork techniques. Susan is a Licentiate member of the Guild of Designer Craftsmen and a practicing contemporary quilt artist. Her exhibits have been seen in the United States and France. Susan contributed the chapters on Special Effects and Fabric Manipulation.

Acknowledgments

The publisher would also like to thank Anne Walker for the supply of equipment for images on pages 28 to 38; Bogod Machine Company for images of Bernina sewing machines on page 34 and 35; The Woodrow Studio Ltd of London, for their donation of fabric. All the samples were made with The Colour Play Palette, and Inspired by Lalique. Special thanks to Bridget Cordy at CDC2020 for making their "Coolblue" Develpment, Brighton, available for photography

The sampler quilt on page 98 and the Log Cabin quilt on page 108 were quilted on a long arm quilting machine by Jan Chandler, Quilting Solutions, Firethorn, Rattlesden Road, Drinkstone, Bury St Edmunds, Suffolk IP30 9TL Tel: 44 (0) 1449 736280 email: cnquirics@quiltingsolutions.co.uk.

Images on page 10 and 11 are by permission of the Bridgeman Art Gallery.

Katharine Guerrier would like to thank the contributors for sharing their special expertise in the field of patchwork and quilting; and to thank her husband George Hudson, for his unfailing support in this and other publications.

Credits

The publishers would like to thank the following quilters for the inclusion of their quilts:

Irene MacWilliams for *Stars*, page 7; *Dominoes, Ocean Currents, Life Goes On*, p. 17; *Diagonal Illusion*, p. 156 (top right); Ann Fahl for *Symphony of Color*, p. 7; *The Walking Bridge*, p. 65 (middle); Deirdre Amsden for *Colorwash Cubes*, p. 7; Becky Knight for *Thinking of You*, p. 8; *Indian Shiny*, p. 65 (right); Mary Kent for *Mary's Quilt*, p. 9; p. 172 (left and middle); Natalia Manley for *Into the Light*, p. 17; Nancy Breland for *Morning Glory*, p. 68; Sally-Anne Boyd for *Arvieto*, p. 68; Valerie Ann Snowdon for *First Try*, p. 70 (left); p. 226 (left); Joan Tunstall for *Feathered Stars*, p. 70 (middle); Jean Grimshaw for *Indigo with Red*, p. 70 (right); Sara Impcy for *Kitchen Curtains*, p. 156 (top left); *Cold and Frosty Morning*, p. 156 (bottom left); Valerie Hearder for *Settlement: Displacement*, p. 156 (bottom right); Marianne Mohandes p. 157 (left); *Another World*, p. 157 (right); p. 206 (middle); p. 200 (middle); Margaret de la Croix for *Lavender Fancee*, p. 157 (middle); p. 226 (middle); Anne-Marie Troup for *Poppy*, p. 172 (right); Debbie Cook for *My Poorly Foot*, p. 200 (left); Josephine Bardsley for *Wildflowers*, p. 206 (left); p. 251 (middle); Jacqueline Holland for *California Blues*, p. 226 (right); p. 241 (right).

Index